Ra

Radical Strategy

Second Edition

How to use strategic conversation
to win in an age of hostile competition

Tony Manning

ZEBRA

ZEBRA

Published by Zebra Press
(a member of the New Holland Struik Publishing Group (Pty) Ltd)
PO Box 3103, Halfway House, 1685
Tel: (011) 315 3633
Fax: (011) 315 3810

First published in January 1997
Second edition June 1998

DTP and design A1 Graphics
Cover design Crazy Cat Designs

Reproduction by A1 Graphics
Printed and bound by National Book Printers, Drukkery Street, Goodwood, 7460

ISBN 1-86872-106-X

For Kim
Who left a silence that's deafening
And for Sandy and Lee
Who walk the lonely road with me

THE META PRINCIPLES OF RADICAL STRATEGY

1. Strategy connects the values of an organization with those of its customers.

2 Strategy must enable the organization to make a difference that matters to a critical mass of 'right' customers.

3. Focus, value, and costs are the keys to competitive advantage.

4. Imagination and human spirit inspire maximum performance. These are products of both individual contribution and symbiotic relationships.

5. It may be easy to clone a product, but it's impossible to clone a community. So, a vital goal of strategy is to create and sustain a unique community.

6. Purpose is the glue that holds a community together, drives teams to seek their potential, and provides the context in which individuals can apply their imagination and spirit.

7. Shared ideas lead to shared meaning. The more openly and honestly ideas are shared, the greater the level of trust will be, and the more ideas will be shared.

8. People value work that makes them valued. When they make strategy, they matter. And they own the outcomes.

9. Strategic management is conversation. It informs, focuses attention, triggers fresh insights, lights up the imagination, energizes people, and inspires performance.

10. Corporate conversation provides a context for personal and group learning. Your message must be complex and challenging, or no one will buy it. It must also be simple, clear, and believable, or you won't sell it.

Contents

Preface

... we obviously have little control over global economic trends, currency fluctuations and devaluations, natural disasters, political upheavals, social unrest, bad weather or schizophrenic stock markets. We do, however, have complete control over our own behaviour ...

— Roberto Goizueta, chairman The Coca-Cola Company[1]

As we let go of the machine models of work, we begin to step back and see ourselves in new ways, to appreciate our wholeness, and to design organizations that honor and make use of the totality of who we are.

— Margaret J. Wheatley, *Leadership and the New Science*[2]

When Roberto Goizueta became chairman of Coca-Cola in 1981, the company had a market value of $4 billion. When he died in 1997, it was worth $152 billion.

What was his secret?

How did this Cuban-born chemist make Coke a money machine? How was he able to coax double-digit growth from a 100-year-old product, in a market that analysts said was saturated?

The answer, I believe, is deceptively simple. It was captured in his quote:

> *This is a very simple business. When we complicate it, we really mess things up.*

Goizueta focused his team's attention on three things: shareholder value, leveraging the Coke brand, and extending his distribution reach. Period. If more firms followed his lead, they'd do themselves a big favour. (In fact, why don't you copy those words and start debating them with your team today. And from now on, start insisting on simplicity rather than complexity in everything you do: every programme, every project, every system, every task.)

Coca-Cola is a big organization. It operates in more than 150 countries. As you can imagine, the managers have a lot on their plates. But by focusing like a laser on the few things that would make the big difference, Goizueta led Coke to become the world's second most valuable company.

There's a clear message here for executives in literally every other firm in the world. Remember the KISS principle: keep it simple, stupid!

It is easy to over-complicate the strategy process. Hopefully, this book will help you un-complicate it. If you take away nothing more than Goizueta's words, I'll be happy.

My purpose in these pages is threefold:

1. To help cut through the clutter of issues calling for your attention and focus on the few that will make the biggest difference.
2. To provoke you into a radical mind-set.
3. To provide ways of creating your own future.

From the time I wrote my first book, *Communicating For Change*, in 1987, and through all my subsequent efforts – *Business Strategy in the New South Africa* (1988), *World Class!* (1990), and *The Race To Learn* (1992) – I have pursued consistent themes. All those books were underpinned by extensive research, anecdotal evidence, and observation. All remain as relevant today as ever.

Radical Strategy is a new book for a new age. I hope it provokes you to think hard about the context in which we now compete, and to do what you must to exploit today's remarkable challenges.

The first edition was the '*beta* version'. It drew a great deal of response from many people, and their insights and observations have been invaluable.

There are many new ideas in this second edition. My consulting practice gives me access to a wide range of companies in literally every industry (so I have the unique privilege of being able to spend my working days in a real-world business school!). I also give dozens of speeches at major conferences each year, which offers me a unique opportunity to get instant feedback. And I keep up an intensive research programme, reading widely and spending long hours thinking about how the latest concepts and theories apply in the real world of business.

The ideas in this edition of *Radical Strategy* have all been 'field-tested'. The book is shorter than the original version, and, hopefully, more user-friendly. But if you see ways in which I can improve it, please let me know. You can contact me at:

Phone: (011) 884-2635
Fax (011) 884-6006
Cell phone: 082-800-5862
E-mail address: strategist@tonymanning.com

Key themes

The central idea in *Radical Strategy* is that work is a conversation, and the surest way to make any organization succeed over the long term is to manage that conversation well. I buried that idea in the first edition of *Radical Strategy*, but here it's up front and central to the entire text.

What you won't find in these pages is a list of easy ways to improve the way people talk to each other. Nor will I tell you how to create an information technology strategy. Instead, I focus on a totally new approach to making strategy, a radical way of growing your sales and profits against the odds.

Strategy is ultimately as effective as the analysis and creativity that shapes it, the energy and commitment that drive it, and the learning that derives from it. In this age of hyper-competition, 'brainware' is the only edge. To exploit it, organizations must be 'open-minded' or 'porous'. Information must flow in and out of them, and within them, freely and fast. All censorship must be outlawed.

Management thinkers have known much of this for a long time. Experts in other disciplines – social psychology, chaos theory, cybernetics, physics, and information technology – have added powerful insights. Ideas from many directions and disciplines are beginning to converge. However, what's missing in my view is a simple, integrative approach that managers can easily grasp, and that companies can use fast and with little fuss.

Too much of the new debate is still at a theoretical level. Executives are left saying, 'It sounds good, but what the hell do I *do* on Monday morning?'

Conversations need themes. Here are mine:

- However well your company is doing, you have to raise your 'bar of excellence'.
- The quicker you face the world's toughest competitors, the better.
- Radical strategy is more important than incremental improvement.
- Creating a strategic plan is less important than creating the capacity to think and act strategically.
- It is entirely possible to grow your company even while you transform it.*
- What you 'know' – about your industry, your customers, your processes, and so on – is both your biggest problem and your biggest opportunity.
- Dramatic changes and performance improvements can and must be made to happen much faster than you think.
- Many of the best-known strategy concepts are obsolete – and downright dangerous.
- Simple strategies are useless; today, complexity wins. But if you can't explain your business logic simply, you lose.
- For many firms, market share doesn't matter; what really counts is a critical mass of the 'right' customers.
- Growth is vital, but innovation and change drive it.
- The most potent competitive weapons are not finance, technology, or marketing know-how, but imagination and the human spirit.
- The first priority of management is to 'informate'[3] the workplace: to flood people with information and to link them together into the organization's nervous system.
- To empower people is not to enable them to reach their potential inside your organization, but to enable them to leave and do even better outside.
- Paradoxes offer the biggest opportunities for competitive advantage.
- Thinking about the future is more important than ever – and you know more about the future than you think!

---

* In South Africa, 'transformation' is often used to suggest total change in workforce composition, organizational structure, culture, systems, and so on. In fact, the real intention is affirmative action.

Many of these opinions fly in the face of current business wisdom. But that's precisely what strategy is all about.

Throughout this book, I've tried to illustrate key points with actual examples. Most are from foreign organizations, as they are the new competition and it's vital we know what we're up against.

Some of the South African companies mentioned by name are clients of mine, and I have their permission to talk about them. Many are not clients, but what they're doing is well known or has been commented on elsewhere. Often, I don't mention names or even which industry a firm is in, so I can talk frankly about what really goes on in organizations.

Too early to celebrate

Radical Strategy is not a celebration of how smart South African managers are. Some are geniuses. Some local companies are truly world class and are doing wonderful things to improve. Other books tell you about the witty and wise things top executives say, and try to reduce their successes to glib formulas.

A lot of what's dished up elsewhere is simply a re-hash of old ideas. Too often, it's based on anecdote – garnered from whomever was available and would talk – rather than solid fact.

What's more, much reporting is more like a snapshot than a complete movie. If you follow the 'audit trail', it is impossible to link specific strategies to measurable results. The latest recipe turns out to be a convenient collection of stuff that makes for a good story.

Business success is a product of many factors. Decoding it is extremely difficult, if not impossible. What chief executives say they do and what actually happens are often very different. The gap between intentions and practice is wide.

My goal is to provide a cold analysis of where South African business really stands, and what managers have to do. To report on what works in the real world, to cut through the clutter of often-conflicting theories, and to home in on concepts that make a difference.

In spite of the challenges that face every company, some consistently report excellent results. Many management teams have made important changes to their organizations. Annual reports and articles in the press are full of all the right phrases: 'core competencies', 'participative management', 'learning organizations', 'total quality management' (TQM), ISO 9000, 'electronic data interchange' (EDI), 'flattening the hierarchy', 'broad-banding', 'self-managing teams', 'community involvement', 'environmental audits', and so on.

But there can be no arguing that most firms have a long way to go. They haven't confronted the reality of what's ahead, nor have they changed radically enough or fast enough.

The end of easy times

Deprived of choices, South African customers and investors were pussycats in the past. Business was allowed to get away with often-pathetic performance. By almost every measure – innovation, customer service, people development, corporate governance, financial returns – they were far from world class.

Until recently, many companies 'grew' on the back of rising inflation. They simply kept increasing their prices. But now they must show real growth in a *deflationary* environment. And for many this small local market is either saturated or shrinking.

The winds of change are blowing at gale force.

Some companies have seen the need to act and have forged ahead with a vengeance. Improvements will become more widespread as customers travel abroad and learn what they should be getting, as local firms venture into foreign territory, and as foreign firms continue to arrive here. Like it or not, South African companies are learning how tough international competition is.

To argue that you did well 'under the circumstances' is an opinion not a fact. To say that you are 'getting things right but it will take time' is to be dangerously complacent.

There is no time.

Once, South Africa was cut off from the world. We might not easily have been able to trade elsewhere, but nor could nasty foreigners come in here to steal our customers. Now, it's open season.

Once, there were plenty of growth opportunities in the local market. Now, companies find they've hit the limits. With inflation down, they have to sell more just to stay in place – but there aren't enough new customers, and those that there are, shop around and buy on price.

Once, South Africa's economy was based on commodities – mostly gold. Now, it's shifting towards exports of value-added manufactured products and services. But there are countless other producers around the world, and many set standards that we can't begin to comprehend, let alone meet.

Once, many sectors – minerals, agricultural produce, liquor, broadcasting, transport, retail pharmacy, and cement, to name a few – were closed shops. Competition within them was tightly regulated. There was little 'churn', as there was little reason to get out and little or no chance of getting in. Now, regulatory barriers are falling and almost anyone can play.

Once, employers had the upper hand in their relationships with employees. Now the balance has gone the other way – especially for workers with skills.

Once …

Reminiscing may give you a nice warm feeling, but it hardly helps.

A new age of hostile competition is upon us. The way is full of promise, but we'll have to go some to grab it. Shocks are in store. Shocking action will be needed to survive them.

Foreign companies have also had it rough. But watch how fast many of them have turned around or taken off in new directions. The speed with which they have changed and the magnitude of their improvement have been extraordinary. It's a sobering thought, too, that they often had to unravel far more complex arrangements than any South African firm does.

The way forward

To meet the challenges ahead, executives will have to discard many of the fads that occupied them in the past decade, and get down to the new realities of managing in a mad, unforgiving, and pressurized environment. This means that you have to urgently abandon much, or maybe all of what worked in the past, and rapidly overhaul your ways.

As you head into the future, remember to:

- Beware of 'breakthrough' solutions.
- Check the 'audit trail' from concept to results – and if it's not clear and believable, run a mile!
- Stick to the basics and execute them with a vengeance. (Most of your competitors won't, so you'll beat them while they fiddle around.)

Management, says General Electric chairman Jack Welch, is 'looking reality straight in the eye and then acting on it with as much speed as you can'.[4]

The first reality is that rapid, radical – and continuous – change are inevitable if your firm is to survive and thrive.

The second is the need to operate from first principles.

The third is the need to leverage those principles to gain and hold a lead over your competitors.

Strategy is not rocket science. It's common sense and creativity combined. The best business ideas are so obvious that everyone overlooks them, or so extraordinary that no one thinks about them. Either way, it's how you execute them that finally matters.

Kill snakes!

When Ross Perot sold his company, Electronic Data Systems, to General Motors for $2,5 billion in 1984, he became the single largest shareholder in GM and was appointed to the board. But his insider's view made him so critical of management, and so outspoken about the need for urgent change, that he was soon paid another $750 000 and asked to resign.

While still a director, Perot was asked by *Fortune* magazine what he'd do if he ran GM. The feisty Texan had a blunt answer: 'We've got to nuke the system.'

Then he went on: 'I come from an environment where, if you see a snake, you kill it. At GM, if you see a snake, the first thing you do is hire a consultant on snakes. Then you get a committee on snakes, and then you discuss it for a couple of years. The most likely course of action is … nothing. You figure the snake hasn't bitten anybody yet, so you just let him crawl around on the factory floor. We need to build an environment where the first guy who sees the snake kills it.'[5]

That's the kind of environment every South African company needs to build right now.

That's the kind of attitude managers need.
It's time to kill snakes!

Tony Manning
April 1998

Endnotes

1. The Coca-Cola Company Annual Report 1994.
2. Margaret J. Wheatley, *Leadership and the New Science*, San Franscisco: Berrett: Koehler Publishers, 1994.
3. This term was coined by Shoshana Zuboff, professor at the Harvard Business School, in her book *In the Age Of The Smart Machine*, New York: Basic Books, 1984.
4. Carol J. Loomis, 'Dinosaurs', *Fortune*, May 3, 1935.
5. 'Make-or-break time for General Motors', *Fortune*, February 15, 1995.

Introduction

In the end, every individual extracts the most basic sense of purpose from being part of an organization.

— Christopher Bartlett and Sumantra Ghoshal, *Harvard Business Review*[1]

Causally ambiguous resources are often organizational capabilities. These may exist in a complex web of social interactions and may even depend critically on particular individuals.

— David J. Collis and Cynthia A. Montgomery, *Harvard Business Review*[2]

Recently, I was asked to brief the top team of a major organization on what the world might look like in 2005 and 2010. Some of their questions: Which way will the economy go? Who will have the buying power? Where will people live? What will be the effects of immigration and emigration? What'll happen to education? Will crime diminish? Will joblessness rise? Where will the new jobs be? How will technology change the way companies work? And, of course, what about the political landscape?

'We're going to invest a hell of a lot of money,' I was told, 'so we need to be sure what lies ahead.'

We'd all like to know exactly what the future holds. But while there are many useful clues, surprise is the only certainty. So while managers must ask these questions, and must plan today for tomorrow's results, it is even more important that they *build the kind of organizations that will survive whatever comes at them.*

Who are you kidding?

'Nothing is so easy as to deceive oneself,' said Demosthenes. 'For what we wish, we readily believe.'

A senior executive in one of South Africa's biggest corporations recently showed me a graph illustrating the outlook for his company. Economists had drawn a line that rose for two years, then fell sharply for a long time. But management had another view. Their trend line kept rising.

'Why the difference?' I asked.

'The chairman wants the line to go up,' was the answer.

This isn't an isolated case.

Early in 1997, the head of a motor manufacturing company showed me his sales and market share forecasts. His line, too, went up. When I asked why, he told me about new vehicle launches, price cuts, better service, and so on.

'That's all good stuff,' I said, 'but has it occurred to you that if I had this conversation with any of your competitors, they'd all tell me the same things. What makes you think you'll gain share when they're all improving like crazy?'

Shortly afterwards, *Finance Week* ran a story on prospects for the motor industry. The accompanying chart pointed to serious delusions of success. The collective market share of the companies in 1997 was naturally 100 per cent. Their projected share for the year 2000 was ... 173 per cent!

Dealing with these human fallibilities is something management must deliberately work at. You have to short-circuit a powerful, natural inclination.

For strategic debate to have value, the process must be open, honest, and challenging. But as Harvard psychologist Chris Argyris warns us, 'defensive routines can act to distort reality without our being aware of the distortion'.[3] Executives who've worked together for years think they can read each other's minds, and decode what their colleagues are saying. If they're golfing buddies, they're unlikely to fight hard for their own views, or to demand clarity from the other. 'Facts' are presented and accepted without a fuss. Team-building exercises can paradoxically weaken a team because the members learn how to 'play the game'.

But the problems run deeper. In every group, it's okay to talk about certain things, while others are forbidden territory. You can declare that sales will go up, but don't dare suggest that they might fall. You can discuss shortcomings in Purchasing, but not in Marketing. The result will be a vicious cycle of self-deception. 'Something that is not discussable,' says Argyris, 'by definition, makes even the undiscussability undiscussable.'[4]

Good times are dangerous times. When things are running smoothly there's no pressure for change: people feel no need to challenge the status quo. Confronting the future is easier in times of crisis. Trouble makes us more sensitive to changes in the environment and more willing to talk about tough action. But even in emergencies it's common to see a lot of 'wheel-spin' as managers skirt issues and put off what they know they must do.

Being nervous about the future is no reason not to think about it. There will always be hurdles ahead, and you'd better get ready for them. They won't go away just because you refuse to see them. Better to pay attention now and to take whatever measures you must, than to be caught off guard later.

Welcome to the relationship revolution!

It's incredible. As we hurtle through the 1990s towards the future, an old symbol has suddenly become famous. In fact, in 1995 it became the most important symbol in the world.

Here it is:

@

When I was a kid, we used it to do sums: 'Four bags of mielies @ four-and-sixpence equals ...' Today, that symbol captures the most powerful ideas in commerce.

Consider some of the questions it raises:

- Where is your head 'at'? (Hippies used to ask that back in the '60s; the rest of us took 30 years to wake up!) What occupies your people's thoughts? What excites them? How much time do they give to innovation? How many way-out ideas do they dream up?
- Where is your organization 'at'? Hopefully, it's on a mental plane that your competitors can't even imagine. Physically, it could be anywhere on the planet. And it could include lots of 'outsiders'. (Nike doesn't make shoes; it promotes a brand and manages logistics. Dell doesn't make computers; it buys in just about everything but marketing.)
- Where is your customer 'at'? Who are they? Where are they located? What are their needs, wants, values, and buying behaviour? How are they changing? What will satisfy them tomorrow?
- Where is your strategy 'at'? How radical is it? How effective is it? Is it clear to all who need to know it? How aggressive are you about executing it? Do you have the resources? Where to from here?
- Where is your value delivery system 'at'? How effective is it? How much effort are you making to change or improve it?
- Where are your suppliers 'at'? Are they doing all they could to help you add value and reach your growth goals?

The list goes on. These are the questions that every manager in every organization needs to think about right now. And that's the symbol you should plaster on your walls, discuss in your meetings, and design into your business model.

The cogs that used to make the world go round are rusted tight. This is the age of relationships. *Connections* count. And @titudes matter.

Nobody understands this better than *Fortune* writer Thomas Stewart. His 1997 book *Intellectual Capital* was one of the first of a flood of publications on the knowledge revolution. The central message:

> *Networking is lots more than a metaphysical idea, a technological phenomenon, or a hot industry. It is the most important development in management since Du Pont, General Motors, and others invented the modern corporation – with its headquarters officers and staff, multiple divisions, and functional departments – before World War II.*[5]

Some executives will no doubt seize on views like this to justify bigger investments in information technology. They'll give up on their efforts to get more out of their people, and turn instead to the gizmos that hold such high promise:

computers, fibre-optics, satellites, digital video, electronic whiteboards, groupware, the Internet, intranets, and extranets.

But before you switch from 'high touch' to 'high tech', take note of this observation from Michael Schrage, one of the seers of the IT industry:

> *The so-called 'information revolution' itself is actually, and more accurately, a 'relationship revolution'. Anyone trying to get a handle on the dazzling technologies of today and the impact they'll have tomorrow, would be well advised to re-orient their worldview around* relationships.[6] (my stress)

Dazzling new information technologies all have one purpose: to enable people to interact more effectively. Just as a computer's value depends on the speed with which the bits and bytes flow and connect, and on the machine's ability to reveal new truths, so does a firm's value hinge on this traffic and transformation.

What happens in a computer is, in effect, an extremely rapid 'conversation'. What happens in an organization – and between an organization and other stakeholders such as suppliers and customers – is also conversation.

The new value creation process

The value chain concept is now well-known and widely used. But like so many other concepts, it came from the Industrial Age. It allowed managers to unbundle activities – creating ideas, buying, making, selling, and service – that naturally followed one after the other. But when things become messier, when they do not naturally follow in an orderly and predictable sequence, you need another way to think about your business.

'In today's highly competitive environment,' says Robin Cooper in his book *When Lean Enterprises Collide*, 'sustainable advantages are like Nobel Prizes – extremely rare. They are rare because to achieve a sustainable advantage requires a complex clustering of events that together create an insurmountable barrier to emulation.'[7]

Competitiveness is a product of five functions (Figure i):

1. **Sensing.** You have to be aware of what's going on 'out there' and interpret the signals. Seeing the future ahead of your competitors gives you a head start over them. But simply collecting information is not enough; *insights* are what count. 'Peripheral vision' is vital; but it is only as valuable as your ability to translate economic trends, new laws, shifts in buyer behaviour, changing needs, fashions, and tastes into new products and processes.

   Capturing the profit in these insights takes more than knowledge of the external world. You also have to know what's possible 'in here' – your organization's capabilities. Companies greatly influence customer demand. Successful innovation is always a collaborative effort. Firms like Nike and Sony excel in both R&D and marketing.

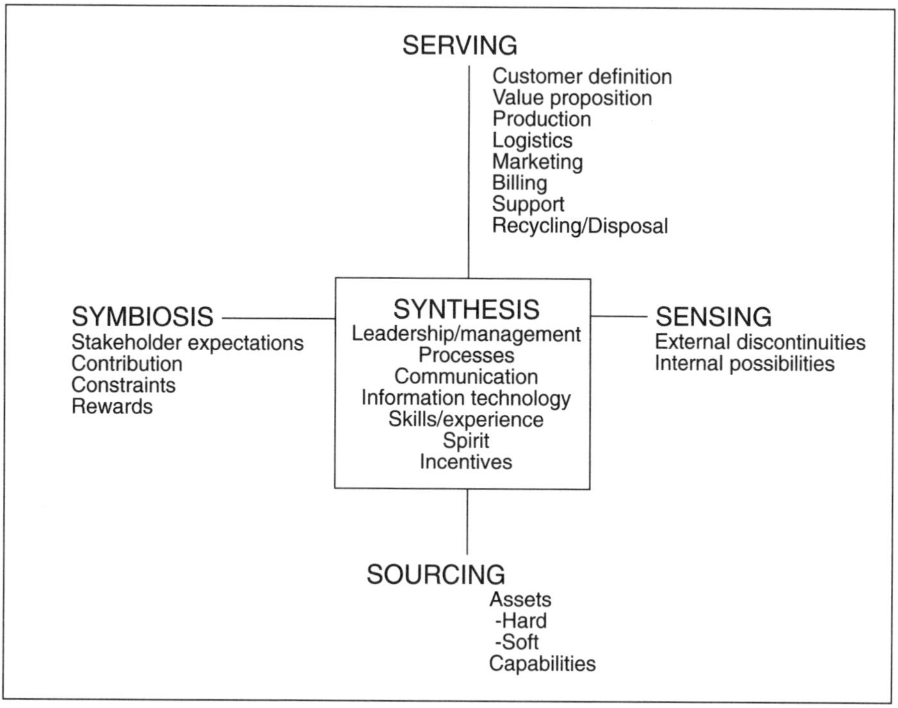

Figure i: *Value creation in the Information Age*

2. **Sourcing.** Satisfying any need requires resources. You need 'soft' inputs such as skills, capabilities, and finance, as well as 'hard' ones like raw materials, components, and plant and equipment to keep a business alive.

   Most are outside of the firm now, and more will be in the future. So the first requirement is to define the resources you need and identify the best suppliers. Then to communicate and strike deals across boundaries.

   Needless to say, these tasks become more complex and difficult as you reach out across industry and national borders, and as convention, custom, and language intrude.

3. **Serving.** Companies survive and thrive on the courtesy of their customers. Every company is in the service business. How well you do hinges on whom you choose to serve and how you do it. This value delivery process defines your value proposition. It is central to the design of your business model.

4. **Symbiosis.** Every organization has multiple stakeholders – not just customers, but also suppliers, distributors, investors, society, and others. What you do for them affects what they will do for you. How well you perform in terms of sales, profits, or growth depends on how intimately you understand them and on the depth of your commitment to them.

Stakeholders comprise an organization's 'ecosystem'. And just as the plants and animals in a natural ecosystem flourish when their relationship is symbiotic, so it is with organizations. Win-win relationships are the essence of competitive excellence.

Think of stakeholders as voters for your success or failure. Ask why they should vote *for* you rather than *against* you. Too often, there's no good reason. But effective executives create reasons. They use the strategic conversation to keep the votes coming.

5. **Synthesis.** Insights, ideas, resources, and activities must be linked in order to exploit opportunities. Organizations exist to make these connections. They arrange information into concepts, processes, and, ultimately, products.

   Of the five functions, it's synthesis that puts some companies at the top of the pile and keeps them there and consigns others to the dustbins of business history. It's this task that is most important, most difficult – and most *neglected.*

   'In the high-value enterprise,' says former U.S. Secretary for Labour Robert Reich, 'profits derive not from scale and volume but from continuous discovery of new linkages between solutions and needs.'[8] Yet it's precisely in these linkages that most companies come unstuck.

   The most obvious linkage is between a company and its customers. But there are many others. Work must be integrated across functions, departments, and business units. Learning from one area must be shared with others. Political power must be managed and trade-offs must be made. Problems and opportunities must be seen and dealt with in a balanced way. Investments in one place must be balanced against returns elsewhere.

   Synthesis is more than just coordination of the firm's thrusts. The Oxford dictionary describes it as 'combining of elements into a whole'. Applied to business, it gives you more than you set out with. It's the process by which you turn an angry customer into a loyal friend, tap a salesman's experience to refine a product, or use a supplier's views on component design in your own production system.

   Synthesis put Lee Iacocca on the road with the Ford Mustang. It turned 'un-sticky' glue in a 3M laboratory into Post-It notes. It gave us Polaroid instant film, the Sony Walkman, Black & Decker's Snakelight torch, and Windows 95. In fact, any great product you can think of is a result of synthesized insights, ideas, resources, and action.

   Synthesis makes possible the growth and profitability of companies. Virgin Atlantic Airlines is more than just a Richard Branson dream. Coca-Cola's success is due to a lot more than the extraordinary leadership of Roberto Goizueta from 1981 to 1997. Swatch is more than just a fashionable product. Daimler-Benz is more than factories and engineering skill.

   Winning companies stand out for a simple reason – they couple opportunities and actions more effectively and timeously than their competitors.

> The laggards might see the same customer needs, buy from the same sources, and offer equal service, but to use a famous line from television's A-Team, their plan doesn't come together.
>
> This could be because of a flaw in the plan. More likely, it's a result of poor execution and, by implication, of poor conversation.
>
> My involvement in hundreds of strategy discussions suggests that while many executives might see the same opportunities, and while they may have access to similar resources, only a few make the intellectual connections that will make them rich. Few act on what they see. Fewer still are able to get the right things done at the right time.

Unlike the linear value chain, the 'Five S' model shows the complex nature of value creation in the Information Age. It embraces the fact that value is more than a neat sequence of actions; that insights, experiments, learning, and knowledge are messy overlaying factors. And the more confusing and competitive the business arena becomes, and the more firms focus on their core competencies, the more relevant this model becomes.

Value is a concept. It's a product of resources, imagination, attitudes, and actions – of how you see the world, of how you think, and what you do. If ever it could be created in step-by-step fashion, it would be very difficult to do in this time of accelerating change and hostile competition.

Value may be born in many places – in the mind of a customer, in the R&D lab, in a front-line encounter, in a formal meeting or a passage chat between colleagues at work. It's added in countless ways – by designing products which are easy to assemble well and service efficiently; by manufacturing to Six Sigma quality; by providing the skills which let people handle questions and fix problems, by hiring for attitudes and rewarding initiative.

Value might be a product that gets you from A to B, makes toast, or stops pain; or a service that saves lives, fixes things, or provides information. But no customer just buys the 'what'. They also buy the 'how'. Satisfaction is as much an *outcome* as the *process* that leads to that outcome.

Who captures the value?

Not that long ago, advertising agencies claimed to know more about customers than their clients did. Now, companies like Unilever, Woolworths, and SA Breweries Beer Division are the experts, thanks to their huge investment in market research and their contact with customers. Others have intimate relationships built up over many years. Pick 'n Pay's scanning technology tells management, sale by sale, how promotions are working. Hollard Direct, Microsoft, and Vodacom all have call centres which give them a window on the customer's world.

Not long ago, wholesalers played an important role in getting many products from manufacturers to retailers. Now, manufacturers deliver direct.

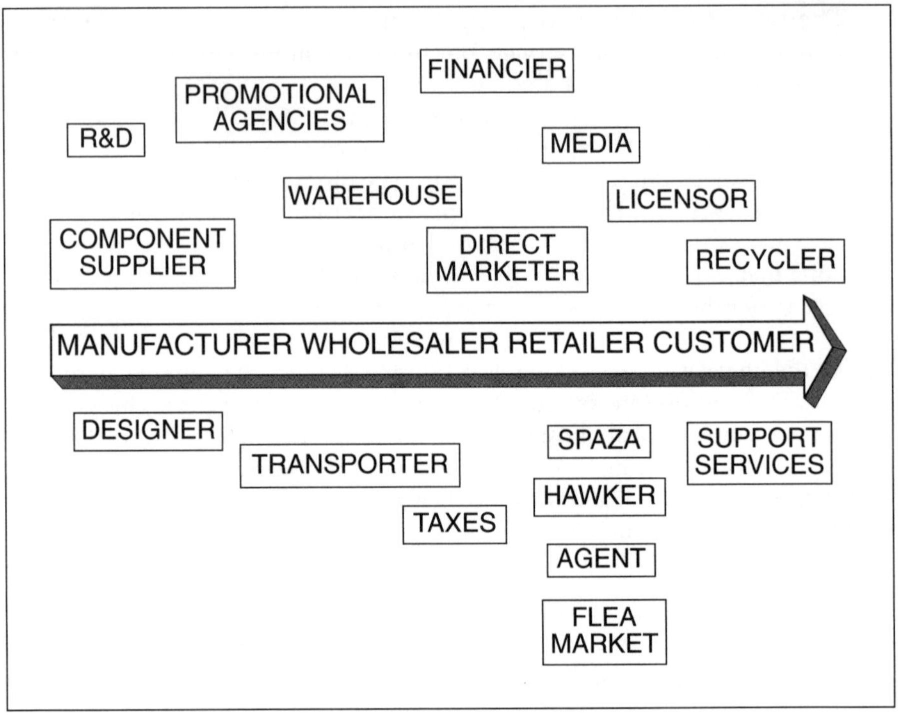

Figure ii: *Who captures the value?*

Not long ago, companies tried to do as much as possible 'in-house'. Vertical integration of every value-adding activity was a popular strategy. Now, companies focus on their core competencies, and outsource everything else.

The point is, value creation is now widely dispersed. Many players take a slice of the income in most corporate ecosystems. Profits are shared according to the power of the various players (Figure ii).

Theatre owners share their profits with Computicket. Airlines share profits with travel agents. Car makers share profits with design firms, component suppliers, ad agencies, media, transporters, dealers, finance companies, insurers, the AA, fitment specialists like Tiger Wheels and Battery Centre, petrol companies, used-car dealers and even with scrap merchants. And when increasing competition forces down prices and prompts discount deals, the customer takes a bigger slice, too.

You may be able to choose who should capture the value created by your business – and how. But you can easily lose control of the process. If you're not alert, some canny innovator will work out how to divert your revenue stream his way. Chances are it's happening right now. Your profits could vanish in the blink of an eye.

The goal, of course, should be to design the process yourself. To decide, up front, who should do what and who should get what in return.

Disciplined collaboration

Organizational boundaries are shifting. 'Our company' used to describe a neat social group and the boxes and lines on organograms used to make sense. Now, the talk is of 'corporate ecosystems' and 'virtual organizations'. And while you still need to manage what happens inside your company, you also need to extend your influence. Your 'infomocracy'[9] needs to include outsiders who help you create and deliver value.

The question is, does your organization share information at the clock speed of a clunky 286MHz computer or of the latest Pentium? That, in turn, leads to other questions:

- What is shared?
- Who gets the information?
- How is it shared – meetings, phone calls, e-mail, etc.?
- What is the style of sharing – i.e., open and honest, robust, challenging, inspiring, etc.?
- How easy is it for people to 'drill down' through the corporate memory and to access and link data?
- How is new information added?
- How are raw facts and figures and meeting reports turned into insights?

Then, there are issues of discipline and control. Organizations exist to focus and coordinate the actions of their members and to seek synergies. People cannot just be left to 'do their own thing'. Information provides the glue that unites them in pursuit of a common purpose. So here are some more questions:

- What are the 'rules' that guide behaviour?
- How are results measured?
- What feedback mechanisms exist?
- What rewards and sanctions apply?

The answers tell you about your organization's health and its prospects. The metaphor of work as conversation suggests that most companies need radically different ways of shaping strategy and of turning it into action. Thanks to IT, you have infinite possibilities for doing both in ways that no one has thought of.

In the cut-and-thrust of daily work life, some things need to be said while others may go without saying. Some of your organization's progress will come through explicit learning, some through tacit learning.[10] The value of your company tomorrow depends entirely on how you capture, use, and store information today. The results you get hinge on the conversations you hold, and the way you hold them.

Knowledge multiplies and becomes more valuable with use. As Schrage points out, new information technologies force people to define where and how they add value. When you 'go digital', you need to know where information must flow and how it'll be used. This demands that you think about your value delivery system as never before. Your information needs must be dictated by your customers and people, not by the latest technology on offer.

Geoff Mulgan, director of a London-based think-tank called Demos, terms human interdependence 'connexity' – a wonderful word for our age! In his book by that title he writes:

> *A society in which people lead good lives is likely to be one where there is high mutual understanding, where people automatically pick up signals and nuances, where they understand how another person relates to a third.*[11]

Strategy is made and implemented by human beings. It works when they work well together, and it fails when they don't. Collaboration is vital. Connexity is the key. Technology just offers a smart new set of tools for leveraging human talent and skill.

The way things really are

Concepts like reengineering have great appeal because they sound so logical and systematic. Numbers matter. Machines have a key role in business. But when all is said and done, competitiveness depends on people. So as you consider ways to shape up, keep in mind what you have to work with.

Begin with a view from Thomas Moore, a psychotherapist. He should be required reading for strategists. In his book *Care of the Soul*, he writes:

> *Today professionals are preoccupied with the 'dysfunctional family'. But to some extent all families are dysfunctional. No family is perfect, and most have serious problems. A family is a microcosm, reflecting the nature of the world, which runs on both virtue and evil. We may be tempted at times to imagine the family as full of innocence and good will, but actual family life resists such romanticism. Usually it presents the full range of human potential, including evil, hatred, violence, sexual confusion, and insanity. In other words, the dynamics of actual family life reveal the soul's complexity and unpredictability, and any attempt to place a veil of simplistic sentimentality over the family image will break down.*[12]

Companies, like families, are complex and unpredictable. They disappoint us when we try to place a 'veil of simplistic sentimentality' over them. The people within them act in strange and often toxic ways. Individuals may be lazy, devious, and dishonest. Many revel in playing politics. Teamwork is a wonderful idea, but despite the huge efforts and investments that organizations have made to foster it over many decades, it remains problematic. And teams remain fragile; they come apart for the slightest reason.

It would be great if every worker were positive, dedicated, and honest, and better still if they all pulled together in the same direction. But real life is not that simple.

Individuals have their own agendas. Different things motivate them. And today, the best of them have many choices.

Ideally, you should only employ people who have lots of job options. They probably have talent, and the fact that they choose to work with you counts for a lot. They're *volunteers* and are likely to deliver far more than mere 'conscripts'.

In most firms you don't have the luxury of 'zero-basing' your workforce. You have to build on what you've got. But for all the flaws you may see in your present team, there's probably a positive side to it that you haven't seen. In the appropriate context, even the most ordinary people can reach extraordinary heights.

Successful strategy depends on your ability to tap the imagination and spirit of every person in your team. That, in turn, requires that you make your dysfunctional organization as functional as possible.

There is no perfection. There is no 'right way'. Business is a messy activity. The best you can do is set out with a clear purpose to try lots of things.

It's tempting to separate hard questions of strategy from soft issues of spirit. And of course, conventional wisdom does – so *planning* is seen as one task, *implementation* as another. Often, they're given to different people.

In fact, imagining the future and making it happen are two sides of the same coin. Purpose and process are equally important.

When you accept this and begin to manage both, you'll see a surprising change in both attitudes and performance in your organization. People will do the right things to the highest standards. Ideas will come from the most unexpected quarters. And your most ambitious goals will become ones that can be realized.

The human resource

Radical strategy is not invented by people with a 'more of the same' mindset. Nor does strategy drive itself. The best strategy in the world won't be effective if spirited people do not make it happen.

As in judo, balance is vital in business. Enthusiasm can often compensate for a shaky strategy; but doing the wrong things with great energy simply takes you down the wrong track faster. A workaholic culture kills people and companies when it has no purpose; dabbling half-heartedly at breakthrough ideas is equally useless.

The need to manage both strategy and spirit, and for balance between them, is illustrated in the following matrix (Figure iii). I would argue that this is the most important business model you'll ever see!

- **'NO-HOPERs'** are business basket cases. These companies – and people – go nowhere slowly.
- **'NERDs'** are rocket scientists. They use every available tool, from consultants to computers, to shape and sharpen their strategies. But they're thinkers, not doers. All brain, no brawn. Or to put it more bluntly, they're wimps!

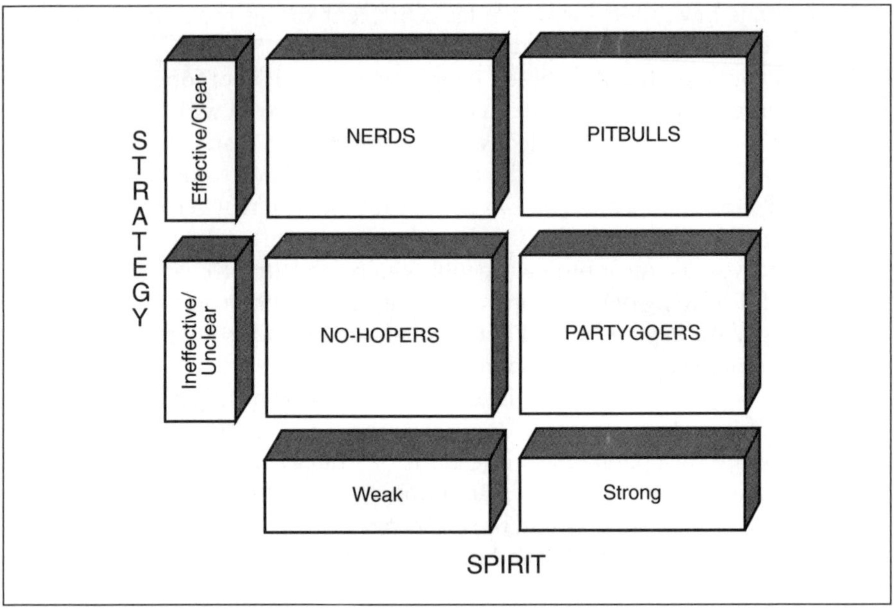

Figure iii: *Strategy and spirit*

- **'PARTYGOERs'** have more energy than they can use, so they use it frantically. They flap around without a clear goal, seizing a challenge here, fighting a fire there. Busy, busy, busy! What happened yesterday? 'I don't know, but hell, I was busy.' What's going on right now? 'I can't talk; I'm too busy.' What's next? 'I haven't thought about it; I'm too busy.'

- **'PITBULLs'** are 100 per cent sure of their direction and 100 per cent committed to getting there: 'There's the intruder; kill the bastard!' No ambiguity at all. Great strategy, underpinned by great spirit.

  Of course, the analogy is not quite right, because dogs of this breed are not known for their brains, and might conjure up notions of inflexibility or of a brutal, 'rip the flesh off the enemy' mindset. But I chose it because of its symbolic impact. It makes the point.

  When I use the idea in workshops, people instantly get the message that a winning company needs both strategy and spirit; they quickly start talking about becoming 'the pitbulls of our industry'.

  Some teams have gone so far as to create T-shirts and other items linking their own company name and slogans to a picture of a vicious dog. One CEO regularly asks his colleagues: 'Are we acting like pitbulls? Is our strategy still clear – and right? How's the spirit among our people?'

On the one hand, you're most likely to arrive at an effective strategy if your people really want it to happen, if they're well informed and voluntarily apply their intellect to the task. (*So spirit drives strategy.*)

On the other hand, you can only implement your strategy with the support of your people. The energy level in your organization rises in direct proportion to their sense of purpose, involvement, respect, and power. (*So strategy ignites the spirit.*)

Check your strategic capability

Following are some key attributes of highly competitive companies. Rate your company on a scale of 1 to 10 (1 being poor, 10 being excellent) on each of them. Identify *one* attribute which is a special strength in your company. Describe how it came to be, why it makes a difference, and how you can build on it.

STRATEGIC CAPABILITY CHECK

1.	Common purpose	1 2 3 4 5 6 7 8 9 10
2.	Customer focus	1 2 3 4 5 6 7 8 9 10
3.	High energy level (spirit)	1 2 3 4 5 6 7 8 9 10
4.	Clear philosophies	1 2 3 4 5 6 7 8 9 10
5.	Consistent messages	1 2 3 4 5 6 7 8 9 10
6.	Comfortable with ambiguity	1 2 3 4 5 6 7 8 9 10
7.	Involvement/empowerment	1 2 3 4 5 6 7 8 9 10
8.	Teamwork	1 2 3 4 5 6 7 8 9 10
9.	Alertness to opportunities	1 2 3 4 5 6 7 8 9 10
10.	Symbiotic partnerships	1 2 3 4 5 6 7 8 9 10
11.	Curiosity/learning	1 2 3 4 5 6 7 8 9 10
12.	Innovation	1 2 3 4 5 6 7 8 9 10
13.	Speed/agility/flexibility	1 2 3 4 5 6 7 8 9 10
14.	Ability to execute plans	1 2 3 4 5 6 7 8 9 10
15.	Effectiveness in leveraging strengths	1 2 3 4 5 6 7 8 9 10
16.	Lean processes	1 2 3 4 5 6 7 8 9 10
17.	Performance measures/incentives	1 2 3 4 5 6 7 8 9 10
18.	Rapid feedback of results	1 2 3 4 5 6 7 8 9 10
19.	Effective, user-friendly systems	1 2 3 4 5 6 7 8 9 10
20.	Availability of resources	1 2 3 4 5 6 7 8 9 10

TOTAL SCORE (POSSIBLE 200 POINTS) ____________

Note that most of these factors involve soft rather than hard issues. There's a simple reason: in the Information Age, corporate performance hinges increasingly on skills and knowledge, and on cultural traits like attitudes, ambition, energy, commitment, and perseverance. You can have the finest buildings and equipment in the world, but without these 'invisible assets', they're worthless.

Strategy is change management

Managing change is a hot topic. But while managers talk of strategies for change, few think of strategy *as* change.

But what else is it? Why does your company need a strategy, except to chart its course into a choppy future? If tomorrow is different – and it will be – can you survive by doing more of what got you this far?

Change is implicit in strategic management. Planning, power, and process are inter-twined. Problems arise when you try to separate them, when you try to allocate neat chunks to different people.

There are four steps to managing change effectively (Figure iv):

Step 1: Create dissatisfaction with the status quo.
Step 2: Debate possible futures.
Step 3: Act to learn.
Step 4: Review and revise.

Step 1 shakes the organization free from the past. Until this happens, no progress is possible. People won't let go and do things differently, or do different things, without compelling rational and emotional reasons to do so. Involving them in scanning the environment is a powerful way to begin. Bob Pike, an American training expert, taught me, 'People always believe their own data.' When you ask for their views, they'll usually conclude that 'more of the same' is not an option.

Step 2 gets them thinking about the future. When they collaborate in shaping your company's purpose, buy-in is almost automatic. It's 'their' purpose; you don't have to sell it.

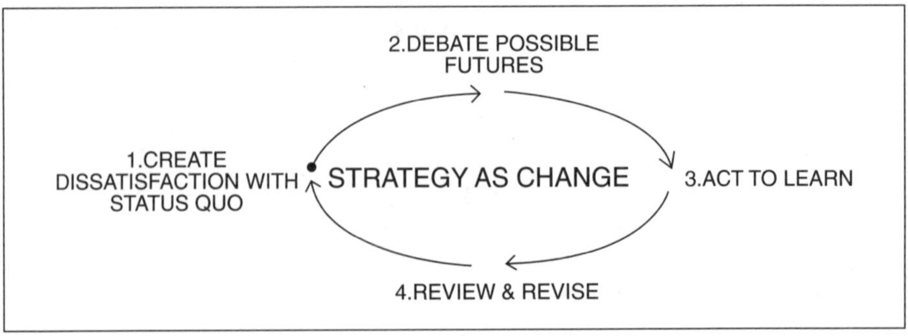

Figure iv: *The cycle of change*

Step 3 turns purpose into action. When people do, they learn. When they act, they discover what's possible, and theory becomes reality. Inevitably, they find they can achieve much more than they thought. They raise their own 'bar of excellence'.

Step 4 asks: Where are we now? What did we learn? What else can we do? This reflection almost always creates more dissatisfaction with the status quo. The process fuels itself.

Understanding strategy as change forces you to take it out of the executive suite and make it a company-wide activity. It lets you integrate many activities that would otherwise be tackled separately, sequentially – and fruitlessly. Most important of all, it keeps you focused on moving ahead, on acting out the future.

Most managers still see planning and implementation as separate activities. First they plan, then they act. And they're surprised when things don't pan out as expected, or take a long time to get moving.

But it's obvious why problems crop up.

Strategic debates are seldom simple affairs. Information and ideas fly around. Arguments go back and forth. Positions are taken and tested. Side issues are raised. 'Trial balloons' are flown. From a complex mix of facts and feelings, a rich tapestry is woven and hopefully a central theme emerges.

Then it's back to the office to sell a one-liner to the troops!

What follows is perfectly predictable. When the boss announces the new plan, they nod (usually because it's damned dangerous not to!) then get back to business as usual.

These 'outsiders' haven't heard all the nuances of the debate. They haven't seen the body language, felt the passion, or smelled the fear. They get the orders, but not the context. Their own mental models are incomplete.

They are required to act with speed and dedication, and though the *what* and the *how* may be clear, the *why* isn't.

The culture trap

Let's get one thing straight right now. No matter how poorly you might have scored, I'm not about to suggest that you start fixing things by trying to change your organization's culture. That's usually the first line of attack – and almost always the wrong one.

Clearly, culture is a cause of the results you get. But it's also a consequence of how you act (Figure v).

Corporate change agents promote the idea that you have to change culture to change results. But psychologists have known for over 100 years that the way to change a person is to change what they do; what they think and feel will follow.

Alcoholics Anonymous helps people stop drinking by encouraging them to drink less day after day – not by lecturing them on the negative effects of drink-

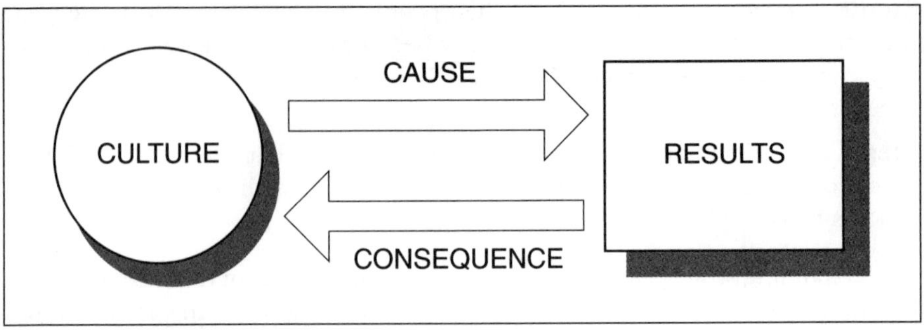

Figure v: *Culture as cause and consequence*

ing. The surest way to fix a fear of heights is by flying, rock climbing, or venturing up tall buildings. If you're nervous about public speaking, you have to make speeches to gain confidence.

Executives would profit by taking note.

Starting right now, your focus should be on *managing key elements of your corporate conversation: your business purpose, the few goals and actions that will get you there, the need for rapid and radical change, and what you learn at each step*. If your current culture is healthy, you'll make it healthier. If it's not, this is the surest way to bring about the results you want.

Expect the best, prepare for the worst

To be worth anything, a strategy must be robust. It must stand up to the rigours of the real world. So if you're responsible for strategy you must test and torture your thinking, challenge your most deeply-held assumptions, and be prepared to change direction when it's clear you're on the wrong course.

And you must do this over and over again, because comfort creeps up and smothers us all too easily.

Complacency kills. No manager in his right mind goes looking for trouble. The best managers keep scanning the environment, keep asking 'what if?' and keep stirring things up.

It's easy to be successful in good times. But to do keep doing well when the going gets rough is beyond many executives.

One reason is that they're surprised by economic downturns or competitor tactics. They miss the signs, ignore them, or deny them.

A second reason is that their strategies simply aren't robust enough. The assumptions they're based on may not be sound. Critical decisions are badly conceived and, when the going gets rough the wheels fall off. Exogenous shocks cause people to lose their focus, stab at problems that seem to most urgent, and defend the status quo rather than pursue innovation and growth.

All indications are that South African executives can plan for better times ahead. The shackles that bound this economy have largely been removed. Cut free of apartheid, we can attack new markets, attract new partners, and access the finance, information, and technologies we so badly need.

But wise managers will expect stiffer competition, sudden shifts in customer demand, outbreaks of violence, currency shocks, interest rate and inflation swings, political surprises, legislative hassles, and more.

They'll plan for *change*, not for *continuity*.

They'll look forward to the future, but prepare at the same time for the obstacles they're sure to hit along the way.

Planning vs. strategy

Ironically, the value of strategic planning is being questioned at a time when strategy is more important than ever. But where *plans* used to be the goal, what counts today is the *ability to think and act strategically*.

Imagine that you are about to embark on a trip down a stretch of dangerous river. Ask yourself what you'd prefer on your boat: a detailed map of the rapids, rocks, and waterfalls plus a precise plan for getting through the treacherous waters; or a team of resourceful, responsive people whom you can rely on to do the right thing at the right time?

Say you opt for the plan. You study it carefully until you know every twist and turn and obstacle in the water. You work out every move in advance. You hit the water confident that if you act out your script, you'll get through alive.

But what if the water level has dropped since your map was made? What if rocks are exposed, making the rapids more dangerous? What if whirlpools now churn the surface? Can you stick to your plan and survive? Of course not. You know where you want to go, but you're going to have to make up the 'how' on the spur of the moment.

Nor are you helped by the fact that you're surprised, drenched, and terrified after the first bend. Or that your team is thrown into confusion when members discover that the plan isn't playing out as it was supposed to.

Tom Peters, that most astute observer of corporate behaviour, tells his seminar delegates that 'the winners just try a lot of stuff'.

Architect Buckminster Fuller ascribed his success to a simple approach: 'I just invent, then I wait until man comes around to needing what I invented.'[13]

When Chrysler's product development team was working frantically on the Neon subcompact, no one was sure how things would go. 'With the exception of having faith that we would find a way,' says Robert Marcell, head of the company's small car team, 'we really didn't know how we were going to get there.'[14]

A successful entrepreneur told me: 'I just put my head down and go for it. I'm not interested in what "might" happen in the future. I can't wait that long. I don't even read a newspaper, because they just tell you the bad news, why you shouldn't do anything.'

This kind of unstructured, entrepreneurial approach works more often than strategy theorists admit. But that doesn't mean you should abandon planning.

No organization's future can be left in the hands of people who only have gut feel to guide them. It wouldn't be sensible to tell a meeting of investment analysts, 'We have no idea where we're going, but it should be okay.' More is needed. Strategy makes the future a matter of choice, not chance.

Some companies need detailed plans. Some circumstances demand them. You can't sink a mineshaft on a whim; nor can you build a new factory, launch a new car, or restructure a company of any size without careful thought.

But it's not always necessary to write down a plan. Nor is it a good idea to try and steer any organization by micro-management. One reason is that things change. Another is that you cannot anticipate every contingency. And third – and perhaps most important – you'll drive your people crazy.

In my experience, most fat strategic plans are a huge waste of time and money. More goes into these documents than comes out of them. This happens because the process is flawed, managers use the wrong concepts, or they can't turn intentions into action.

Organizations exist to leverage the magic of their people. Strategy should facilitate this process, not impede it. The *way you make strategy* is as important as the *strategy you make*.

Fortunately, there's one 'lever' that can make a dramatic difference. It's called *strategic conversation*, and it's without doubt the most powerful management tool available. When you use it well, many things are possible. When you don't, too much seems impossible.

Strategic conversation guides and inspires people to high purpose. It also grows them as a resource. It is the missing link in what we know about managing knowledge work.

Are leaders listening?

Late in 1997, *Fortune* brought together 50 European CEOs to share ideas on how they were coping with change. In a report afterwards, two comments appeared on one page in the magazine, suggesting two ways of dealing with the future.[15] Which one do you think makes most sense?

> *So how do you get executives from 128 countries to work together? If you're Göran Lindahl, CEO of ABB Asea Brown Boveri, you put them through a vigorous diversity programme aimed at airing their prejudices.*

> *ABB's former CEO Percy Barnevik used to say, 'I'm in the business of showing overheads.' That's because he used to spend 250 days a year presenting his vision of the company to its far-flung employees.*

My guess is that most South African executives would grab the first one. After all, don't we have the mother of all diversity problems?

And look around right now. Teams from many companies are bungee jumping off the Victoria Falls bridge, shooting rapids on the Tugela River, climbing poles, clambering over rocks, building rafts, and letting their inner-most feelings hang out in 'value-sharing' sessions.

Team-building is a growth industry. Companies spend fortunes on it.

But while all that activity is going on, *where are the leaders with their overhead slides?*

When – and that's a big if, not a given – those teams have bonded, where are they supposed to go? Do they know? Are they inspired by that purpose?

Do they know 'what counts around here'? Do they know what's expected of them?

If you say they're empowered, do they know what that means? Do they know what's not negotiable?

If I were abseiling off a cliff, I'd want the biggest, strongest person holding the rope – not the smartest or the one I liked best. If I were sent on a survival course, I'd want people who could catch food. And as to sharing values, that must surely rank way behind knowing the details of my company's strategy.

Teams fail, not because the people in them don't get on, but because *they don't have a common understanding of their context or a common purpose.* Percy Barnevik understands this. While he was hands-on at ABB (he was appointed chairman in 1996, and now heads Investor, another Swedish company and a major shareholder in ABB) he never stopped preaching the corporate gospel. He knew that time on the road was more important than time in the office; that he had to be the company's No.1 message carrier.

Noel Tichy, a professor at the University of Michigan Business School, says that the best leaders reduce their business concepts to a 'teachable idea'. And of course, they are themselves committed teachers.

Here, for example, is General Electric chairman Jack Welch at work:

> *Jack Welch ... is one of the most dedicated teachers I know. For fifteen years he has made biweekly visits to GE's Crotonville executive training centre to enter into dialogue with thousands of his employees each year. His schedule is also filled with hundreds of video conferences, meetings, factory visits and workshop sessions. For Welch, every organizational process from strategic reviews to budget meetings to the annual general managers meeting are teaching and learning events.*[16]

Steve Miller, group managing director of Royal Dutch/Shell, says, 'Everything we do is a teaching opportunity.' Since 1997, he has spent more than half his time working with grassroots employees to transform the organization.[17]

In the same way, other admired leaders are relentless communicators. They know the value of the strategic conversation. They take personal responsibility for spreading their gospel.

How do South African executives rate against these fanatical travellers and teachers? Is their time spent on the right things?

In my experience, most don't rate at all. Most think they can drive their companies from behind a desk. To see them in a classroom is unusual, to say the least. Their time is spent on the high-level stuff: doing deals, networking with their peers, poring over the numbers.

A quick sum tells you there are about 220 working days in a year. That Barnevik spent more time than that travelling and talking tells you about the value he attaches to aligning his people behind a clear purpose. South African leaders who argue, 'I'm too busy for that', should think long and hard about their real responsibilities.

When they stay home and juggle their to-do lists, they waste an invaluable resource: themselves. They ensure that their people won't be aligned behind a common goal and won't develop as fast as they might; that empowerment remains no more than a good intention, and that their firms won't be as responsive or as innovative as they need to be.

The leader's priorities shape the organization's priorities. When the boss's focus is wrong, everyone else's will be too.

New thinking for a new time

Managing a company is a serious and difficult business. Every day brings new challenges. Threats lurk around every corner. While long-term planning is essential, short-term, immediate action is also needed. And while it makes sense to think about key issues in an orderly, structured – perhaps sequential – way, you also need to think 'out of the box' to gain a meaningful lead over agile competitors.

Here are three areas in which new thinking is needed:

First, managers need to understand that imagination and the human spirit are the two most important competitive weapons. This means that they need new kinds of people and they need to manage them in new ways. That, in turn, demands fresh ideas about organizational structure, information technology, incentives, and so on.

Then, they need new ways to think about strategy. Every executive worth her salt 'knows' the formulas for gaining competitive advantage. But are they sound? Are there other ways to win? If so, what are they? And how do you put them into action?

Managers also need what Peter Drucker calls a 'theory of business' to help them make difficult decisions.[18] Without one, they'll get sucked into a vicious cycle of self-defeating debate. Self-doubt will kill decisiveness. Second-guessing themselves will become a deadly drag on their performance. Like a buck caught in a hunter's light, they'll stopped in their tracks.

- They need a clear sense of what's happening in their environment.
- They need a clear sense of purpose.
- They need a clear sense of what causes business success.

The world is hard to understand. Pressures, problems, and possibilities come at us from all directions. The role of business in society is under the microscope. An endless stream of management fads is terribly confusing.

The only way to deal with all these matters is to hold your assumptions to the light, and to question them ruthlessly. To ask 'why' before you ask 'how'. To let go of what you know and to embark on a journey of discovery. To have the courage to think new thoughts, to go to new places, and to do new things. In short, you need to question your past, understand your present, and imagine your future (Figure vi).

'The reasonable man,' said Bernard Shaw, 'adapts himself to the world; the unreasonable one persists in trying to adapt the world to himself. Therefore all progress depends on the unreasonable man.'

Charles Handy calls this 'the age of unreason'. Seen through new eyes, it becomes an age of infinite opportunity.

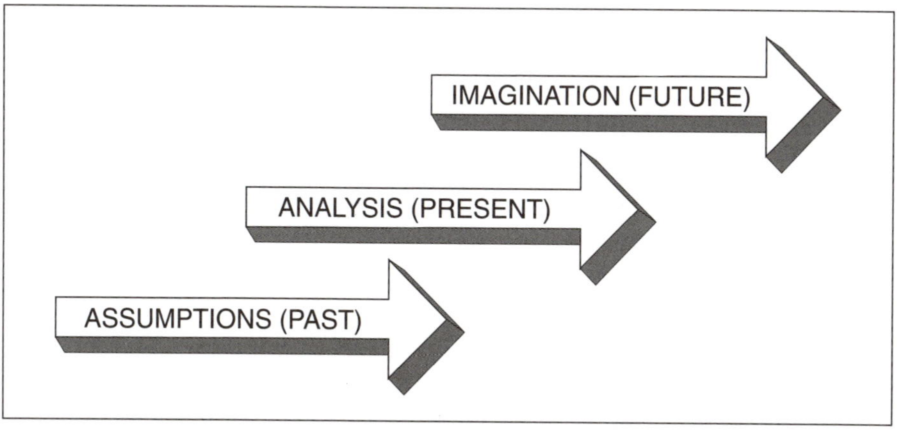

Figure vi: *Thinking about radical strategy*

Six basic questions

It's easy and tempting to make a meal of strategy. Any planning process can be drawn out and over-complicated. There are many places to start and even more ways in which to progress.

But when you get down to it, every strategist in every company must answer the same basic questions:

1. What's happening outside – problem or opportunity?
2. What can we do inside (innovation) to exploit the change?
3. Whom do we serve, and how should we do it?
4. What resources do we need, and how can we get them?
5. Which stakeholders affect our performance, and how can we win with them?
6. How will we pull it all together?

Answer these questions, and you have the makings of an effective strategy. Skip them or fail to think through them carefully, and you're sure to lose out.

These six questions deserve constant attention. Things change, so today's best answers quickly turn out to be wrong.

Focused messages

Think of strategy making as communication. Think of the topics you need to cover for the process to have value. Here's a 'map' (Figure vii):

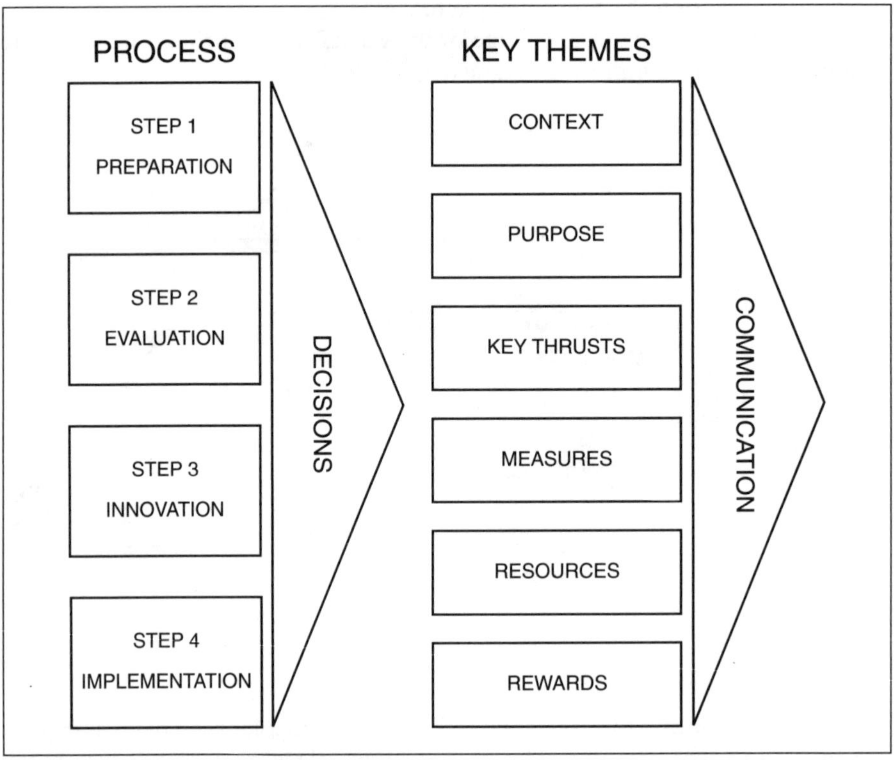

Figure vii: *Decisions and messages*

The process has four steps:

Step 1: **Preparation.** Define what you expect to achieve. Agree who'll be involved and how. Decide what information you need, and collect it.

Step 2: **Evaluation.** Analyze your environment. Gather and interpret customer and competitor information. Develop key assumptions about what lies ahead.

Step 3: **Innovation.** Seek breakthrough ideas. Decide which few will get your attention and resources.

Step 4: **Implementation.** The action stage. Get out there and experiment.

Each of these steps leads to certain decisions. Those, in turn, suggest a set of key themes – or core messages – which you need to communicate both inside and outside your organization:

- **Context.** What's happening in your world. What it's likely to look like in the future. Problems and possibilities.
- **Purpose.** Why your organization exists, and what you aim to do.
- **Key thrusts.** The few actions that will get you where you want to go.
- **Measures.** How you will check your performance.
- **Resources.** What you need to succeed.
- **Rewards.** What's in it for everyone who counts.

All the information-gathering and decision-making that goes into strategy has one purpose: to tell your team what to do, what to become obsessed about, what to focus on like a laser.

Begin with the view that strategy making is essentially about communication, and you will dramatically simplify – and clarify – how you go about it from now on. Many issues that may not have made sense suddenly do. And best of all, your to-do list gets shorter.

The two most important words

The two most important words in business are 'critical mass'. They're well-known and widely used, but their importance is constantly ignored. They make all the difference between winning and losing. If more executives remembered this, more firms would be more successful and fewer would get into trouble. Here's why:

- For every individual some opportunities in life matter more than others. One person wants to be a golfer; another likes gardening; a third wants to build a dental practice or climb Kilamanjaro. You can't be good at everything. Faced with a range of opportunities, you have to choose. Some of your goals will rank higher than others. You have to decide where your critical mass of opportunity lies.
- Your goals must matter. They must offer a critical mass of some kind of reward: a feeling of achievement, income, a step towards a larger goal. If what you get back is not significant enough, reaching for it will be pointless.
- No matter how important a particular result might be, the fact is that if you don't go for it with enough resources – money, thought, effort, or whatever – you'll fail. There has to be a critical mass of input to get a critical mass of output.

These facts hold true for study, sport, hobbies, social relationships – and business. There are no short-cuts. Peak performance does not come through taking occasional stabs at a project. Skimping and winning don't fit together.

Companies survive and grow when they capture and keep a critical mass of customers. This, in turn, requires that they apply a critical mass of money, imagination, energy – or whatever other resource – to their goal. Without enough resources or customers, failure is certain.

Choosing the best opportunity for your firm is an entrepreneurial decision. It requires insight and imagination. It also demands hard choices and serious commitment. Your aim must be to:

- Identify those opportunities that offer a critical mass of returns (money, learning, reputation).
- Focus a critical mass of resources at them (skills, time, energy, imagination, money).
- Build momentum fast, to own a critical mass of stakeholder 'votes' (customers, distributors, suppliers, developers of related products and services).
- Develop and sustain a critical mass of the assets and capabilities that will lock in customers and ensure a long-term relationship with them (knowledge, processes, reputation).

These are not merely good ideas; they are inviolable principles. Defy them, and your chances of success plunge.

But look around, and see how many companies are doing something else. Little wonder that so many fail so fast. They may be successful now, but they won't last.

Strategic thinking should be both logical and creative. Yet a lot of what passes for it is quite the opposite.

From the inevitable to the irrational

Often, at the start of a strategy workshop, I can see where the process should lead. No matter how creative the participants get, and no matter how widely the debate ranges, it's quickly apparent that a handful of issues demand attention.

The first task of the strategist is to see what is inevitable for his business.

This sounds odd, given the need to stand out from the crowd and the infinite number of ways you might do it. But while it's a fact that any business must do *many* things to survive and grow, there are always a *few* things that make the big difference.

Get the basics right and everything else more or less falls into place. Manage the big issues and the small ones manage themselves.

Coca-Cola understands this, hence its focus on 'acceptability, availability, affordability'.

McDonald's understands it, so the key words in the world's biggest fast food company are Quality, Service, Cleanliness, and Value.

Woolworths talks 'simplicity of display, operational efficiency, and retail theatre'.

Many companies have yet to learn this vital lesson. They waste time and money trying to develop needlessly complex strategies. They overlook what's really important, and try to finesse their way into the future. They should spend more time asking:

> 'Who are the few customers that will give us the best returns?'
> 'What are the few things that matter to those customers?'
> 'What few things must we do that will make the biggest difference to them?'
> 'Which few people in our firm make the most impact?'
> 'Which few projects will give us the biggest payoff tomorrow?'
> 'Where are the leverage points in our organization?'

What it all comes down to, of course, is making the famous 80/20 rule – the Pareto principle – work for you. Something we all know but consistently and even persistently ignore. Even as the idea of core competence grows in popularity, companies stay firmly in 'spray and pray' mode!

But getting the basics right isn't enough. It doesn't take forever for smart competitors to see and master them. So the next task of the strategist is to define what everyone knows to be irrational, and to start doing some 'dumb' things (Figure viii).

INEVITABLE ⟵⟶ IRRATIONAL

Figure viii: *Inevitable + irrational = radical*

- Richard Branson did this by creating Upper Class on Virgin Atlantic Airways (First Class service at Business Class fares), and offering to drive passengers between the airport and their homes or offices.
- Bell Equipment teaches mechanics to pilot helicopters, so they can reach broken machines fast and cut customers' downtime costs.
- Amazon.com reinvented bookselling by offering a choice of 2,5 million books via the Internet, many at discounts of 40 per cent.
- Facts & Fiction has coffee bars in its stores where book lovers can read in comfort. (Not long ago, bookshops used to seal many books in cellophane, in case customers soiled them!)
- In a well-developed market for deep-fried chicken, Nando's got hot with its flame-grilled birds and peri-peri sauces.
- Though Levi's focuses on the mass market, it offers custom-fitted denim jeans through its 'Personal Pair' stores.
- Hyundai sells cars over weekends and services them at night.
- When Microsoft launched its Internet Explorer browser, the only way to get it was *free* off the Internet; here was one of the biggest new product releases of all time, and you couldn't go into a store and buy the product!

Your goal should be to have your competitors wake up every day sweating and swearing. You know you've got it right when they say things like:

'Holy smoke!'
'Damn!'
'They're not supposed to do that!'
'Don't they know how stupid that is?'
'They just don't understand ...'
'Bastards!'
'They'll destroy the industry!'
'Not fair!'
'What on earth is going on?'
'What the hell can we do?'
'Why didn't we think of that?'

When they call the Competition Board, or call you to 'talk reasonably about this', you know you're on the right track. Radical strategy is surprising, unpredictable, risky, absurd – and ultimately very expensive – to anyone on the receiving end.

But that is exactly its point.

Take charge!

As human beings, most of us are where we are in our lives more by accident than design. Sure, we might set out with great ambitions and good intentions. But most of us get dragged off course by unexpected events and by people with other agendas.

The world is full of managers who are frustrated surgeons or actors. We imagine climbing Kilimanjaro, but settle for a stroll around the block. We dream of living in a big house near the ocean, but wind up in a city apartment. We see ourselves married to a gorgeous soul mate, but family pressures see us stuck with an ugly slob we can't talk to.

Companies too, get jerked around. Without a clear sense of purpose and the will to stay their course, every problem has the potential to stop them in their tracks; every opportunity becomes the priority.

Company behaviour is a product of both design and accident. If you look back through an organization's history, it's often hard to tell how or why a particular course was chosen. Sometimes success or failure results from a single, clear decision: more often, a host of factors made it happen.

As I've pointed out, you can't decide every move in advance. And as I'll show, luck is as crucial a factor in the success of companies as of individuals. Strategy and serendipity both play a part.

But you're most likely to get where you want to go when you act as a result of *choice*, not *chance*. And chance comes to those who are prepared. Luck hits those who step into its path.

Most organizations would do better if they set out to do things *deliberately* rather than by *default* (Figure ix). They would target and chase the most profitable customers. They would focus their R&D spend in areas with the greatest potential. They would avoid accidents and environmental pollution. They would build sound community relationships ahead of the need to have society on their side.

The strategy process helps you identify the deliberate actions that will help you reach your organization's potential. It should also equip your team to respond deliberately to events.

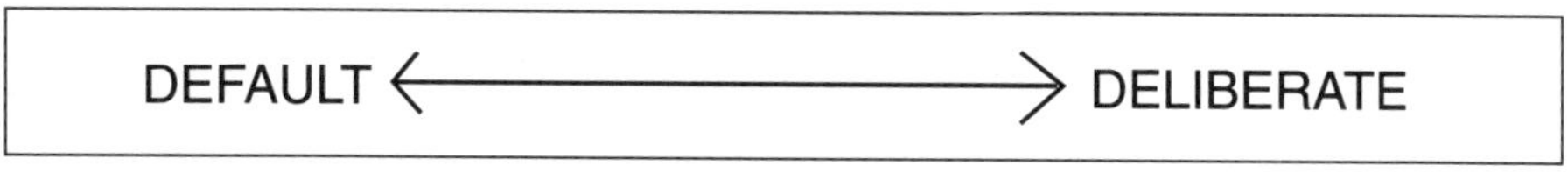

Figure ix: *Avoid default results, aim for deliberate choices*

Assumptions about strategy

Like any thinking tool, every business model is based on specific assumptions. When you evaluate a new concept or framework, it's important to know what its underlying assumptions are. Many management fads sound plausible but make no sense. A lot of the 'solutions' that managers so eagerly try to use are based on flawed thinking or conditions that no longer prevail. If you want to compare concepts, you need to know what assumptions they are based on.

So here are my assumptions about strategy. Each one leads to a logical conclusion.

Assumption No. 1: Strategy must prepare an organization to deal with an uncertain future.

Assumption No. 2: Strategy is change – a process, not a plan.

Assumption No. 3: The First Principles of Business Competition are mandatory.

Assumption No. 4: Imagination and the human spirit drive performance.

Assumption No. 5: Synthesis is the most important competitive skill.

Assumption No. 6: What's talked about is measured ... what's measured is managed.

Assumption No. 1: Strategy must prepare an organization to deal with an uncertain future. It must change the organization's mind and its behaviour. Most importantly, it must change people's underlying assumptions – the real drivers of performance.

Conclusion: To be effective, organizations must constantly change both how they think and what they do. Practice and performance must occur concurrently. The surest way to bring about change is to change what people *talk* about – in other words, the corporate conversation. This requires that you encourage new information flows.

New information must be allowed into the organization – and be shared internally – and old information must be let go. People must learn to question, to challenge, and to argue constructively. If changing assumptions is the goal, 'robust' conversation must be the rule. This is what 'organizational learning' is about.

Assumption No. 2: Strategy is change – a process, not a plan. Every organization must change constantly to meet changing circumstances. For change to happen, a critical mass of people must support it.

Conclusion: Strategy is an ongoing process – a way of corporate life – in which people from across the organization are involved in dialogue about their purpose, their future goals, their performance, and their learning. This conversation leads them to:

- Confront the realities of their environment and their current performance.
- Think creatively about possibilities.
- Test their potential through action.
- Reflect on – and learn from – their progress, thus renewing themselves and building the capacity to keep progressing.

Assumption No. 3: The First Principles of Hostile Competition are mandatory. Whereas almost every concept of strategy is optional, and may be used or not, depending on the whim of managers, these three rules are iron-clad and apply across organizations and industries:

1. If you don't make a difference, you don't matter.
2. You can't make a difference to everyone.
3. You have to keep changing and improving.

Conclusion: To be effective, an organization must aim a critical mass of resources at a critical mass of opportunity (customers). Then it must rapidly reinvent the value/cost proposition. The focus decision is a tough entrepreneurial choice and is probably best made at a high level. Value and costs must be managed at all levels of the organization.

Assumption No. 4: Imagination and the human spirit drive performance. Since every competitor can understand the First Principles – and is likely to apply them – it's the way they're executed that makes the difference. Ideas give you a head start but action gets you to the winning post.

Conclusion: Strategy and spirit – idea and action – are two sides of the same coin. Good ideas and powerful insights can come from many places in an organization. Involving people in 'high-level' conversations about strategy takes them from *feeling* important to *being* important. It not only taps their knowledge, experience, and imagination, it also helps them understand the context in which they work: what must be done, and why.

Assumption No. 5: Synthesis is the most important competitive skill. Organizations must sense challenges and opportunities, source whatever they need to perform, serve customers, and foster symbiotic relationships with a portfolio of stakeholders. But it's the synthesis of these activities that leads to advantage. The ability to 'pull it all together' makes the difference outside in the marketplace.

Conclusion: Organizations must pay more attention to communication, coordination, collaboration, and to community. And the key to all of these lies in *conversation* – in what people talk about and how they do it. To manage the corporate conversation is to manage information flows. A fast, open, and 'robust' exchange of information and ideas must be the goal.

Assumption No. 6: What's talked about is measured ... what's measured is managed. An organization's conversation determines what it will focus on, how it will act, and thus what it will achieve.

Conclusion: Conversation provides a context in which people work. Much depends on whether it is nourishing or toxic. Conversation affects the trust level in your organization. This, in turn, determines how readily people share information and ideas, how they help each other, and how committed they are to your strategic goals. Corporate conversation is too often left to chance. By managing it, you can gain an enormous competitive advantage.

Conversation is a human process, but it may be greatly aided by technology. Every business process must be considered from both a human and a technological point of view. By defining your organization's key themes – the few most critical messages that people must hear – you concentrate attention where it will make the most difference.

If you accept these assumptions and conclusions, why not test your strategizing practices against them? If you have other assumptions, what are they – and can you justify them? Do you have well-considered reasons for pursuing the path you're on? Do you know why you use your current thinking tools?

Endnotes

1. Christopher A. Bartlett and Sumantra Ghoshal, 'Changing the role of top management: beyond strategy to purpose', *Harvard Business Review*, November–December 1994.
2. David J. Collis and Cynthia A. Montgomery, 'Competing on resources: strategy in the 1990s', *Harvard Business Review*, July–August, 1995.
3. Chris Argyris, *Strategy, Change, and Defensive Routines*, New York: Pitman, 1985.
4. Joel Kurtzman, 'An Interview with Chris Argyris', *Strategy & Business*, Issue No.10, First Quarter, 1998.
5. Thomas A. Stewart, *Intellectual Capital*, London: Nicholas Brealey Publishing, 1997.
6. Michael Schrage, 'The relationship revolution', Merrill Lynch Forum, 1997.
7. Robin Cooper, *When Lean Enterprises Collide*, Boston: Harvard Business School Press, 1995.
8. Robert B. Reich, *The Work Of Nations*, New York: Alfred A. Knopf, 1991.

9. This term was coined at PeopleSoft, a leading producer of enterprise resource planning software. See Paul Roberts, 'We are one company no matter where we are. Time and space are irrelevant', *Fast Company*, April–May 1998.
10. Ikujiro Nonaka and Hirotaka Takeuchi, *The Knowledge-Creating Company*, New York: Oxford University Press, 1995.
11. Geoff Mulgan, *Connexity*, London: Chatto & Windus, 1997.
12. Thomas Moore, *Care of the Soul*, New York: HarperCollins, 1992.
13. Quoted in *I Seem To Be A Verb*, Buckminster Fuller with Jerome Agel and Quentin Fiore, New York: Bantam Books, 1970.
14. 'Chrysler's Neon', *Business Week*, May 3, 1993.
15. 'The European path to revolutionary change', *Fortune*, November 10, 1997.
16. Noel Tichy with Eli Cohen, *The Leadership Engine*, New York: HarperBusiness, 1997.
17. Richard Pascale, 'Change how you define leadership, and you change how you run a company', *Fast Company*, April–May 1998.
18. Peter F. Drucker, 'The theory of the business', *Harvard Business Review*, September–October 1994.

1

THE NEW CONTEXT

1

South Africa meets the Real World

When the rate of change inside exceeds the rate of change outside, the end is in sight.

— Jack Welch, chairman General Electric Corporation

Our world has changed: all of the old knowns are now unknowns.

— Athol Fugard, South African playwright [1]

Remember those extraordinary scenes in 1994.

A praise singer in Parliament! Fidel Castro chatting in the sun to FW de Klerk! *Umkhonto we Sizwe* members lustily singing *Die Stem*!

What the hell was going on? What on earth did it all mean?

South Africans were brought up on the sight of solemn Afrikaners in morning coats and Homburg hats, defenders of the last white outpost in Africa, trying desperately to be symbols of civilisation. But suddenly there was a new flag, a female Speaker of the House, Boer bureaucrats working for communist cabinet ministers, and lots of noise.

For decades, the world shunned us. Yet on May 11, 1994, our return to favour was sealed. The six Impala jets that trailed colourful plumes of smoke over Pretoria were Nelson Mandela's jets. His inauguration was a global event. The freedom of his people made it possible to believe in the freedom of all people.

On that day, South Africa played host to the greatest gathering of world leaders since the funeral of U.S. president John Kennedy. Luncheon guests at the Union Buildings included Hillary Clinton and Al Gore, Prince Philip, Yasser Arafat – and, of course, the fading Fidel Castro. Who would have guessed they'd ever sit in the same place, let alone in this place?

The world we knew was history. Our paradigm had been turned on its head.

The things which some had taken so seriously – and defended at such cost – didn't matter any more. Our values and beliefs, our institutions and organizations, our symbols and our systems were all up for examination.

Now, every aspect of this nation is being reinvented. From education to housing, from health care to road building, from employment to legal processes, and arts and entertainment, all are up for grabs.

The extraordinary changes sweeping across South Africa are part of much greater changes across the world. Everything we know about everything is in flux. Suddenly, the door to a new era has opened. This is an age of the most daunting problems – and mind-blowing opportunities.

We can build whatever we want. But what we now need to grasp most urgently is that the only thing that stands between where we are and where we want to be is *where we have been.*

Our future is hostage to our past. If we can't let go, we won't get going.

Losing ground

'Once South Africa joins the global marketplace,' warned strategist C.K. Prahalad on a visit here in early 1996, 'the pace of change is not going to be dictated by you.'[2] How right he was. Other players with their own agendas make the rules. Countries and companies that want our customers don't 'play fair'.

Studies of national competitiveness tell us that a secure home base is vital for firms wanting to build global presence. But day by day, South Africa becomes less comfortable for business.

The country's macro-economic policies don't help corporate competitiveness. Crime and violence overshadow every decision. Political hiccups impede vital investment. Serious social ills traumatize communities and send scarce talent running. Administrative inefficiencies – often bordering on chaos and collapse – raise costs all around. And while government, labour, and business tussle over strategies for economic growth, local firms lose ground to brutal foreign competitors.

- For most of its history, South African Airways shared its lucrative international routes with only a handful of airlines. Today, some 60 carriers fly to this country.
- The four local tyre-makers used to have this market to themselves. Now, as many as 100 different makes of tyre are on sale.
- A short while back, seven motor companies operated behind high walls erected by government. But tariffs are falling, the Motor Industry Development Programme (MIDP) has encouraged competition, and customers are buying down. Fifteen brands of heavy truck are already here, making this one of the most competitive markets in the world. Exotic sports cars aside, about 25 marques are represented here – more than 360 models in a small market!
- Until the change of government, there were few management consultants in South Africa. Now most of the big global players – McKinsey, Gemini, Braxton, Bain – are here.

- The hotel industry used to be dominated by Sun International and Southern Sun, with City Lodge, Protea Hotels, and the Kaross group occupying niche markets. But now these locals share the market with some 47 foreign groups. Inter-Continental is back in a link with Southern Sun. Hyatt and Sheraton have arrived, and Singaporean and Russian hoteliers are investing in new developments. Dutch group Golden Tulip has opened its first hotel in Cape Town. Days Inn plans to have 75 hotels in southern Africa in a decade. Hospitality Franchise Systems, the world's largest operator, is on the way, and other companies are scouting around.
- KFC is already number one in the fast food market. McDonald's is expanding much faster than anyone expected. Domino's Pizza has plans for 164 units.
- Around 70 foreign banks have arrived here. They all want the same profitable customers, so they're falling over each other in niche markets like merchant and investment banking, corporate finance, and serving high net worth individuals.
- After the 1996 'big bang' on the Johannesburg Stock Exchange, the cosy club of stockbrokers was invaded by banks. Local banks have bought brokers and established equities trading subsidiaries. Global giants like Merrill Lynch, SBC Warburg, NatWest, Deutsche Morgan Grenfell, Flemings, and UBS have all done deals with firms already established here.

To make matters worse, smuggled goods pour through the country's borders. Contraband textiles, sports goods, and consumer electronics are on sale everywhere. Though efforts are being made to close the loopholes, crooked traders will be a competitive threat for years to come.

With few exceptions, South African companies are not ready to deal with this invasion. External factors aside, they are held back by their systems and structures, their policies and their processes.

A lot of their technology is outdated. Their factories are creaky. Many management practices are rooted in the past. There's a huge – and growing – shortage of skills, particularly at middle management and supervisory level.

Most crippling of all, however, is the *attitude* of so many local executives.

They simply are not 'killer competitors'. Years of 'inward industrialization' kept them focused inwards. Protectionist policies blinded them to the new realities of global competition. They cling to obsolete strategic concepts. They shy from the tough choices that effective strategies require. They hope 'things will come right'.

To put it bluntly, they're out of their depth. It seems they just don't want to win badly enough. They assume that if they just hang in there and make a few changes, all will be well.

But one thing is sure: business results will not come just because you turn up. Nor will faster economic growth rescue flagging firms. Delivering improved sales and profits will get harder every day. Ground lost now may never be recovered. Time wasted is opportunity squandered.

Playing to win

Having grown used to a certain level of competition, South African managers think everyone plays the same way. But while we were absent, things changed.

It's crazy to assume that the competitors you face tomorrow will behave just like the old lot. They won't. They clearly have a very different approach to competing than you're used to or comfortable with.

Former Coca-Cola chairman Roberto Goizueta knew this all too well. Listen to him in an interview with *Fortune* magazine:

> *They say, 'Do you sleep well at night with all the competition?' I say, 'I sleep like a baby.' They say, 'That's wonderful.' I say, 'No, no I wake up every two hours and cry.' Because it's true, you know. You have to feel that restlessness.*[3]

McDonald's came here to own the hamburger market, not to fulfil some lofty social role or to play second fiddle to a local firm. British Airways is not here on a warm-up mission. Dell Computer isn't just testing the waters. Barclays Bank is not passing through. General Motors, Volvo, and Peugeot won't drive off in the morning.

Locals on the move

Foreign firms are not the only cause of increasing competition in this market. Many local companies have worked hard to shape up. Also, there are more players in many fields.

- All the local motor manufacturers continue to invest in new infrastructure, rationalize their dealer networks, and improve their customer service.
- Once, steakhouses had a secure place in the restaurant industry. Now, diners have a choice of South African, Italian, Indian, Thai, Chinese, Mongolian, or French cuisine, as well as seafood, health food, pub grub, and much else besides. Chains like Nando's, Steers, and Spur are truly world class. (And they're expanding overseas to prove it!)
- Virtually overnight, retail food malls have mushroomed in many suburbs. They offer consumers a plethora of options. Randburg's Waterfront, for example, has almost 60 restaurants, coffee shops, and pubs. The Thrupps Centre in the Johannesburg suburb of Illovo has 11 venues, and there are another five over the road. There are at least 24 restaurants in Sandton City and adjoining Sandton Square and more than 30 in Cape Town's V&A Waterfront.
- 'Wheels' banks like Wesbank and Bankfin used to have their segment to themselves. Suddenly they must fight for deals against non-traditional competitors such as BMW Financial Services and Ford Credit. The Imperial and McCarthy groups – both major motor distributors – have acquired banking licences.

- A non-bank – Edgars – is the biggest issuer of credit cards in the country. Pick 'n Pay offers banking products at its checkouts. Shoprite Checkers sells insurance policies. Mergers between banks and life assurers promise to transform the financial services sector further and faster.
- From about 20 radio stations a few years ago, there are now more than 125. SABC-TV and M-Net compete with DSTV. A new free-to-air television service will add to viewers' channel choices. (And here as elsewhere in the world, TV broadcasters face growing competition from cinemas, computer games, and the Internet.)
- In the lodging business, conventional hotels are challenged by furnished executive apartments. Guesthouses are flourishing – in Cape Town alone, it's estimated that there are more than 200. Any number of portfolios of lodges, inns, and private game reserves compete for guests. Conference centres with accommodation are popping up everywhere.
- Training firms fall over each other with courses on virtually everything. They stray into management consulting territory by claiming expertise in strategy, culture change, and productivity and quality improvement. The consulting field is also swamped by large numbers of executives who were retrenched, took early retirement for tax reasons, or were given packages to make way for affirmative action appointees.

Every manager talks nostalgically of a time when there were fewer competitors, when competitors 'played the game', and when competitive strategies and performance standards hardly changed from year to year. But wishing for a return to the past is no way to face an increasingly dangerous future.

The rapid proliferation of competitors means that new markets are being created and old ones are being redefined. Today's safe haven is tomorrow's soft target. And as companies feud more aggressively for customers, even the cosiest niche becomes harder to defend.

South African firms face enemies on all fronts. Unfortunately, you don't have a choice as to whether you'll take them on or not. You have to expect that they'll attack you here. And you have to challenge them in foreign markets if you want the really big opportunities. So facing them can either faze you or fire your spirit.

Aggressive new competitors present a daunting challenge to a country that has for decades been obsessed with itself. But there's more to worry our managers. Even as the competitors change, the very nature of competition itself is changing. The game of global business becomes daily more difficult and dangerous for everyone.

Hail to our champions!

Of course, some local firms have been anything but complacent, and many have made serious assaults on world markets.

SA Breweries Beer Division has become the world's fourth biggest brewing group. Pepkor is the leading mass-market retailer in Britain and Liberty Life is the biggest property centre owner there. Sappi is one of the world's biggest pulp and paper producers.

Ogilvy-Mather, Rightford Searle-Tripp, Makin is a star in the international O&M crown, and was voted International Agency of the Year in 1996 by *Advertising Age*. (Another South African agency, Hunt Lascaris TBWA, earned the accolade in 1993 and was voted one of the world's top 10 agencies in 1997.)

The R3,5 billion Columbus Steel project makes this country one of the top three stainless steel producers in the world. Billiton International, a Gencor offshoot, has become one of the world's top aluminium producers.

There are many other examples in many other industries.

Bell Equipment exports articulated dump trucks, sugar cane loaders and transporters, and timber harvesters and transporters to about 40 countries – facing down such global giants as Caterpillar and Komatsu. Consani Engineering has captured 26 per cent of the R1,2 billion-a-year global tank container market. Avroy Shlain Cosmetics has not only become the largest direct-sales firm in the beauty business in South Africa, but also sells to many other countries. Cape-based Carol Boyes sells half her decorative stainless steel cutlery overseas. Retail franchises like Biggie Best, Sweets From Heaven, and Nando's are expanding fast across the world.

All these companies started selling in foreign markets when sanctions were in place and local problems handicapped them in every possible way. Now, with the barriers gone, anything is possible.

So far, few South African brands have been exploited in major markets. Names like De Beers and Outspan have been promoted internationally for years. Others like Thelema (wines), Conservation Corporation (game lodges), M-Net (television broadcasting), and Naartjie (children's clothing) are becoming known. But for most the going will be hard and costly.

The suggestion that there could be opportunities to use the 'South Africanness' of local products to sell them elsewhere is a long shot. You might be able to add some cachet to jewellery, wine, fruit, curios, or safari clothes this way, but not to much else. As we'll see, building a brand takes more than just waving a flag.

South African firms that are making it good internationally have business models that deliver world-competitive products and services. They are good not because they are South African, but because they know what it takes to play the global game and they have the guts to go for the big opportunities.

The transformation challenge

Given South Africa's history and the needs of this nation, companies are under the spotlight. They are the most powerful social units. Most are owned and run by whites, so their actions inevitably appear to be racially biased. Most of their employees are not white, and they enjoy relatively few privileges.

'The new South Africa is as divided as ever,' commented *Newsweek* during the visit of U.S. president Bill Clinton in March 1997. 'If whites feel their comfortable world disappearing, blacks complain that their country isn't changing fast enough.'[4]

The view that (white) capital is pitted against (black) labour is easy to sell, and will continue to be the theme of many interest groups. There are enough South Africans with a socialist leaning to ensure that business and 'the people' will not be on the same side for a long while yet.

What's more, all signs are that the pressures on business will grow.

The Mandela presidency was defined by reconciliation. His successors will be more intent on levelling the playing fields and delivering a better life to the masses. In a 1996 interview with Millennium magazine, deputy president Thabo Mbeki sounded this warning:

> *... there are some partners who treat the national partnership as though it were entirely a vehicle for their own promotion without regard for reconciliation. These are our captains of industry. They indicate zero about what they are going to do.*[5]

Late in 1997, he told *The Economist*: 'The reality is that the legacy of apartheid still defines present-day South Africa. Transformation would take time, but the white population I don't think has quite understood the importance of this challenge.' The article concluded with 'his message to South African whites, who still hold most of the country's economic power: *if they do not change things voluntarily, he will not hesitate to force them to do so*'[6] (my italic).

The more money foreign investors pump into the Johannesburg Stock Exchange, the greater will be the pressure on local firms to boost their profits. At the same time, they face new demands to transform themselves to reflect the diversity of South Africa's population. And they must deliver in both areas in the face of intensifying competition (Figure 1.1).

Business faces challenges that appear to be mutually exclusive. The profit/transformation paradox will paralyse many of them, and has the potential to tear some apart. The greatest risk is not that they will try to make progress in both areas and fail, but that they will settle for an either/or course.

But make no mistake about it: the fact that these two matters are both in sharp focus does not mean you can choose one ahead of the other. Nor does it help to whine about a shortage of black skills, the fears and insecurity of whites, or the difficulty of changing the complexion of your company in a hurry.

White managers can easily summon facts to support their call for slower change. Skilled whites are leaving. It doesn't make commercial sense to lose experienced people. Laws enforcing transformation are, by definition, racist. Legalized change will add unnecessarily to costs.

But, while raising these issues may seem sensible, it's hardly helpful. The fact is, if you want to do business in South Africa, your company has to abandon its white bias and put black people into positions of power. And you have to do it in no time at all.

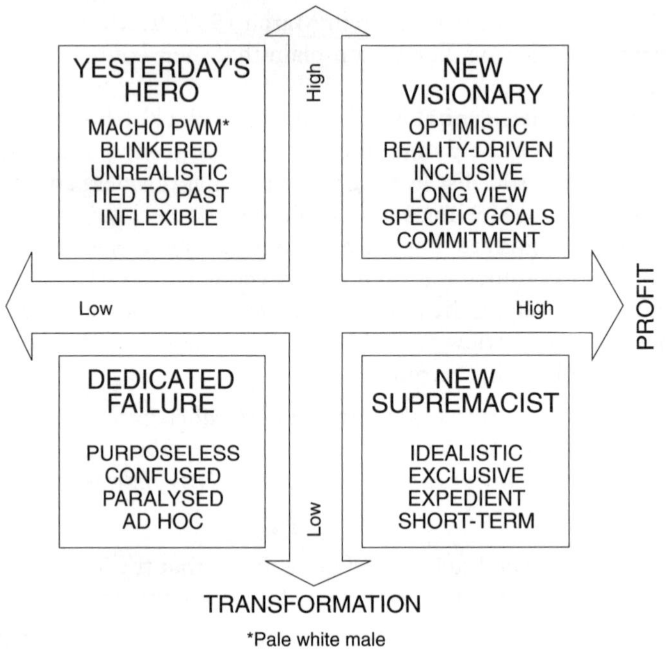

Figure 1.1: *The profit/transformation paradox*

To date, few companies have made significant progress on the affirmative action front. Lots have tried hard – and tried many things – but with few exceptions the results have been disappointing. The popularity of black empowerment deals is confirmation of how hard it is to change things *inside* organizations.

It's tempting to point to highly publicized disappointments at firms like National Sorghum Breweries, New Age Beverages, and JCI as proof that blacks can't crack it in big business. However, one could as easily point to the failure of many white-run firms. And before we get stuck in a debate, we should step back and question some of our assumptions.

For example, we 'know' that it takes a long time to prepare a manager for a top post. (A study by Gordon Donaldson and Jay Lorsch of the Harvard Business School said it took two to three decades to become a general manager heading a large division of a big U.S. company, and that most CEOs of *Fortune* 500 firms were over 50 years of age!)[7] We 'know' you have to work your way slowly up a corporate ladder, spending time in a variety of jobs to give you the skill and perspective you need at the top.

And how do we know these things? Because that's what happened in the past. Because that's how most of the present crop of managers became successful. Because that's conventional wisdom.

But what if we're wrong on all counts? What if the real problem is not that *people develop slowly*, but that *organizations develop them slowly*?

How else do you explain the success of international business heroes like Bill Gates or Richard Branson? Or of locals like Sir Ernest Oppenheimer; Bill Venter, chairman of Altron; or Dimension Data's Jeremy Ord? Where do most entrepreneurs discover their potential?

More to the point, how do you explain the success of Nail chairman Dr. Ntatho Motlana, of Saki Macozoma at Transnet, of Zwelhake Sisulu and Molefe Mokgatle at the SABC*, of Mamphela Ramphele at the University of Cape Town – or of Trevor Manual as Minister of Finance? None of them came to their large and complex organizations with a long and successful track record in management. None was given time to learn the ropes. All were thrown in at the deep end and told, 'Sink or swim!'

This is not to suggest that we should toss out all we know about management development, and simply fill every top job with unproven people. Nor does it mean that the best way to grow people is to leave them to work out how things work. What it does say is that we must stop clinging to what we know and start opening our minds to brand new possibilities. That we accept both the urgency of the transformation challenge, and the utter inadequacy of our current thinking on the subject.

The tools we have tried so far have not worked. One that has been poorly used – conversation – is undoubtedly our next best choice. So best we get on with it. It's time to talk.

The lost communications war

South Africa's future is in the hands of its managers; it's time for their wake-up call. But it's also in the hands of workers and their trade unions.

Conflict in the workplace has cost this country dear. Executives still spend too much time trying to resolve differences with their workers, for too little improvement in quality, productivity, or service. Time spent toyi-toying might have wrung some concessions from employers, but it has been a costly distraction.

Of course, 'hygiene' factors do affect performance, and workers' lives must be improved. The South African workplace was – and in many cases, still is – marked by inequality and unacceptable treatment of people.

But heartless though it may sound, companies are not social clubs. Firms have to satisfy not just their workers, but customers, investors, and other stakeholders too. And that task is getting harder by the minute. Until this message sinks in, every job is at risk.

---

* Stepen Mulholland, former chief executive of Times Newspapers and now a columnist for the *Sunday Times*, recently apologized for doubting Sisulu's capabilities. 'Along with other critics, I have been proved comprehensively wrong,' he wrote (*Business Times*, February 22, 1998). 'It gives me great pleasure to admit this and to acknowledge that Sisulu has established himself to be an effective, pragmatic and brave chief executive officer … Effective because he made clever appointments such as those of Molefe Mokgatle, head of television …'

This is no time to delude ourselves. Silly propaganda will get South Africa nowhere. Political tap-dancing will do us in.

Every citizen needs to understand precisely what we're up against, and precisely what's needed to move forward. It should be a national goal to be recognized as the country with the best workplace conditions, the best-prepared workforce, and the best work ethic in the world.

It could be argued that getting this message across is government's responsibility. And indeed, government should be the lead player. But it's too much to expect politicians and bureaucrats to do what's needed as fast as it must be done. Pretoria has its own agenda; business must deal with real-time issues.

If companies today face serious challenges in a difficult environment, they have to accept a great deal of responsibility for having *shaped* that environment. By their actions – or *inaction* – over many years, they have contributed to the situation we're now in.

Who else can be blamed for the low level of workplace training that has come to be normal? Who else should have paid attention to relationships in the workplace? Who else could have altered people's understanding of commerce?

The fact is, *business has been remiss in not communicating its point of view.*

Business has not explained, clearly and with vigour, how important the economy is, how the economy works, what competition is all about, and why each individual must play a role in defining the future.

A decade ago, in *Communicating For Change*, I advocated that companies should teach their people about these matters. But while some companies did try programmes like 'Justice For All' or the National Productivity Institute's '6M' game, most did little or nothing.

Trade unions and left-leaning politicians, on the other hand, worked hard at the propaganda game. They used every means possible to win hearts and minds, including posters, T-shirts, marches, songs, and *toyi-toying*. Some people even used violence.

Companies in this country have been in a communications war. The advent of democracy did not bring a cease-fire.

To survive and thrive in the age of hostile competition, firms must radically change what they do and how they do it. So best they stop complaining about being held hostage by their workers and stop reacting to demands, and instead start *proactively* managing perceptions and building new capabilities.

Many of the changes that are needed will be both painful and provocative. Now is the time to win people over to your cause. And at the risk of boring you, let me say it again: the only way to do that is through conversation.

Hopes, fears, and realities

South African business must cope with many difficulties. Government will not make life easy. But as players in a global community, both groups have to act in ways that fit with the emerging international paradigm.

'World opinion' might be a vague and meaningless term, but as Francis Fukuyama pointed out in *The End of History and The Last Man*, 'The apparent number of choices that countries face in determining how they will organize themselves politically and economically has been diminishing over time.'[8]

Simply put, we have a pretty good idea of what works and what doesn't.

The basics of good business are the same whether you're in Beijing or Bloemfontein. Of course, there are nuances, but the core issues hold for big firms and small, wherever they are and whatever industry they're in.

No company anywhere can ignore customers, deny the need for innovation and speed to market, or say no to quality. The best practices for getting results in all these areas are universal.

As world trade grows, and as technology exposes every organization to greater scrutiny and pressure – from buyers, investors, 'greens', local communities, governments, and many other influential groups – your margin for error narrows.

You compete on global terms or you die.

Government, too, has to 'toe the line'. Pretoria has to behave 'reasonably', or its objectives will never be met.

Rash moves over trade policy, taxation, privatization, or foreign exchange controls will bring instant punishment. With more than $1,3 trillion zipping across the planet each day, and with investment funds in the hands of fewer and fewer fund managers, economic risks have grown.

As was evident in mid-1996, when a confluence of factors hurt confidence in South Africa, 'the big money' flies away with a few computer keystrokes. 'That amorphous thing called the market', as Trevor Manuel put it in his first press conference after being appointed minister of finance, has awesome clout.

Donald McCloskey, professor of economics and history at the University of Iowa, calls this 'the Gulliver effect'. This quote, from an article in *Scientific American*, explains:

> *Isolationists should take a lesson from Jonathan Swift and realize that economics without the rest of the world is scientifically bankrupt. When Gulliver awoke from his nap in Lilliput, the little folk had tied him down with tiny threads. 'I attempted to rise, but was not able to stir; for as I happened to lie on my back, I found my arms and legs were strongly fastened on each side to the ground; and my hair, which was long and thick, tied down in the same manner. I likewise felt several slender ligatures across my body, from my arm-pit to my thighs; I could only look upwards.*[9]

South Africans hope for a better future, and the prospects are real. There are reasons to fear what lies ahead – and for business to fear what government might try. But the reality is that everyone is in this together, and we're in it with the rest of the world. Politicians may promise wonderful things, but then they have to do roughly the right things.

Contrary to what many people fear, and what some socio-political commentators warn about, it doesn't matter a great deal which political party runs South Africa in the future.

The more integrated this country becomes with the rest of the world, the more our leaders will have to play the global game.

There are many issues that will affect business. Politics should not be at the top of any executive's list.

Instead of worrying about what Pretoria might do, executives would do far better to ask what they must do. And then to get on with the job at hand.

Waiting for Elvis

Although there's plenty of proof that Elvis Presley died, many fans around the world are sure he's in hiding and will someday reappear. They live in hope. The facts are against them, but blind faith makes that irrelevant.

South Africans, too, are hope junkies.

Our fickle spirit rises and falls from moment to moment; our mood swings with the news; we set great store by side-shows.

From mid-1995, big wins in rugby, cricket, and soccer had us convinced we could beat anyone at anything. A low-flying Boeing put a lump in our throats. Widespread rain and a sudden spike in the gold price made us feel bulletproof.

There's no denying the symbolic value of these events. But reinventing this nation will take a lot more than waving our flag or belting out *Shosholoza*. Winning the Olympics was never going to make us healthy, wise, or rich.

Yet South Africans in general are awfully complacent. They seem to think that if they do nothing they'll be okay. Many haven't even noticed the dangers that now threaten them.

My earlier books all warned of more difficult times ahead. In talks and seminars, I have consistently emphasized the need to think and act differently. Yet almost daily I meet top people who're stunned by the speed and magnitude of the changes now swirling around us.

The real surprise is that they're so surprised.

The tragedy is, they respond so slowly.

No time to waste

South Africa is being reinvented. Our country is a work in progress. There is much to be done in a short time with limited resources.

Unfortunately, there are few handy models on which we can base our future. There is no precedent for what we are attempting. The world in which we live is very different to the one in which other countries found success in the past. We have to learn as we go.

Euphoria after the 1994 general election lulled many people into a false sense of security. For a while, things looked rosy. South Africa was the flavour of the times, and everyone wanted to be our friend.

Now, our window of opportunity has closed. This is just another small emerging market.

It is also part of Africa, a continent known to be a tough place for business. And for all the talk of an 'African renaissance', there's too much news of war and political strife, of poverty and disease, of crime, corruption, and crumbling infrastructure.

That said, it's important to note that South Africa is not 'just another African country'. It is far and away the most industrialized country on the continent. Many politicians and bureaucrats are both well trained and competent. Much of our infrastructure is very sophisticated. Things do work. You can do business here with relative ease.

But we are at a critical moment in our development. You might call it a 'breakpoint', or as Intel chairman Andy Grove would put it, a 'strategic inflection point'.

Government must deliver on many fronts, even while many of its functions are in disarray or close to collapse. There is a real danger that many of the problems have reached critical mass, and will never be resolved – especially when there is a serious shortage of competent administrators.

Sooner rather than later, those in public service will have to quench their predilection for caucusing, conferencing, and carousing, and make things happen. Vital structural changes cannot be put off forever. And as the days tick by, those changes become more difficult to make.

Business too, faces a moment of truth. On the one hand, there are suddenly a host of new problems to cope with. On the other, there are too many opportunities.

For the first time in decades, companies have access to global markets and resources. But with our new-found access to the world comes the world's access to us. When I published my book *World Class!* in 1990, its message was easily ignored. Today, every firm faces the need to become world class overnight.

South African managers have been isolated for too long. They talk about the need for change, but most are changing too little, too late. They deny the need for radical change, and instead opt to improve so slowly that they can easily be overtaken. And they justify their lethargy with the tired argument that change takes time and must be meticulously planned.

Especially disabling is the fact that many South African companies use strategy concepts that will make them less, not more, competitive. And too often, their implementation programmes are so complicated that no one can make them work.

South African companies don't have time to waste on vague experiments. They can't afford to skip from fad to fad, or to seek the perfect answer before acting. They must urgently get into the shape that will let them compete in a hyper-competitive world. They must move purposefully and fast.

Justifying inertia

'A lot of guys will blow out soon when the new SA comes,' warned Murray & Roberts chairman David Brink in a 1993 interview. 'When we have an ANC government, pressure on management is going to be enormous.'[10] And so it is, from many quarters. But what are most managers doing about it?

The short answer: too little, too late!

In difficult times it often seems safest to do nothing. 'Keep your head below the parapets' sounds sensible. But inertia and drift are lethal. Getting things right is often less important than getting them done.

South African managers will find plenty of reasons to hold back and wait for proof that 'we are different', or that the economy really is on the mend. They'll wait in vain to be rescued by extraneous forces. Listen for excuses like these:

- 'Crime and violence are too high.'
- 'We're crippled by the skills shortage.'
- 'The civil service – and the country's infrastructure – are collapsing.'
- 'We can't operate while unions run the country.'
- 'We're worried about affirmative action.'
- 'We can't afford new technology, with the rand as weak as it is.'
- 'We can't be sure inflation will stay down.'
- 'We can't see past 1999, when the next election is due.'

These are all perfectly legitimate worries. But every company faces them. And if now's not the greatest time ever to get on with building your business, when might the magic moment be? Timing is all-important in strategy, but waiting too long is lethal.

Every company I know would gain from a greater sense of urgency. Yet it's incredible how many managers are content to move slowly, and how many seem set on doing as little as possible as late as they can.

It's time they learned the simple truth: you can't *bekruip* the future. While you're sneaking up on it, it is likely to overwhelm you.

Fast forward!

Managers are fond of saying that change takes time. They point to firms that have been stuck in transition for years, and 'still haven't got it right'. But watching the failures doesn't tell us what's possible. You can make massive changes incredibly fast, and many companies – including large and complex ones – have shown the way.

My experience shows that when companies talk change, most err by setting deadlines too far into the future. So they inadvertently build slack into the system. They allow the wheels to spin.

Instead of stressing urgency, plans give people 'enough time'. Instead of painting a broad-brush picture of the final destination, and letting others fill in the details and invent solutions on the run, change leaders try to start with everything worked out, everything in place. Instead of focusing on the few things that will make a big difference, they keep people busy with the plethora of small and interesting activities that chew up resources and don't add up to anything significant.

What really takes time is not the act of change, but preparing to change. Mostly, executives spend too long talking about the need for change, why it'll be complicated and costly, and precisely how they'll pull it off. This is a luxury no one can afford.

The fact is you can make your *next* meeting more pleasant, more productive, and more instructive; your sales assistant can smile at the *next* customer who walks through your door; your machine operator can make the *next* product perfectly; your clerk can fill in the *next* form without error.

In days, weeks, or months, rather than years, you can make your organization a different place. First, you have to decide to do it. Then, you need to explain to your entire team why it's the only way and what you expect of them. And then you have to make it clear that there's no room for slack, no tolerance for people who get in the way of progress – and you have to *demonstrate* that you mean it.

Of course, there's more. Training, equipment, and so on are all critical. But first comes your attitude. First comes your ambition. First comes the question: just how serious are you about change?

Listen to this advice from the authors of *Lean Thinking* (and of *The Machine That Changed The World*):

> *Once you dive in, if nothing dramatic is accomplished in the first week of working on a problem activity – typically halving of required effort, a 90 percent reduction of work-in-progress, a halving of space requirements, and a 90 percent drop in production lead time – you've either got the wrong sensei or you are not really a change agent.*[11]

Womack and Jones came to this conclusion after studying many major companies around the world. Surely, you cannot be different. Surely you cannot ignore their message if the companies you compete with today – or certainly will encounter tomorrow – are in such aggressive mode.

Every day, international business reports tell of mega-changes at the world's most successful corporations. This one chops 10 000 jobs; that one dumps a favourite technology; a third exits a market where it earned vast sums in the past. Global business leaders know that 'no pain, no gain' is an uncomfortable truism. But it seems to be lost on South African organizations. Many are engaged in deal-making; but where are the harsh moves that foreigners are prepared to make? (In saying this, I am not advocating job cuts. I'm simply pointing out how serious global competition is, and what local firms are up against.)

Of course, the one factor that's absolutely critical to such quantum change is leadership. That, more than anything, makes the difference. And that, sad to say, is what is absent in so many organizations.

The unhappy fact is, there has been too much misinformation about what good leaders do. And now, under sudden pressure for transformation, many executives are way out of their depth. They avoid hard decisions, skirt serious questions, and protect people and systems that hold them back.

What's needed, on the one hand, is for leaders to become teachers. But on the other, is for leaders to provide discipline.

Contradictory though it might sound, what's absolutely necessary in this time of participation, consensus, empowerment, and all those good things, is for tough leaders who light a blowtorch under the organization's backside.

That might not be nice. That might not be a popular view. But you'd better believe it – because it's reality.

A test of character

South African executives will be tested to the limit in coming years. They'll be faced with making their companies competitive against great odds. Personal and family issues will be of growing concern.

The nation has enormous potential, but realizing it will take special qualities of creativity and courage.

Every manager can complain about the difficulties of operating in this environment. Everyone has had to deal with sanctions, trade union action, unpredictable government policies, high inflation and interest rates, and a host of other factors. Every company has faced pretty much the same set of challenges.

But some have come through far better than others.

While many held back, cursed, and complained, a few drove forward aggressively – Derek Keys and Brian Gilbertson at Gencor, Christo Wiese at Pepkor, Les Boyd at Amic, Graham MacKay at SAB Beer Division, Bas Kardol and Steven Koseff at Investec Bank.

Another group showed that medium-sized firms can be a powerful engine for growth in tough times – Robbie Brozen at Nando's Chickenland, Patrick Enthoven and Miles Japhet at The Hollard insurance company, Stuart Cohen and Laurie Chiappini at Specialty Stores Group.

The years ahead hold great promise. Many of yesterday's excuses for lousy performance have gone. If the men weren't separated from the boys by South Africa's internal hassles, they surely will be when they try to compete in the global arena.

To lead change, you have to change yourself. You have to rediscover and reinvent your own identity as well as that of your organization.[12] Unless you are prepared for the introspection, the pain, the costs, and the risks this will bring, your potential will remain a mystery.

Now is the time to test yourself.

Endnotes

1. 'Reflecting on a handful of pumpkin seeds from a beautiful land', *The Sunday Independent*, December 17, 1995.
2. In a speech at the BMW-sponsored Innovative Thinking conference, Cape Town, March 28, 1996.
3. 'A conversation with Roberto Goizueta and Jack Welch', *Fortune*, December 11, 1995.
4. 'The color of fear', *Newsweek*, March 23, 1998.

5. 'Thabo talks tough', interview with Hugh Murray and Ingrid Uys, *Millennium*, May 1996.
6. 'Who is Thabo Mbeki?' *The Economist*, November 1, 1997.
7. Gordon Donaldson and Jay W. Lorsch, *Decision Making At The Top*, New York: Basic Books, 1983.
8. Francis Fukuyama, *The End Of History And The Last Man*, New York: The Free Press, 1992.
9. Donald McCloskey, 'The Gulliver effect', *Scientific American*, September 1995.
10. Interview with Nick Binnedell, *Embark*, November 1993.
12. James P. Womack and Daniel T. Jones, *Lean Thinking*, New York: Simon & Schuster, 1996.
13. Robert A. Burgelman and Andrew S. Grove, 'Strategic dissonance', *California Management Review*, Vol. 38, No. 2, Winter 1996; Richard Tanner Pascale, *Managing On The Edge*, New York: Viking, 1990.

2

The Age of Hostile Competition

All advantages erode. As competitors copy an advantage it is no longer an advantage. It is a cost of doing business.

— Richard D'Aveni[1]

To truly secure a segment ... you must expel all other competitors and establish yourself as the dominant market leader.

— Geoffrey Moore[2]

Never underestimate a hungry, purposeful, committed company.

— Eckhard Pfeiffer, president Compaq Computer [3]

'WELCOME TO THE REVOLUTION!'

This 1993 headline in *Fortune* referred, of course, to the extraordinary changes sweeping the planet and affecting companies everywhere. And in the article that followed, Thomas Stewart wrote:

> *We sense that the changes surrounding us are not mere trends but the workings of large, unruly forces: the globalization of markets; the spread of information technology and computer networks; the dismantling of hierarchy, the structure that has essentially organized work since the mid-19th century. Growing up around these is a new information-age economy, whose fundamental sources of wealth are knowledge and communication rather than natural resources and physical labor.*[4]

As Alvin Toffler and many others predicted, the Industrial Age is giving way to the Information Age. Knowledge workers are ascendant. And most executives are thoroughly confused about how to leap from the past to the future.

Throughout history, change has been uncomfortable for the people living through it – 'too soon', 'too fast', 'too much'. Contrary to what most people might think today, says Eisenhower biographer Stephen Ambrose, 'the generation that had to deal with the greatest changes, in business, commerce, war, and all other aspects of human life lived in the first half of the nineteenth century, not the second half of the twentieth'.[5] However, the pace, magnitude, and complexity of events since the late 1980s have been truly breathtaking. The closing years of the second millennium bring special pressures and problems. Corporations and their executives face challenges for which few are ready.

Following World War II, many national economies grew strongly on the back of new consumer demand and infrastructural rebuilding. Then in the 1970s, the brakes were applied. Rocketing oil prices were rapidly followed by rising inflation, growing trade union power, and falling consumer demand. Having learned that they could pump up sales and profits just by turning up at work each day, managers suddenly discovered that 'business as usual' was a thing of the past.

If that was a nasty shock, the next decade was even worse. In the blink of an eye we've seen political systems crumble, societies disintegrate, economies integrate, and yesterday's best technologies become obsolete.

Managers everywhere stand at the edge of an abyss. Behind them is familiar terrain. The paths are well worn, the natives friendly. Ahead is a sudden drop to a strange place.

Dangers lurk out there, ones they cannot see and don't understand. A haze lends gentleness to the view. They are told there are great rewards ahead, but they secretly know that reaching them will be an awesome task.

It's hard to imagine that a mere century ago we knew nothing of antibiotics, nuclear power, jet planes, computers, or plastics. It boggles the mind to think that as much new text is produced each day as was produced from the time writing was invented, to the start of the nineteenth century.[6] And who wants to face the fact that while we've learned so much, we are still so vulnerable.

Major challenges, necessary changes

Today's organizations operate in a climate of increasing turbulence and surprise. Many are poorly prepared to deal with the wide array of challenges they face. Even smart managers are paralyzed by the new realities.

Here are some of them:

- The rate, scope, and complexity of change are growing.
- Socio-political and economic uncertainties threaten the unwary.
- Competition is escalating rapidly – more players (often from outside your industry), faster innovation, more aggression.
- The power of many stakeholders (consumers, environmentalists, health and safety activists, workers) is rising.
- Technology is transforming the way products and services are created, delivered, and bought – and the way organizations work.

In this tough new environment, you have to:

- Sense, provoke, manage, and sustain change.
- Balance (often-conflicting) stakeholder interests.
- Give customers 'more for less'.
- Cut concept-to-cash time.
- Preserve key strengths from the past while building new advantages for the future.
- Increase workforce diversity and manage new relationships.
- Improve teamwork and collaboration.
- Create external alliances (perhaps with competitors) to access new capabilities.
- Exploit new technologies.
- Grow your profits.

Paradoxes and possibilities

To complicate things further, this is also the age of paradox. Executives face a stream of dilemmas both outside and inside their organizations which present them with uncomfortable choices.

The natural inclination is to adopt an either/or point of view. Often this is just not practical or acceptable. Besides, simplistic choices – electing to do this or that – may shut out rewarding possibilities.

Paradoxes are part of managerial life.[7] There simply is no escaping them. You have to:

- Produce profits today – and invest for tomorrow.
- Plan for the long-term – and act in the short-term.
- Minimize risks – and seek opportunities.
- Commit to a direction – and change direction.
- Centralize some decisions – and decentralize action.
- Encourage teamwork – and individual initiative.
- Provide discipline – and allow for experimentation.
- Manage from the top down – and from the bottom up.
- Be a specialist – and a generalist.
- Compete aggressively – and collaborate with your 'enemies'.
- Drive value up – and costs down.

Paradoxes paralyze some firms and energize others. They may throw you into confusion or let you surge past your competitors. The way you respond to them will have a profound impact on your performance, and may prove to make all the difference between success and failure.

Mastering tensions – between future and present, vision and opportunism, premeditation and spur-of-the-moment action – has always been a mark of successful companies. But as the bets, the risks, and the possible payoffs all get bigger, it becomes even more critical.

Recognizing that you live in a paradoxical world is a first step towards managing the future. Raising your awareness of paradoxes has to become a habit. But at the same time, you need a clear and consistent theory of business to guide your actions.

Making decisions in this environment grows increasingly difficult. What's more, though you'll seldom have all the information you need, you have to act with lightning speed to seize opportunities and stay ahead of your competition. And you have to do many things, all at once.

As F. Scott Fitzgerald noted in *The Great Gatsby*, the test of a first-rate intelligence is 'the ability to hold two opposed ideas in the mind at the same time and still retain the ability to function'. It's an ability that's vital in today's competitive environment.

Why Bill Gates is worried

Pick one company that should have an assured future, and you'd probably name Microsoft. The giant software maker's growth has been truly astonishing. Worth more than $200 billion by February 1998 (vs. $95,8 billion for IBM), it became the second most valuable company in the world in just 20 years. Only GE is bigger.

Most executives would give anything to run a company this successful and with prospects this exciting. Yet co-founder and chairman Bill Gates knows the danger of complacency.

A swarm of start-ups vie for tomorrow's customers. New technologies are announced every day. Wars are fought over standards.

You might think that Microsoft has a key weapon in its fight for the future – its DOS and Windows operating systems are in close to 200 million computers around the world. Its 'industrial strength' NT system has become the *de facto* standard for tens of millions of corporate users. And its CE system is found in almost every palmtop product – a segment with huge potential.

This installed base is a powerful advantage. Microsoft earns most of its profits from selling the applications (Word, Excel, PowerPoint, and Publisher, and bundled suites like Office) that run on DOS and Windows. But nothing is forever. The blistering growth of the Internet, the rising popularity of Java (a programming language developed by Sun Microsystems), and the potential of 'network computers' from the aggressive companies like Silicon Graphics, threaten to make DOS and Windows unnecessary for many users.

If Microsoft is slow to introduce new 'killer apps' (computer industry jargon for 'killer applications' or breakthrough products) its lead will quickly vanish. Market needs will be defined by someone else.

This problem is not unique to the computer industry. Upheavals in the macro-environment change the way all industries work. That, in turn, puts pressure on every company – forcing them to change faster and more radically than at any time in the past.

Executives complained of chaotic conditions throughout the 1970s and 1980s. But as they swung into the 1990s they discovered that much of what they'd done suddenly didn't matter. Much of what they'd learned was irrelevant. Many of the new management theories they'd so eagerly seized were of little or no help.

The average company survives a mere 35 years – about half the lifespan of a man in most industrialized countries. Companies are terribly frail and vulnerable. And in the future we're likely to see them come and go increasingly quickly.

'My goal,' says Gates, 'is to prove that a successful corporation can renew itself and stay in the forefront.'[8]

That is a challenge indeed.

Collisions in the competitive arena

Industries (for want of a better term) evolve in predictable phases (Figure 2.1):

Phase 1: Innovation
Phase 2: Fragmentation
Phase 3: Consolidation
Phase 4: Breakaway

In **Phase 1**, an entrepreneur invents a new offering. There's nothing like it, so he has the market to himself. Customers try his product, but don't know what

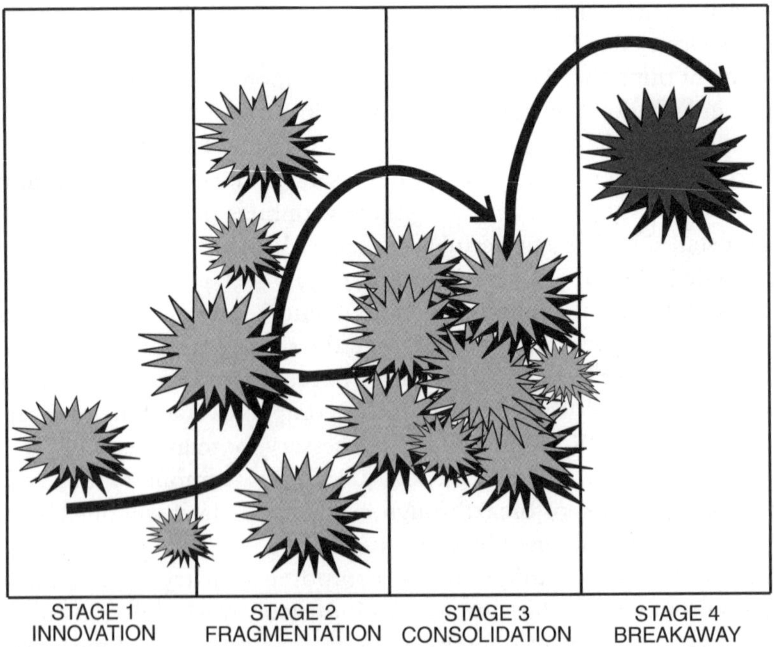

Figure 2.1: *Collisions in the competitive arena*

to expect; its value is unclear. The entrepreneur can charge a reasonable price and earn healthy margins.

In **Phase 2**, other players arrive on the scene. They see the opportunity that's been created. The pathfinding work has been done for them. Customers like the idea of having a choice.

This early, there's plenty of space in the market. New entrants can do the classical marketing thing: position themselves apart from each other. They can hype their differences and earn good money. But as they battle for position, chaos and confusion become the order of the day. Prices are driven down and margins start to erode. Some old players disappear, and new ones snatch sales.

In **Phase 3**, things start to settle down. Suppliers and buyers work out what 'value' means – and it begins to mean roughly the same to all of them. A 'dominant design' emerges as they agree on standards, adopt the same business models, and deliver the same features and benefits.* The edges of the industry start to harden. Attitudes, too, start to harden. The industry has a new mental model, and for a time it contains 'irrational' behaviour and lets companies earn enough profit to keep them in the game.

In **Phase 4**, someone decides that enough is enough, or grasps the fact that the industry is looking inward instead of outward. It may be one of the incumbents, or an outsider. They break away. And a new Phase 1 is born.

This cycle of life and death is repeated over and over again. A few firms manage to survive the turbulence. Most die young.

Of course, the pace and intensity of competition vary from industry to industry. In some cases, Phase 3 is a comfortable place to be. But it's less and less so. Accelerating change and a plethora of possible players tend to make this the *worst* place to be. All too often, price is the key determinant of which offering customers choose. So margins take a beating.

Many firms now in Phase 3 want nothing more than to stay there. They'd like more take-home pay, but they're wary of rocking the boat, and perhaps too lazy or unimaginative to try anything radical. What they don't realize is that today's profit sanctuary is tomorrow's grave.

As a strategist, you face a clear challenge: how to make a difference that matters in the mind of the customer. How to create not just new products or services, but *a new business model* – and a new and meaningful *value proposition* – that will give you the high ground.

What can you do to break free of the pack, and to capture and keep new customers and profits?

Then, how can you *stay* ahead when strategies suddenly diverge and then slowly converge, when breakthroughs give way to blandness, when you and your competitors all seem set to survive by doing the same things in the same way?

* For an excellent view of the process, see James M. Utterbuck's book *Mastering the Dynamics of Innovation*, Boston: Harvard Business School Press, 1994.

These are the questions that face you now. They demand urgent attention. They demand radical strategies – and, therefore, *radical approaches to strategy.*

Industry shakeouts

Around the world, industries ranging from autos to airlines, from chemicals to computers, from phones to pharmaceuticals, are now in the throes of an awesome structural revolution. The earth is moving under every executive's feet.

Industry boundaries are shifting and blurring. Traditional competitors may not be the ones to fear. The players on your radar screen may be the wrong ones to watch.

Cafés have to worry about garage convenience stores. Banks are threatened by supermarkets that offer financial products at their checkouts. TV broadcasters, cinema owners, and music publishers worry about the Internet.

In this messy new world, yesterday's 'key factors of success' quickly become today's key triggers of failure. Yesterday's 'core competences', affirms Tom Peters, become today's 'core incompetences'.[9]

Being the best player in the wrong game is useless. Far from making a company more competitive, incremental improvements can kill it. Doing the wrong things with increasing skill, energy, and enthusiasm gets you nowhere.

But the problem goes further. 'By virtue of being excellent in one knowledge domain,' says Harvard professor Dorothy Leonard-Barton, 'an organization is relatively unreceptive to ideas from others.'[10] Ironically, the harder you work to improve in a particular area, the less likely you are to embrace innovations from outside that would really make a difference.

Competitiveness is a global obsession. Everywhere you look, companies are cutting costs, re-jigging their architecture, upping their R&D spend, hiring smarter people, spending more on training and development.

Restructuring is an everyday affair at the world's most prominent companies. Though many have made vast changes, they still aim for massive improvements. Consultants worldwide report that reengineering is still the greatest concern of most managers, even though it has been badly misused and is widely blamed for hurting staff morale and loyalty.

A single issue of the *Wall Street Journal Europe* recently carried stories about major changes at SmithKline Beecham, Mercedes-Benz, Electronic Data Services, Saab-Scania, Varta, Time Warner, Multimedia, ICI, and Royal/Dutch Shell.[11] One copy of *Business Week* reported on troubles at McDonald's, Motorola, and Kimberley-Clark; and of tough times facing Asia's carmakers and Russia's Dialog Bank.[12]

Companies everywhere are learning in the hardest way that only the most drastic action will keep them alive. In some cases, that drastic action involves a 'slash and burn' attack on staff numbers. In others, it means closing factories and offices and relocating people. It may also include abandoning once-core product lines, switching distribution channels, making heavy investments in new technology, or selling valuable equipment at fire-sale prices.

Driven by the need to gain critical mass in resources, capabilities, or markets, companies do whatever it takes to fight another day. If you want to play their game, you have to be prepared to play tough. In this age of hostile competition, there's just no easier way.

Sometimes, you can't play if you can't pay

Niche players serving some customers may get by for a while on limited investment. But to be really successful on a global basis in virtually any industry, costs a fortune.

Breakthrough products don't come cheap. Start-up costs are huge. Distribution and promotion to customers across the world quickly runs up big bills. Operations chew funds.

It can cost $5 billion to bring a new car to market; $350 million to develop a new pharmaceutical drug; $150 million to launch a new washing powder.

In high-tech manufacturing, a paradox shuts out many players. 'Moore's Law' (named after Gordon Moore, founder and chairman of Intel) says that the number of transistors that can be put on a silicon chip doubles roughly every 18 months, while the cost falls in half. 'Rock's Law' (named after Arthur Rock, a venture capitalist and Intel director) says the cost of plant and equipment doubles every four years.

Capital spending to produce Intel's Pentium chip was $5 billion – five times the cost of the earlier 486 and 50 times that of the 386. Because of growing technological complexity, a 1983-vintage chip took 20 days to make, while it takes up to 60 days to make a Pentium.[13]

Firms that make these big bets want a big payoff. The trouble is, competitors are snapping at their heels. So cutting concept-to-customer time is a key strategy in the race for the future; but just getting there first is no guarantee you'll last.

Big ideas have become hard to come by and often too costly for single firms. 'Going it alone' is now a viable option in very few fields. Staying 'at the leading edge in a particular market segment,' says IMD professor Derek Abell, 'now demands an array of competences and resources that goes beyond the capabilities of any single firm'.[14] Companies have learned that it pays to collaborate with the opposition. So old enemies in many industries now gang up to pool cash and share ideas:

- Nissan, Fuji, and Isuzu share production of crankshafts.
- Hewlett-Packard and Canon are fierce opponents in the inkjet printer business, but since the 1970s they've worked together on laser printers: Canon makes the engines while HP delivers control chips and software.
- BMW makes engines for Rolls Royce.
- Microsoft recently took a big stake in long-time rival Apple Computer.
- While Kodak and Fuji lock horns in an acrimonious legal and political battle, they worked closely together – with rival camera makers Nikon, Minolta, and Canon – to develop the Advanced Photo System, a new 35mm cassette film.

As South African firms re-enter the world, and find themselves head-to-head with this new breed of competitor, they'll have to make giant improvements in their price/performance capabilities. Strategic alliances will be especially important in this process. Many firms have already forged valuable links. Others need to see that creating partnerships is essential for survival and growth.

Many foreign firms will prefer to come into this market in some kind of alliance, rather than as direct investors. This way, they'll lessen their risks in what they see as a potentially unstable place. Some will choose black partners to send a politically correct message.

Alliances will be beneficial in that they'll plug South Africa into the mainstream of world ideas. It's hard to over-estimate the impact this will have on the way we do business. But other aspects of strategy need attention.

To understand them, you need to see business in its new context – a global context. For competition now comes from unexpected quarters: not just from the player next door, but from across the planet; not just from firms within your industry, but from others with a totally different view of things.

Power shifts

It seems only yesterday that Japanese manufacturers of almost everything were held in awesome regard by the rest. Their designs were better, their manufacturing processes were widely copied, their quality was the benchmark, their costs were lower, and their customer focus was legendary. Few people saw American or European factories making a comeback.

But watch, for example, how American carmakers raced back to set new standards of design, quality, and productivity, recapture market share – and turn yet another paradigm on its head. Chrysler, technically bankrupt in 1991, currently makes more profit per vehicle than anyone else does. The passenger car chief at Mercedes-Benz says Ford is the industry benchmark for production.[15]

The same dramatic turnaround has been evident in many other industries. Company after company has looked into the abyss and clawed its way back to health and prosperity.

But it's not just American companies that have become more competitive. Faced with accelerating competition, organizations everywhere have shaped up with blistering speed.

It's evidently possible to become a winner against the odds. It is possible to deal with the shocks of the new business arena, and at the same time to re-tool for the future. And you can change your organization much faster than you've been led to believe.

It all depends on how you think – and how badly you want to win!

Drivers of competition

Numerous forces drive the mega-changes that challenge today's managers. Five of them demand special attention:

1. **Globalization.** Former Harvard Business School marketing guru, Ted Levitt, alerted managers to the 'globalization of markets' back in 1985. While some companies quickly seized the idea, many got burned trying to 'go global'. But now, everyone's doing it.

   The spread of capitalism and democracy has opened massive markets in central Europe, east Asia, Latin America, and Africa. Cross-border trade has become easier as regulatory barriers to foreign investment have eased, telecommunications and transport costs have fallen, and capital markets have opened up.[16] New media such as satellite TV homogenize consumer tastes and let marketers use 'one sight, one sound, one sell' across borders and cultures. Rising labour costs force companies to leave their home countries and relocate production in cheaper places. At the same time, they seek to put marketing activities close to customers – wherever they might be.

   By staying local and avoiding the hurly-burly of global competition, companies inadvertently hurt themselves: learning is slow and there's little pressure to improve products or processes. Firms that grow complacent on their home turf suddenly find outsiders eating their lunch. Their customers buy from the invaders, and profits dry up.

   Globalization and competitiveness feed off each other. As more companies reach beyond their home bases, competition increases everywhere. That, in turn, forces more firms to go exploring.

2. **Deregulation and privatization.** Governments worldwide are selling off companies and changing the laws that frame industries. Barriers that protected manufacturers and service providers are falling. Life has become a free-for-all for firms that once could do virtually as they pleased.

   This process is forcing painful and costly change on South African companies. Regulators are rewriting the rules that govern industries from broadcasting to gambling, from agriculture to diamonds, from motor vehicles to health care, textiles, and taxis.

   South African Airways is still far and away the biggest airline here, but not the only one. (Flitestar was the first casualty of local air combat.) Combi-taxis have taken passengers and profits from Putco. Spoornet's trains vie for contracts with a swarm of large and small truckers. Cellular phones have forced Telkom to improve its service. The SABC faces numerous other broadcasters.

3. **Overcapacity.** For the past three decades, producers of virtually everything have been on a buy-and-build spree. Factories have sprung up everywhere, often supported by governments keen to create jobs. With the spread of capitalism, companies in many developing countries have become mainstream producers. At the same time, new and improved technology and strong productivity programmes have boosted output.

   But worldwide recession at the end of the 1980s made buyers cautious – and price-conscious. Turmoil in Asia a decade later caused more unease. And population growth in many countries is slowing sharply.

From 1996 to 1998, steelmakers added capacity twice as fast as demand grew.[17] Car companies can produce 100 million vehicles a year, while they sell about 70 million. It's the same in many other industries. Too many producers serve too few customers. Computer chip prices fell 60 per cent in 1996 because manufacturers overestimated market demand. Pulp prices fell by 50 per cent between January and March that year. A General Electric fridge that sold for $509 in 1953 went for $399 in 1997 – after inflation.[18]

The result is that manufacturers of everything have been forced to slash costs. Factories are shut; huge amounts of equipment lie unused; short shifts and overtime cuts reduce working hours; skilled people are laid off in huge numbers.

But it's not just manufacturers who are under pressure. In 1982 it cost $1 200 to $1 400 to ship a container of goods out of South Africa to the Far East vs. $200 to $400 today. Airlines battle to fill their seats. Hotel occupancies are down. New office blocks stand empty.

Bringing supply and demand back into balance will be a long and costly process. Meanwhile, companies that ignore the situation will be badly hurt. 'Lean and mean' is not just another option for management fad fans; it's the only way to go.

4. **New technology.** Advances in technology are transforming products and processes. Information has become the most vital corporate resource.

   In a discontinuous world, rapid innovation is vital. 'Fast prototyping' is the new management religion. Engineers use CAD/ CAM systems and virtual reality to design new products. Factory robots speed up production and make zero defects the norm.

   At the same time, electronic mail and sophisticated databases 'demassify' markets and let firms build one-to-one interactive relationships with customers. Advances in telecommunications send messages – and money – zipping across the planet.

   Exploiting the new technologies takes time and money, new skills, and new kinds of organizations, all of which create a great deal of unease. Along the way, the industrial landscape is irrevocably altered. Yesterday's rules of competition no longer apply.

   Software producers who give away their programs on the Internet may have no idea how they'll earn money, but they're changing the economics of global commerce.

   Designers who cram more and more transistors onto computer chips are driving a profound shift in human potential.

   Smart materials, smart cards, and smart products promise to change our concept of 'value' in ways that none of us can imagine.

5. **Blurring technological boundaries.** Until recently, it was quite clear where one technology ended and another began. But no longer. Now, they converge, overlap, and blend. The knowledge that 'belonged' to one specialization is now shared with others.

Technologies are combined to enhance each other and to create new functionalities. Hardware, software, and service are bundled together to add value in a growing array of products. Adventurous customers seek new satisfactions from non-traditional sources and suppliers are forced to redefine themselves. Success in any industry hinges on access to instant and in-depth knowledge of other industries.

- Most motor cars are marvels of both engineering and electronics. It's become a cliché that the average car contains more computing power than went to the moon in 1969. (A BMW has seven kilometres of wire in it and more than 50 'controllers'.) But car manufacturers also need sophisticated expertise about aerodynamics, materials, temperature control, light refraction, and so on.
- A Gillette Sensor razor blade glides across your skin, thanks to a built-in strip of lubricant. Developing it took not only knowledge about steel, but also about plastics and chemistry.
- 'Smart' toothbrushes have bristles that change colour with use, to tell you when it's time to buy a new one.
- A typical video recorder or stereo unit is part electric motor, part computer, part infrared sensor.
- Camera-makers must understand chemistry to make new kinds of glass. They need metallurgical skills to develop or exploit new materials for their shutters. They also need to know about the motors which not only wind film but also adjust lenses for light and focus; and they must understand 'fuzzy logic', a technology that works with the exposure meter – another knowledge area – to tell those motors what to do.

The post-industrial revolution will last into the next century. The changes I've mentioned affect your business right now and will present both problems and opportunities in the future. If you and your team aren't watching them and analysing them, you should be. They will affect the way all your stakeholders act, and prescribe your industry's profit potential.

They will either fuel your growth or ensure your failure.

The quick and the dead

Two factors will test management in the immediate future: stormy economic conditions and increasing competition. There's white water ahead. As rapidly as the global competitive temperature has risen in recent years, it will now go up even faster.

Companies everywhere are on steroids. They're leaner, fitter, smarter, and increasingly aggressive. Markets are now being sliced into smaller and smaller niches as marketers strive to hang on to customers. Value is being reconfigured and delivered in unexpected ways. The value that companies used to capture is now shared with numerous stakeholders. Control of the value-creating process is shifting.

The new mantras of lean production and mass-customization drive down costs while simultaneously making firms more responsive. After decades of promises, there's at last a critical mass of technology at work, and it's starting to deliver. Work is being transformed. New skills are needed, and the people who have them can make new demands. So they have to be managed in new ways.

Of course, customers are taking advantage of all the attention. They're not only increasingly tight-fisted, they're also incredibly fickle. They want more and more for less and less. They have so many options, they don't need to buy from anyone who can't promise great quality at the best prices. In the hyper-competitive new business arena, brands quickly become commodities.

South African companies are re-entering the global arena at the best of times and at the worst of times. Suddenly, huge new markets have opened to them. The opportunities are incredible. But with few exceptions, they aren't ready to compete. Many are in for nasty shocks.

Those new markets are *everyone's* targets. Every niche is over-crowded. Companies are falling over each other to dazzle customers with breakthrough products and services. The record number of mergers and acquisitions worldwide and the frenetic pace of reengineering and restructuring should set alarm bells ringing.

Competing in the 1990s and beyond is not like competing in the 1980s. Competing in the big wide world is not like competing in the cloistered confines of yesterday's South Africa. To survive the rocks, whirlpools, and waterfalls that lie ahead will be an awesome test indeed.

Success will depend partly on imagination and strategy and to a great extent on mental toughness, perseverance, and raw energy. This nation's prospects rest on the speed with which South African companies grasp the new global realities and embrace the new rules of competition.

More than anyone understands, our future will be made by business leaders who get up day after day and shove their way into the future.

The winners will be brave, bold, and brash. Insight, innovation, and imagination will be their weapons. Speed and surprise will give them the advantage.

Dinosaurs don't dance

The companies most likely to grow in the future will be flexible and fast. Agility is a measure of organizational wellness, just as temperature tells you about the health of a human body.

Critical to competitiveness, say consultants Steven Goldman, Roger Nagel, and Kenneth Preiss, 'is the need to minimize the concept-to-cash time for creating and exploiting customer opportunities. The marketplace rewards companies that can do this routinely; it punishes those that cannot.'[19]

- '... every product and service is changing,' warns Tom Peters. 'Going soft, softer, softest. Going fickle, ephemeral, fashion ... No corner of the world is exempt from the frenzy.'[20]

- 'Today's innovation is time-based competition,' say George Stalk and Thomas Hout of the Boston Consulting Group. 'Demanding executives at aggressive companies are altering their measures of performance from competitive costs and quality to competitive costs, quality, and responsiveness ... In doing so, they are literally running circles around their competition.'[21]
- '... reducing product life cycles and fragmenting demand can yield powerful advantages for those causing these changes relative to those forced to react to them,' says IBM's B. Joseph Pine II. 'Leading companies have created processes for low-cost, volume production of great variety, and even for individually customized goods and services.'[22]
- 'Our philosophy is that the key to achieving competitive advantage isn't reacting to chaos,' says Silicon Graphics CEO, Ed McCracken, 'it's producing that chaos. And the key to being a chaos producer is being an innovation leader.'[23]

The record shows that it's not always the firm that invents a new product that gains the upper hand. Imitators and fast followers often take over as the long-term leaders. Toshiba's VHS passed Sony's Betamax; Canon overtook Xerox in the small copier market; IBM beat Apple, Commodore, and Tandy in small computers; Diet Coke raced past Diet Pepsi.

What kinds of companies 'routinely' capture and hold valuable markets?

Not the slouches. Not those obsessed by their proud heritage. Not those determined to preserve their culture or averse to writing off sunk costs.

Distinguishing your firm from your competitors through positioning – the goal of most strategies – will continue to be an important goal. Long-term commitment will always be necessary. But as technological advances speed up, product life-cycles shrink, customers shop around, and new competitors show up everywhere, how you do things turns out to be as important as what you do.

Outpacing your competitors counts as much as outflanking them. Your ability to execute a constantly shifting strategy fast and well makes all the difference on the corporate battlefield. Fleet-footedness and flexibility must be built into your organization.

Kevin Kelly, editor of *Wired* magazine, makes the point well in his book *Out Of Control*:

> *The key insight uncovered by the study of complex systems in recent years is this: the only way for a system to evolve into something new is to have a flexible structure. A tiny tadpole can change into a frog, but a 747 Jumbo Jet can't add six inches to its length without crippling itself. This is why distributed being is so important to learning and evolving systems. A decentralized, redundant organization can flex without distorting its function, and thus it can adapt. It can manage change. We call that growth.*[24]

Designing tomorrow's organization is obviously helped by knowing who the customer will be and how he'll behave, what competitors will do, what the economic landscape will look like, and so on. However, the first requirement is not more knowledge, but less attachment to what you already know.

Less reliance on facts. A deep-down desire to make a difference. And above all, a 'just do it' attitude – the secret not just of Nike, but also of 3M, Rubbermaid, Benneton, Honda, Kyocera, and many other global leaders.

Flexibility. Passion. Energy. Enthusiasm.

These are the traits to seek in the people you hire. They're also the way to describe your organization if it's to be around in ten or 15 years' time.

Endnotes

1. Richard D'Aveni, *Hypercompetition*, New York: The Free Press, 1994.
2. Geoffrey A. Moore, *Inside the Tornado*, New York: HarperCollins, 1995.
3. Marshall Loeb, 'Leadership lost-and regained', *Fortune*, April 17, 1995.
4. Thomas A. Stewart, 'Welcome to the revolution', *Fortune*, December 13, 1993.
5. Stephen Ambrose, 'When was the real techno-revolution?' *Forbes ASAP*, December 2, 1996.
6. Arno Penzias, *Harmony*, New York: HarperBusiness, 1995.
7. Anthony D. Manning, *The New Age Strategist*, Johannesburg: Southern Book Publishers, 1988.
8. Bill Gates with Nathan Myhrvold and Peter Rinearson, *The Road Ahead*, New York: Viking Penguin, 1995.
9. Speaking in The Tom Peters Seminar, Amsterdam, December 1994.
10. Dorothy Leonard-Barton, *Wellsprings of Knowledge*, Boston: Harvard Business School Press, 1995.
11. *Wall Street Journal Europe*, February 24–25, 1995.
12. *Business Week*, March 9, 1998.
13. 'A big bet made Intel what it is today; now, it wagers again', *Wall Street Journal Europe*, June 9–10, 1995.
14. Derek F. Abell, *Managing With Dual Strategies*, New York: The Free Press, 1993.
15. 'Mercedes says Detroit sets pace', *International Herald Tribune*, March 6, 1995.
16. 'Everybody's favourite monsters: a survey of multinationals', *The Economist*, March 27, 1993.
17. 'Steelmakers to curb plans for more capacity', *Financial Times*, March 6, 1998.
18. 'Jack cracks the whip again', *Business Week*, December 15, 1997.
19. Steven L. Goldman, Roger N. Nagel, Kenneth Preiss, *Agile Competitors And Virtual Organizations*, New York: Van Nostrand Reinhold,1995.
20. Tom Peters, *Liberation Management*, New York: Alfred A. Knopf Inc., 1992.
21. George Stalk, Jr., and Thomas M. Hout, *Competing Against Time*, New York: The Free Press, 1990.
22. B. Joseph Pine II, *Mass Customization*, Boston: Harvard Business School Press, 1993.
23. Interview with Steven E. Prokesch, 'Mastering chaos at the high-tech frontier', *Harvard Business Review*, November–December 1993.
24. Kevin Kelly, *Out Of Control*, New York: Fourth Estate, 1994.

3

The End of Industry

Markets are complex, ambiguous, and fast-changing abstractions which are given meaning in the minds of managers by processes of selective attention and simplification.

— George Day, *Wharton on Dynamic Competitive Advantage*[1]

... people communicate across and around traditional hierarchical organizational boundaries if their mutual interest in a particular subject matter is strong enough ...

— Howard Reingold, *Virtual Community*[2]

Since any element in a company's value chain can be produced by an independent external party specializing in that activity, companies no longer compete just with other companies in their 'industries'.

— James Brian Quinn, Jordan J. Baruch, and Karen Anne Zien, *Innovation Explosion*[3]

What minor competitors could become immediate threats when combined with another business design?

— Adrian J. Slywotzky, *Value Migration*[4]

The first challenge in strategy is to define the future opportunity that will give you a critical mass of results – income, learning, or whatever you aim for. The 'product/market decision' comes before all others (Figure 3.1). You have to decide *whom* to serve, and with *what* product or service, before you can decide *how* to do it.

The results you get depend on which territory you choose to fight in, and how you go about it. The choices you make depend, in turn, on your view of the

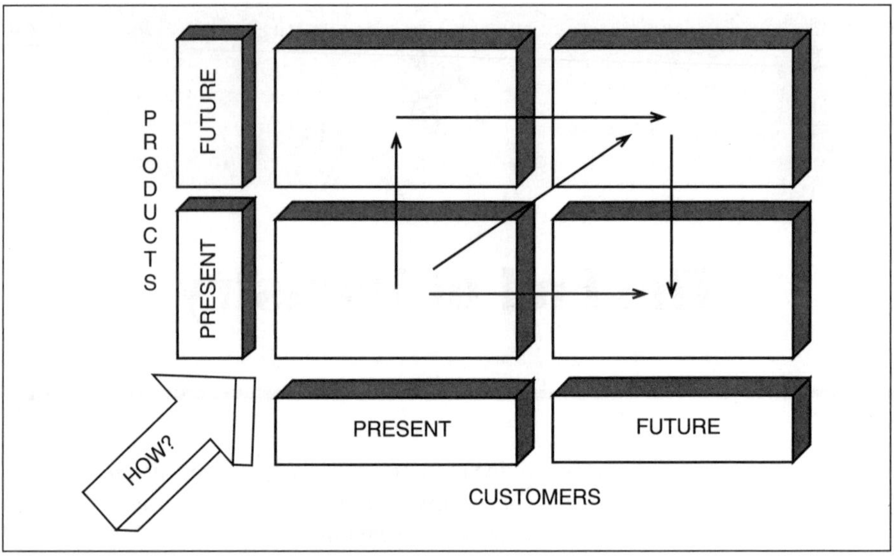

Figure 3.1: *The basic decisions*

opportunities and threats you face. 'Push the envelope' on any one dimension, and you straight away shift into a new opportunity zone.

Here are your broad-brush options:

- Redefine your current customers, or choose new ones.
- Change your value proposition (the product/service you offer).
- Change your value delivery system (your business model).

Surprisingly, many companies are unspecific about where they compete and even less sure about how. (At least they know *what* they sell!) This leaves them vulnerable to players with a clear view of their target; it also means that they might not see those competitors until it's too late.

No more safe havens

What I'm leading to, of course, is an obvious – and ominous – conclusion. Wherever you compete, and however successful you've been in the past, there are dangers ahead.

The new business arena is over-crowded. Future threats to your business are likely to come not just from firms like yours, but from outsiders with none of your baggage, with unlimited ambition, and with access to the best skills on earth.

The risk is that while you try to consolidate your hold on your customers, they will disrupt your efforts by shifting competition to another plane. They will redefine what 'value' means to customers, and they will deliver it in novel ways. And when you try to catch up, they'll dash off in other directions.

In the good old days (which may be *yesterday* just as well as five, ten, or 50 years ago), managers worried about 'raising barriers to entry' into 'our industry'. In the good new days, you need to focus less on keeping others out of your race and more on running faster.

The fact is, competition is a free-for-all. 'Industry' is no longer a concept that keeps invaders at bay.

Industry dynamics

It seems perfectly logical to begin any strategy discussion with a look at 'our industry'. In fact, it's an issue that becomes increasingly irrelevant.

Most people who know anything about strategy cut their teeth on portfolio matrices made famous by Boston Consulting Group (BCG) and General Electric (GE) back in the 1960s and 70s. Most of these have 'industry' as their starting point.

The BCG matrix looks at a firm's market share and its growth rate. The GE matrix looks at overall industry attractiveness and business strength/competitive position. Hofer and Schendel look at the stage of product/market evolution and competitive position. The life-cycle matrix looks at industry maturity and business position. (BCG has thrown out its original matrix, because the assumption it was based on – that cash could be shifted at lower cost within organizations than between them – no longer applies. New tax laws and open capital markets have changed things.)[5]

Michael Porter advises that strategic thinking must begin with an understanding of industry dynamics. His Five Forces model* offers a framework for examining the potential profitability of an industry.

This framework is widely used. But is it still valid? Should you spend time on industry analysis? If so, is there another way to go about it?

As Richard Rumelt has discovered, profit differences *within* industries are on average much greater than those *between* industries.[6] Performance is limited more by management mind-sets than by economics. 'Average' returns tend to hide the fact that there are outstanding players in most industries.[7]

The median ten-year return to investors in the *Fortune* 500 was 14,1 per cent. Computer software ranked first, at 41,8 per cent; airlines were No. 38, at 5,4 per cent. But within the computer software category, Microsoft gave investors a ten-year return of 51 per cent, while Novell delivered just 19 per cent. The 'electronics, semiconductor' category was headed by Intel with a return of 44 per cent while National Semiconductor yielded nine per cent and Advanced Micro Devices lagged at six per cent. 'Beverages' was headed by (who else!) Coca-Cola at 30 per cent, compared to Adolph Coors at three per cent.[8]

* The five forces are: 1) industry rivalry. 2) threat of new entrants. 3) substitutes, 4) bargaining power of buyers, and 5) bargaining power of suppliers

Who's in that industry?

One problem with comparing firms is that almost every category includes companies doing very different things for quite different customers. So while 'airlines' might be reasonably descriptive, 'electronics' or 'retail' may be far vaguer. Companies under the same heading might not compete with each other at all.

James Brian Quinn, a professor at the Tuck School of Business at Dartmouth College, points out that 'the widespread penetration of service technologies has virtually destroyed the boundaries of all industries'. The result is that 'managers can no longer define their corporation as being in a single "industry". Technology demands that they reconceptualize the "industries with which they compete" to include all functional and potential cross-competitors for the services and products they create.'[9]

In summary, then, we have to deal with four facts:

1. Companies don't have to be in 'attractive' industries to make healthy profits. Many firms in mature and boring sectors do extremely well, whereas others in sexier industries lag sadly. *Profits, it's clear, are less a result of industry dynamics than of firm behaviour.* No matter how unattractive a particular industry may seem, there's almost always a manager who will buck the odds and confound the sceptics. Some people, it seems, can wring blood from stones.
2. There was a time when you could define an industry with reasonable accuracy. Now, it's less easy. Boundaries shift and blur extremely fast. Existing or 'traditional' players may offer the greatest threat in an industry; but the greatest danger often comes from 'ignorant outsiders'.
3. It is essential to understand the arena within which you do business. You have to know 'who's who in the zoo', what 'value' means to them, how best to deliver it, and who captures the income from the process.
4. Your objective must be not just to understand the *current* dynamics impacting on your business, but to explore *future* possibilities. Whatever technique you use should help you to see opportunities ahead of others – both customers and companies. It should help you see new ways to serve customers, and new ways to block competitors.

Industry logic

Strangely, while corporate culture has attracted a great deal of attention, *industry culture* has attracted almost none. Yet it provides the context in which companies compete, and it ensures that they compete sub-optimally. Like companies, industries develop their own distinct cultures. Like companies, they start to believe their own propaganda, and they fall foul of their own success.

Economic theory says that there's a 'roughly ideal' strategy for any particular set of market conditions; that companies chasing the same customers in the same environment are likely to do it pretty much the same way.[10]

They might set out with different resources, ambitions, and methods, but over time their strategies converge. Their marketing mix – product, price, place, promotion – becomes remarkably similar. Established players work out the 'rules of the game', and obey them. Though they may compete furiously, and though their respective market shares might rise or fall, there's equilibrium in the market.

Industries evolve and change in response to both internal and external forces. Being human institutions, they develop mental models – or cultures – as they mature.

Insurance companies do things one way, bakers another. The ways of the computer industry are foreign to textile firms. Companies within an industry watch each other, learn from each other, and copy each other.

They reverse-engineer each other's products, and benchmark processes against those of their enemies. When they see a rival launch a new product or cut prices, they scratch their heads and ask, 'How can we deal with that?' They shuffle along in lockstep: Company A improves a product today, Company B catches up tomorrow; Company A cuts prices this week, Company B offers two-for-the-price-of-one next month; Company A appoints new distributors, Company B uses telesales or direct response, or creates an Internet website.

Members of an industry attend the same conventions, read the same publications, and develop their own language. Industry associations form. They define and lobby for members' 'common interests'. Companies poach each other's people, or recruit from universities and technikons that provide training in the same 'discipline'.

Training programmes embrace the same subjects, and 'industry standards' determine who passes, who gets employed or promoted, and who hangs out a shingle. Retired or retrenched executives become industry spokesmen, manage their associations, direct their training programmes – and perpetuate their lore.

Motor manufacturers meet to share information, collect statistics, and lobby government. They hire 'motor men' from each other, rather than outsiders who can't speak their language. They all use the same customer service measures. They all sell and service their products through dedicated dealerships. Their dealers all have problems finding good sales people, and all have a high turnover of these people. They all service cars during the day. Now, whether I walk into a VW dealer or a BMW dealer, a 'team' handles my service problems.

In the same way, bankers, pharmacists, jewellers, golf pros, opticians, mining executives, and many others meet to manage their common interests.

Members of an industry are careful to not disrupt things. Industry paradigms are created, then reinforced. The players appear to compete vigorously, but none wants to be accused of not 'playing the game'. Efforts to improve performance – benchmarking, 'best practices' studies – raise overall industry standards but don't change the relative competitiveness of companies within it.

In many cases, competitors deliberately go easy on each other. They stay out of each other's territory, tone down their advertizing claims, and avoid hiring each other's best people. And although it's illegal, they shift their prices in tandem.

In family life, this is known as incest and it's terribly unhealthy. In business, it leads to customer dissatisfaction and boredom so it's equally dangerous. Besides, as the 'gene pool' shrinks, conformity becomes assured. (I work with many competing companies in many industries, and I'm always struck by the similarities. I hear the same 'tape recording' over and over.)

Understanding the 'glue' that binds an industry and slows its progress is a critical step in breaking free from the pack. By questioning the logic of your industry and challenging its ways, you may be able to redefine value, shift competition to a new plane, and gain a powerful advantage.

Strangely, while corporate culture has attracted a great deal of attention, *industry* culture has attracted almost none. Yet it provides the context in which companies compete, and it ensures that they compete sub-optimally. Understanding the 'glue' that binds an industry and slows its members is a critical step in breaking free from the pack.

The dangers of going with the crowd

You might argue that it makes perfect sense to go with the crowd. By avoiding cut-throat competition, you keep prices at 'sensible' levels, and margins stay satisfactory. Apparently, everyone wins.

But there's an even stronger case for going your own way.

While some marketers may tap into customers' latent needs, the canniest competitors create new needs. They provide products and services that customers never imagined, and deliver them in novel ways. They manage customers' perceptions – and before you know it, your offering may not figure in those perceptions.

Customers are constantly 'retrained' by companies eager for their attention. They're swayed by forces you may not anticipate and can't control. (Consider, for example, the demise of telex when fax came along, the threat to the cigarette industry from health experts, or the switch from mainframe computers to networks and PCs.) And if there's one thing you can bank on, it's that while you strive for 'stability' in your industry, others see the advantages in instability.

Beware those who 'don't understand'

If your strategy is to succeed your competitors must respect it. There's no percentage in taking a knife to a gunfight, or boxing when you're up against a bazooka! Yet most managers are surprised when their enemies don't fight fair.

Innovative insiders are always a threat. The players in an industry do challenge its conventions. For example:

- BMW's Motorplan led the way in offering motorists relief from maintenance costs. Later, the company added free theft and hijack insurance on new vehicles. Both ideas looked like desperate moves to improve sales, but have now become virtually standard practice.

- Nedcor Bank introduced personal banking for a selected group of influential or high net worth individuals. Today, most big banks offer the same service.
- Baker Street Snacks was founded on popcorn, a product for which other snack firms saw no future, by executives who broke away from a market leader to follow their own instincts.

But the bigger danger often comes from 'ignorant' outsiders. When they invade your comfort zone, your proven strategy can quickly become a recipe for disaster. Precisely because they're unfamiliar with your industry's norms, not bound by its history, not locked into old relationships, and not constrained by past deals or sunk costs, the new competitor is able to see things through fresh eyes and act in unconventional ways. Often, all hell breaks loose.

- Billy Rautenbach got the South African agency for Hyundai cars, and within 18 months drove sales to almost 2 000 units a month – as many cars as Ford or Mazda. In less than three years, he snatched close to 10 percent of the toughly-contested South African car market, with just two per cent of the dealers. Rautenbach is a 'business terrorist', defying convention at every opportunity to do the unexpected. He starts with the assumption that whatever the established motor firms are doing must be wrong, then he does just the opposite. He was fanatical about customer service when other car companies just talked about it. Instead of franchizing dealers, he owns all his outlets. Whereas his competitors' dealers all sell *and* service vehicles, Hyundai's sales and service activities are separated. Competitors service cars during working hours – when it suits *them*; Hyundai services cars at night – when it suits *you*. (So a bumper sticker is right on when it says: 'Hyundai kicks butt!')
- Douw Steyn attacked the staid car insurance market with a paperless system and telephone sales. Auto & General's sophisticated computer technology streamlines the way insurance policies are sold and claims are paid. Customers who need repairs are directed to dedicated drive-in assessment centres, so they avoid claim forms and traditional 'three-quotes' hassles. All repairs are done by approved panel beaters – and they're guaranteed for 12 months. Policies can be amended with a single phone call. Premiums are automatically cut as the value of a vehicle falls. Little wonder A&G has grown by a compounded 50 per cent a year since it was founded in 1985, and writes some 100 000 new policies a year. Little wonder, either, that other insurance companies are adopting a similar business model.
- Raymond Ackerman transformed the retailing industry by introducing hypermarkets to this country, and now his Pick 'n Pay group is expanding via franchising. Ackerman opened dedicated butcheries, fish counters, and bakeries in his stores. He upset the highly regulated fuel industry by selling petrol, and tyre retailers were horrified when he started selling tyres. He scared chemists when he loaded shelves with aspirin and antiseptic – and they expect him to open pharmacies in his supermarkets. Retail banks now worry that his financial products will take customers from them.

- After a hostile take-over of Rand Mines, lawyer Peter Flack cancelled lucrative management contracts with mines in the group, empowered mine managers to shop around for specialist services, and promised them big incentives to raise productivity and profits. Established mining houses said he was mad, but with costs rising and profits falling, Gengold and Anglo American soon had to follow him. And as if all that wasn't enough, he then moved towards *branding* gold!
- Irwin Schaffer was taken to court by the Optometric Association when he opened his first Frames shop in 1982 and started selling cut-price spectacle frames. Today, he has a chain of stores in major shopping centres around the country, offering a complete range of optometric services. In the same industry, Eagle Vision optical centres custom-fit lenses to spectacle frames in an hour, instead of the several days traditional 'professionals' can take.
- Corner cafés are an institution in South Africa. But few are known for friendliness, service, or cleanliness, so they're terribly vulnerable to the convenience stores which have suddenly appeared on the forecourts of service stations. Caltex's 'Star Shops', BP's 'Express', and Shell's 'Select' outlets are open 24 hours a day. They're well-lit and well-stocked, clean, staffed by polite people, and equipped with bar-code scanners at the checkouts. Some have in-house bakeries. Many offer wonderful fresh sandwiches, fruit juices, and filter coffee.

In all these examples, the established players could have been agents of change. Their insider knowledge gave them a head start. But it also made them myopic and smug.

What lies ahead?

The problem is not that changes like the ones I've mentioned occur out of the blue. More often, it's that managers simply fail to see the signs. They're so busy managing the present, they forget to look ahead. Strategic blindness is the deadliest of corporate diseases. As Icarus learned, hubris kills.

- Which building society (remember them?) saw ten years ago that banks would steal its home loan clients? (And which bank saw supermarkets as a threat?)
- Which branded consumer-goods company saw the threat of 'no-name' products?
- Which book publisher anticipated the advent of multimedia products like CDs?
- Which typewriter maker worried about PCs?

Structural changes alter the competitive landscape forever. Your ability to detect those seismic shifts, and exploit them early, determines whether you'll be an industry leader, a follower, or a mere spectator.

Competitors generally define the marketspace in the same way. Usually, they cling for too long to their views of customer needs. Customers' perceptions of value shift faster than most organizations can reinvent themselves, and when the link breaks, it's often forever.

While you need to understand today's customers, it's even more important that you anticipate where tomorrow's will be and how they'll buy; for the future is where you'll spend the rest of your life. What's behind you is useful only insofar as it propels you into the future, and lets you stake a meaningful claim there.

Quantum shifts in the environment throw up possibilities for serving new customers in new ways. They also bring new competitors, untrammelled by your logic and equipped with different skills and technologies. Any player who turns an industry's paradigms upside down is bound to cause unhappiness in the short term, but will invariably gain an enormous advantage in the longer term.

New ways of mapping the business arena

Porter's Five Forces model remains a useful tool in some circumstances. But you need to move further, and to enhance your strategic thinking processes. Two new tools will help you 'map' your opportunity arena and explore new possibilities in the 'who', 'what', and 'how' dimensions.

The first one (Figure 3.2) identifies the underlying causes of competitive intensity in your industry. It also provides a useful framework for thinking about what your competitors might do in future.

The drivers of competitive intensity determine how aggressively competitors will play in a particular arena. Understanding this is a first step in gauging how tough things will be, and why. It may also provide useful insights into how to defend your turf or hurt other players.

It's important to work through this model not only from your perspective and from that of your *current* competitors, but also from the point of view of anyone else who might be exploring your territory for opportunities. Used in this way, it will reveal how attractive that territory is, why others might be tempted to attack it – and how you might fend them off.

The second model (Figure 3.3) builds on these insights, and adds detail to your 'industry map'. It helps you step back and take a larger view of your competitive terrain. Once again, it's designed to highlight both current realities and future possibilities.

There are five key issues to think about:

1. The forces driving competition. (From Figure 3.2)
2. The macro context. (External factors likely to cause discontinuities.)
3. Who gets the value? As industries mature and competitive forces shift, different stakeholders capture different value components. (Profits, knowledge, skills, reputation, etc.) Portions of the 'rents' that an inventor gets in the early days are taken by producers, workers, distributors, and others. Knowledge diffuses. Various players build their names on the specific value they add.

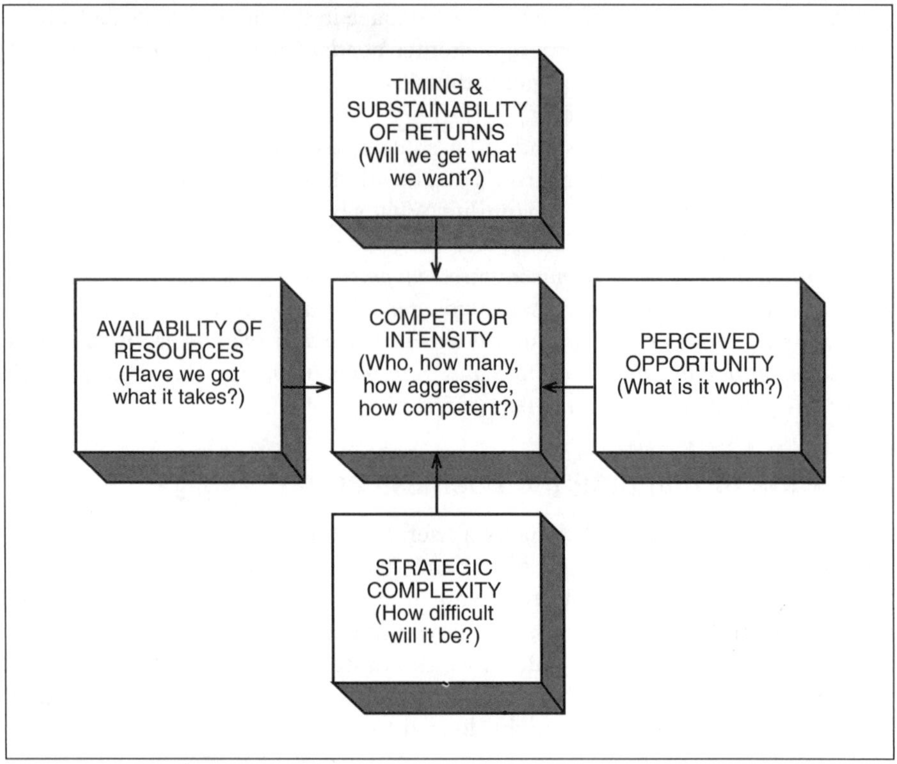

Figure 3.2: *Drivers of competitive intensity*

4. Value-adding processes. (How firms serve customers altogether – their business models.)
5. The key players. (Who's involved in defining and delivering – or *destroying* – value.)

Used together, these new models give you a sound basis for thinking about strategy. Working through them systematically will yield valuable insights. They'll help you map the power shifts and value flows in your business arena. More importantly, they'll get you started on the search for possibilities … for unseen and thus unexploited gaps.

In a complex world, simple competitor analysis is inadequate. Nor is it enough merely to note trends that may affect your firm. A far more explicit picture is essential. Without a detailed map, you won't find your way successfully to the future.

Where you look really matters

In striving to make your firm competitive, you naturally watch your competitors. But while this might be useful, you are more likely to be looking the wrong

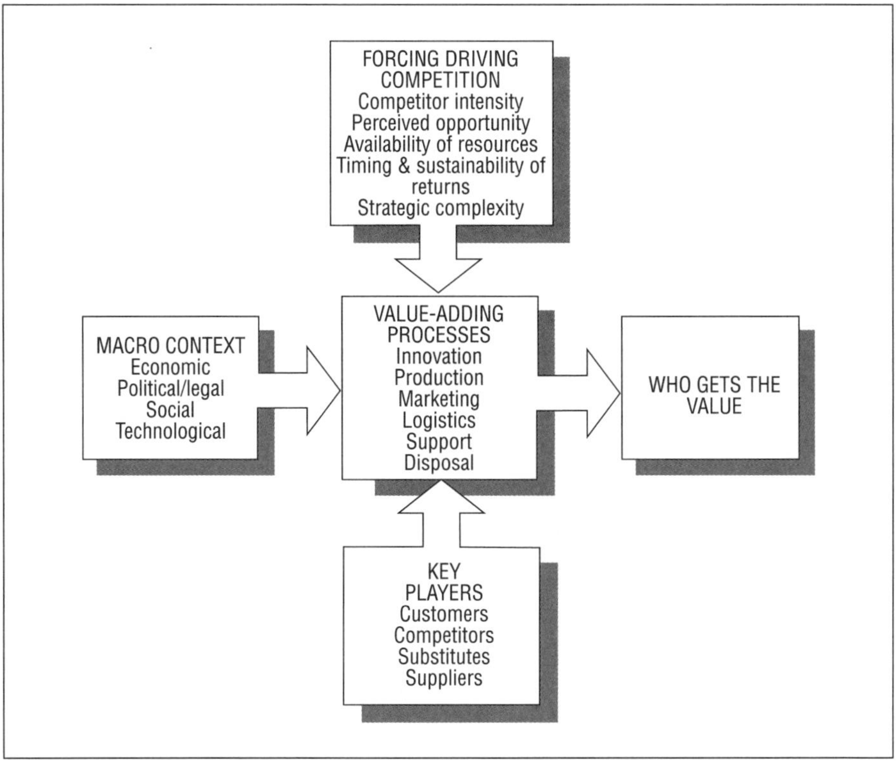

Figure 3.3: *The 'industry map'*

way. The issue is not what your *competitors* are doing, but what your *customers* are doing – or not doing.

Benchmarking has become a fashionable exercise. Firms spend a lot of time studying their competitors. They dissect their business processes in minute detail, and use their enemies' metrics as their own. But to think that you can survive over the long haul by mimicking your competitors is utterly naive. You can never see all of their strategy, so which bits do you copy? What happens when they change? (And sooner or later, someone will!)

And what of customer needs, wants, and expectations? Does studying other suppliers offer insights into buyer behaviour? Does it help you understand better their perceptions of 'value'? And most importantly, does it in any way help you make the radical changes that will let you leapfrog the opposition?

The priority for any firm should be not to outpace competitors, but to change the customer's life. When you get into a race with competitors, you travel the same track as them. Leadership may shift from one player to another, but no one is likely to streak away. In contrast, when you reinvent 'value', you alter not just the rules of competition but the game itself. You radically change the customer's life.

Benchmarking does have some value. Competitors can be a rich source of learning and insights. You should almost certainly measure some of your activities against theirs.

But benchmarking can also prove a dangerous constraint. While it's important to try to understand your competitors, it's stupid to become obsessed by them. It's futile to search for 'complete' answers to their intentions. It's stupid to let them dictate your strategy.

Watch the enemy

Ultimately, you must create the strategy that meets your ambition, fits with your culture, and leverages your resources.

Companies that watch competitors too closely run many risks. Here are some of them:

1. **The risk of misreading their strategy.** Competitive strategy is like an iceberg: some of it is visible and a lot of it is hidden below the waterline. Some companies' strategies are transparent and easy to read. Others are opaque and the bits you can see may be misleading.

   Time and again, for example, salespeople will complain that they can't win because key competitors are cutting prices or offering special deals. But this might be just part of the problem – and a very small part at that.

   In addition to discounting, those competitors could be doing many other things deep down in their business system: improving their products, raising quality and service standards, changing distribution, hiring better people, investing more in training, adopting new technologies, and so on. A highly visible and provocative price cut might, in other words, be merely one of many factors that will give your competitor a much more threatening – and more durable – advantage.

2. **The risk of misreading their intentions.** As human beings, we like to think we can read other people's minds. But of course, it's impossible.

   On the contrary, it's all too easy to misread your competitors' intentions. You almost always have to figure out what they're doing or might do, on the basis of incomplete knowledge. No matter how much information you gather – from their annual reports and brochures, by tracking their adspend and watching their promotions, by clipping press reports, by talking to their customers and suppliers – it's never enough. Even reading their strategy documents may not help. What they say and what they do may differ.

   While it is important to track competitors' behaviour, it is even more important to dig beneath the surface and try to get a sense of where they're going. Present actions may suggest an immediate response; future intentions may require a much more substantial shift in strategy.

3. **The risk of not sensing their spirit.** Just as a motor car engine needs fuel, so does a strategy need the human spirit. Yet most competitor analy-

sis focuses totally on the enemy's strategy, and ignores the spirit that underpins it. Perhaps that's not so surprising. While your competitor's strategy may be fairly easy to decipher, their spirit is less evident. (Does it tell you anything when you see their sales team whooping it up in the local pub? And what do you make of the fact that they're known to be workaholics … to throw great Christmas parties … or to somehow get away with paying their people less than other firms in the industry?)

4. **The risk of focusing on the past.** Where a competitor has come from is much less important than where they're headed. Yet I hear too many executives say things like: 'Their technology is outdated' … or 'They haven't trained anyone for years' … or 'Since they went through the merger in 1978, they haven't been able to get their act together'. These may all be serious handicaps, but they can be nullified by aggressive new moves. It's idiotic to assume that your enemy will keep on doing what they did yesterday.

5. **The risk of assuming that they're stupid.** The 'idiots' down the road didn't get to be dangerous by luck or accident alone. They probably did something right. And they'll probably do more right in the future. If you don't anticipate that, they might kill you.

6. **The risk of assuming that they're smart.** It's wise to assume that competitors will come at you with a killer strategy. But it's also smart to remember that they're fallible. They will do dumb things, their execution will be flawed, and they will do too little, too late.

   (In my years as a consultant, I've seen many weak strategies. I've watched any number of executive teams work laboriously to create a plan, then shelve it and get stuck into 'real work' – until next time. And I've been amazed at how fast managers get bored with what they set out to do.)

There's one other danger in paying too much attention to the competition:

7. **The risk of missing the real threat.** Today's competitor might not be a problem tomorrow. Your worst nightmare could be today's non-competitor. That's where unexpected products and services – new kinds of 'value' – will often come from.

   Competitor analysis tends to focus on the here and now. PC makers watch other PC makers; travel agents watch their peers; book publishers track others in the same field. But in each of these cases, and in countless others, the most significant innovation will be from 'outsiders'. They will change the game. All you'll achieve by watching the 'insiders' is to update your rulebook.

Gathering competitor intelligence is a necessary business function. But far more important is that you focus on your own business, and on transforming your business system to drive the value/cost equation to new limits.

'Tit-for-tat responses to what competitors do may be appropriate,' says Kenichi Ohmae, McKinsey's former Tokyo chief, 'but they are largely reactive. They come second, after your real strategy. Before you test yourself against competition, strategy takes shape in the determination to create value for customers.'[11]

Endnotes

1. George S. Day and David J. Rebstein, Editors. *Wharton on Dynamic Competitive Strategy*, New York: John Wiley & Sons, Inc., 1997.
2. Howard Reingold, *Virtual Community*, London: Secker & Warburg, 1994.
3. James Brian Quinn, Jordan J. Baruch, and Karen Anne Zien, *Innovation Explosion*, New York: The Free Press, 1997.
4. Adrian J. Slywotzky, *Value Migration*, Boston: Harvard Business School Press, 1996.
5. George Stalk, Philip Evans, and Lawrence E. Shulman, *Harvard Business Review*, May–June 1992.
6. Richard P. Rumelt, 'How Much Does Industry Matter?', *Strategic Management Journal*, No. 12, March 1991.
7. Charles Baden-Fuller and John Stopford, *Rejuvenating The Mature Business*, Boston: Harvard Business School Press, 1994.
8. *Fortune* issues on the '1997 100' and 'Global 500', April 28, 1997 and August 4, 1997.
9. James Brian Quinn, *Intelligent Enterprise*, New York: The Free Press, 1992.
10. Richard R. Nelson, 'Why do firms differ, and how does it matter?' in Richard P. Rumelt, Dan E. Schendel and David J. Teece, Eds., *Fundamental Issues in Strategy*, Boston: Harvard Business School Press, 1994.
11. 'Getting back to strategy', Kenichi Ohmae, *Harvard Business Review*, November-December 1988.

4

Technology's Promise

A healthy knowledge market means that employees see that their expertise is valuable and know that others in the organization will cooperate with them when they need expert assistance.

—Thomas H. Davenport and Laurence Prusak, *Working Knowledge*[1]

... left to its own devices, the Information Marketplace will increase the gap between rich and poor countries and between rich and poor people.

— Michael Dertouzos, director MIT laboratory for computer science, *What Will Be*[2]

... looking for value shifts is probably the most important dimension of leadership.

— Michael Dell, chairman Dell Computer Corporation[3]

Dramatic shifts in the 'workscape' are under way. They have extraordinary implications for the global economy, for political and social systems, and for individuals. They're being driven by new ways of doing business, and they are driving even more radical changes in the way business is done. They're changing the way people earn money – and how they spend it.

South Africa has a huge unemployment problem. No one really knows the extent of it. Different definitions of 'unemployment' don't help, survey methods are inaccurate, and the results are often contradictory.[4] The only certainty, according to the International Monetary Fund, is that this is 'the mother of all other crises ... the crisis of crises, upon whose resolution S.A.'s economic, political and social prospects all depend'.[5]

Today some 36 million people are without jobs in the 25 countries which are members of the Organization for Economic Cooperation and Development

(OECD). About one-third of the entire world's working age population is unemployed or underemployed.[6] Unemployment is widely seen as the world's number one crisis.

Companies everywhere are re-designing processes and slashing jobs so they can survive in a hyper-competitive business arena. Joblessness is no longer a cyclical issue that will disappear with economic growth. Long-term systemic joblessness is 'normal'. Nor do the cuts affect just blue-collar workers. Middle management ranks are being decimated and CEOs who don't make a difference are booted out by shareholders.

In the 1990s, the chairmen of IBM, General Motors, American Express, BP, and many other big firms have been pushed out of their posts. Yesterday's job security is a thing of the past. Everyone is at risk.

There are four reasons jobs will stay scarce (Figure 4.1):

1. **The confluence of computer hardware and software with human 'brainware' makes all of us potentially more productive and more creative.** The shift from the Agricultural Age to the Industrial Age took two centuries. The shift to the Information Age has only just begun, but it's changing the way we live and work with lightning speed.

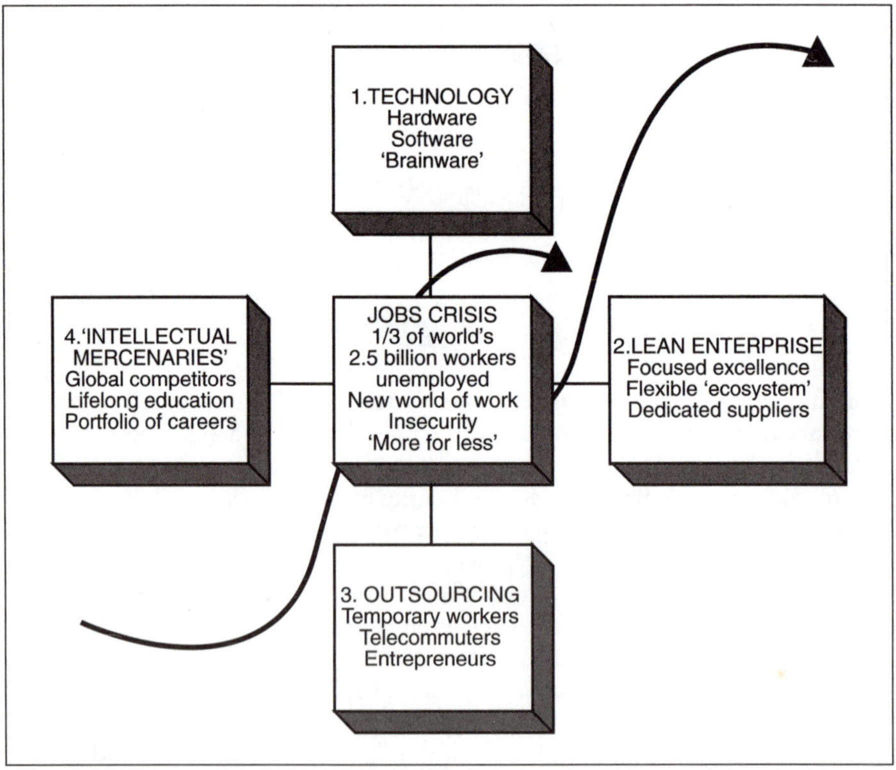

Figure 4.1: *Factors changing the 'workscape'*

Every 18 months the number of transistors that can be fitted on a computer chip doubles every 18 months while the cost halves in the same time. New games pack the power of a 1970s super-computer, and sales of robots grow by ten to 20 per cent a year as firms race to cut employment costs and raise quality.

Along with this hardware, there's a new abundance of mind-blowing software. The shelves of computer stores and book shops are filled with 'shrink-wrapped' applications that offer instant access to vast amounts of knowledge, and leverage our time and talent. Business people, home-makers, and students are suddenly able to perform tasks which were unimaginable only a short time ago, and do them at astonishing speed.

But all this new technology only delivers because there's a growing mass of people who are computer literate, who can use the stuff. 'Brainware' is making the big difference.

Until recently, manufacturing productivity showed continual gains worldwide, while service sector productivity languished. Now, productivity in services – accounting, design, new product development, retailing – is starting to rise.

The new hardware/software/brainware mix will cause it to accelerate exponentially. It will also result in more manufacturing layoffs.

2. **Companies increasingly use a contingent work force to cut costs, increase flexibility, and access the best skills precisely when they're needed.** When recession and new competitive realities forced firms to focus on their core competencies and cut costs, managers learned that while it might be vital to trim the payroll, it's not easy. Job cuts are emotional and legally problematic. Skills are lost. The loyalty of survivors flies out the window.

In future, companies will be reluctant to hire in case cyclical downturns again leave them with too many people. But they've also discovered the value in outsourcing many tasks. It replaces fixed costs with variable ones, and matching production to demand surges becomes someone else's headache. It also provides access to the best skills, and can lead to more innovation. So just-in-time workers have become as necessary as just-in-time production processes.

In the U.S., most new jobs are in low-paying services, or for agencies that supply temps. In every industrialized country, a rising proportion of people work at home or live where they work. Tens of millions of 'road warriors' seldom go into the office.

In South Africa, many companies equip their people with laptop computers, cellular phones, and modems, and demand that they spend more time being productive at home or face-to-face with customers. A growing number of my clients want their people to be 'telecommuters'. Eskom, for example, is vigorously exploring possibilities in the new world of work. The growth of 'virtual companies', 'hot-desking', and 'hotelling' are assured.

3. **Companies compete globally for workers offering skills and/or low-wages.** While you're outsourcing, you may as well shop for the best. Thanks to information technology it doesn't matter where in the world workers are. You can easily reach them via phone, fax, video conferencing system, or jet. Virtual organizations hire them – and let them go – as fast as their needs change.

   ABB Asea Brown Boveri, for example, uses its 'multi-domestic structure' to grab growth opportunities created through shifting labour markets.[7] Other companies take work to workers wherever they may be:

   - Swissair and Singapore Airlines have moved their ticketing operations to India, cutting costs by 50 per cent.[8]
   - European Union laws limit Japanese car sales in Europe. But cars built in Britain are considered European, so Toyota doubled production in Britain in 1994 to beat the law.[9]
   - In 1995, Japanese car firms exported more cars from the U.S. than GM, Ford, and Chrysler; and half of these went to Japan. Of the 380 000 vehicles imported by Tokyo, 25 per cent came from Japanese plants abroad.[10]
   - The German men's clothing manufacturer, Hugo Boss, cuts production costs one-third by manufacturing in Slovenia, Romania, and the Czech Republic.[11]
   - Siemens assembles low-margin electrical components in the Czech Republic, chips in Malaysia, and computers in China.[12]
   - ABB shifted production of engine starters from Heidelberg, Germany, to Brno in the Czech Republic, where labour is one-tenth of the cost.[13]

Firms that set up new factories in foreign countries, even where wages are low, usually hire fewer people. When 1 000 jobs are cut at home, 100 may be created abroad.

Some nations have taken advantage of the opportunities in a networked world. India has become a major software development centre. Egyptian programmers write software for Arab customers, and increasingly for other markets. Ireland processes documents for banks and credit card companies in other countries. Taiwan is the world's biggest producer of PC clones and parts. Barbados promotes itself as a low-cost base for insurance claims and transaction processing, litigation support, and telemarketing. Even Mauritius, traditionally an exporter of sugar and textiles, now also exports software.

As global communication becomes more effective, it'll be easier for South African firms to make use of foreign workers – and they surely will. This will hardly be a matter of choice; it's folly to take on international competitors with free access to the world's best workers without tapping the same advantages. Nor do local labour laws or union militancy help.

By the same logic, foreign firms won't easily be persuaded to invest in fixed assets in South Africa, or to hire large numbers of people; they have too many attractive options elsewhere. Most newcomers have created a presence through partnerships, franchises, or licensing agreements; when it doesn't suit them to be here, they'll vanish overnight.

4. **'Lean enterprise' is the new mantra in virtually every industry.** Lean production was invented and perfected by Toyota, where Eiji Toyoda and Taiichi Ohno worked for years to push the limits of manufacturing efficiency. Its objectives: produce twice as much, twice as fast, with half the resources, at half the cost.

   According to *The Machine That Changed The World*, a landmark study of the global auto industry by a team at Massachusetts Institute of Technology, the 'final manufacturing step ... represents only about 15 percent of the human effort involved in making a car'. Most factory activities are actually services. Integrating the whole requires a 'lean enterprise'.[14]

   Many of today's most popular management concepts – value chain analysis, activity-based costing, core competencies, TQM, reengineering, competing on time – help managers to create such organizations. Streamlining 'unconstipates' the entire system, improves efficiency, and saves money.

   Lean production is not something any company can attempt on its own. Suppliers have to be part of the 'slimming down, speeding up' process. So companies now aim to configure themselves within lean 'ecosystems' in which everyone aims for the same quantum improvements in cost control, productivity, and quality.

   This means that you have to share a lot of secrets. It may also require you to train your suppliers' people, fine-tune their processes, and make them responsible for inventory control, quality, assembly – or almost any other task that you now perform.

   As companies redesign or eliminate processes, they inevitably cut jobs. Low-level people tend to be the first targets, even though they're not the big cost for most companies. But middle managers are also vulnerable; new technology and the trend towards empowerment makes them redundant. And top people who don't sense the need for change, or who can't make it happen, also get shown the door.

Age of the entrepreneur

The global spate of layoffs affects all of society. Lots of young people can't find entry-level jobs. Lots of older people have been laid off at the peak of their careers, with many productive years ahead of them. The victims include not just blue-collar workers, but also administrators, accountants, scientists, and engineers.

So many jobs have been eliminated that large firms no longer offer the career prospects they once did. Today, self-employment is the only way many people can survive. There's a new realization that each of us must take responsibility for our own security, that an organized and comfortable 'career path' is a thing of the past. This puts a new premium on independence. 'Going it alone' has a new respectability.

As a result, the world is on the brink of an entrepreneurial explosion that will transform our lives. A tidal wave of human energy and initiative is being unleashed. Vast numbers of people have the education, the technology, and above all the incentive, to produce breakthrough ideas for their own account. The next few years will see a flood of improvements and inventions – many from people who were regarded as deadwood in the organizations that once employed them.

From Soweto and Sao Paulo to Beijing, Baltimore, and Bombay, highly skilled people are selling their knowledge. They're reinventing their own lives and they're transforming their societies. As work changes so that brain is more important than brawn, their potential grows. And as more governments deregulate their economies the process will gain momentum.

Increasingly, the best knowledge workers are found outside rather than inside organizations. As independent contractors they have a huge incentive to create breakthrough ideas and to sell them to the highest bidder. Companies will have to learn to identify and manage these 'intellectual mercenaries'. Those that exploit entrepreneurial partnerships best will gain an enormous advantage. They'll be able to tap the most relevant core competencies and stay abreast of new knowledge.

After a lot of talk about 'flex firms' or 'adhocracies' (Alvin Toffler), 'hollow corporations' or 'virtual corporations' (*Business Week*), and global networks (Kenichi Ohmae, Robert Reich, and others), it's all coming true. Right now, precisely the talent you need is probably 'out there' – and should probably stay out there as your part-time partner.

The new customer

Customers everywhere have started behaving in ways that threaten most companies. Yet few executives have seen the danger and fewer still are ready to cope with it. Almost daily the press carries stories of well-known companies that are losing out in the market place and of famous brands in trouble.

The 1980s was a decade of conspicuous consumption. The 'me generation' could easily identify with the statement by Gordon Gekko, hero of the movie *Wall Street*, that 'Greed is good!' Individuals demanded more and more of the good things in life, sending the value of luxury goods firms soaring.

Those who couldn't afford to collect watches, fountain pens, or a string of thoroughbreds lifted their spirits with labels from Gucci, Dunhill, or Ralph Lauren. Those with real money went shopping for original Picassos, Atlantic City casinos, London properties like Harrod's or the Dorchester, or Hollywood film studios.

Enthused by this free spending, companies discovered they could expand fast by financing themselves with cheap junk bonds. They went on a buying binge, snapping up competitors, diversifying into new territory, expanding capacity.

But what went up came down with a crash. As the go-go decade closed, the 'value decade' opened. Customers became concerned about getting the most for their scarce cash. Tight budgets triggered a deep down-shift in social values. Buyers expected more for less. Quality and service were more important than ever – but so was low price.

Responding to the new mood, Sharon Stone turned up at the 1995 Oscars in a $30 Gap T-shirt. Many famous couturiers were forced to launch mass-market ranges of their ramp clothes. A headline for Honda's luxury Accura motor car in the U.S. said, 'These days, even the most powerful luxury statements are being made more quietly.'

In a sharp move away from the high-priced end of the car market, Mercedes-Benz announced the 'affordable' C-class series, which has since become a worldwide hit, and later moved even further down-market with the compact A-class model.

Even Intel couldn't escape the new frugality. Faced with growing demand for cheap PCs, the company announced early in 1998 that it would launch a new line of low-priced chips called Celeron. 'Intel inside', one of the branding success stories of the 1990s, apparently has its limits.

Brand wars

On April 2, 1993, Philip Morris (the world's biggest cigarette maker) cut the price of Marlboro (the most recognized brand in the world) by 40 cents a pack. Wall Street saw the 20 per cent discount as an ominous sign.

Investors fled, wiping $13,2 billion from the company's market value that day. Other consumer-goods firms like Procter & Gamble, Quaker Oats, and H.J. Heinz were also the victims of stock sell-offs; the top 25 consumer-goods companies lost a total of $50 billion in market value.[15] The big three U.S. cigarette producers lost close to $7 billion in an ensuing price war.[16]

'Marlboro Friday' is etched in marketing history as the day brands lost much of their appeal. But signs of trouble had been evident for some time.

A 1988 survey showed that 45 per cent of customers were prepared to pay a premium for some brands; by 1992, just 37 per cent felt the same way.[17] Part of the blame lay with marketers themselves.

In the 1950s, major firms in the U.S. spent 90 per cent of their communications funds on advertising, and just 10 per cent on activities such as couponing, contests, and other price-oriented incentives. By 1990, advertising got 25 per cent and below-the-line spend took 75 per cent.[18]

But there were other factors at work. The functionality of competing products converged. Their quality improved and price became less important as a stamp of assurance. Customers changed their ways and started shopping more aggressively for 'good value'.

Major retail chains improved their margins by selling house brands – many of which were made in the same factories that produced costlier branded goods. (The U.K.'s Tesco boasts that its own-label products 'aim to be at least as good as, if not better than, branded products'. The company launched 2 500 new own-label products in 1995 alone, including 500 health and beauty items.[19] Sainsbury's own cola accounts for some 60 per cent of that chain's soft-drink sales.)[20]

In 1985, less than a third of shoppers thought store brands were equal in quality to national brands; by 1993 half thought that way.[21] Altogether, Sainsbury's gets a massive 54 per cent of its sales from own-label products, while Tesco gets 41 per cent.[22]

In the U.K., the market share of private label grocery products peaked at 26 per cent in 1994 (they account for 15 per cent of supermarket sales in the U.S.) Half of the top 500 grocery products are losing ground to private labels. Prices for products such as baked beans, breakfast cereals, fruit juices, and sliced bread have fallen by up to 20 per cent in real terms since 1993.[23]

Pressure on prices and costs

This pattern is consistent with the way people shop in other countries. Faced with abundant choices, customers buy from a range of products within a category. They'll pay extra for treats or where quality matters.

On the other hand, where they can get away with skimping, they will. And as they discover that more and more own-label products serve them just as well as big brands, it's easier for them to bypass famous names.

Shifts in marketing and buyer behaviour impact all the way up the value chain. The housewife spends less in the supermarket ... the supermarket gets tough on the grocery manufacturer ... the manufacturer puts the squeeze on suppliers of everything from raw materials to packaging, transport, and advertising. The ad agency in turn leans on film production houses. They demand a better deal from script-writers and editors. And when those creative people go shopping, what can they do but cast around for the best price?

Brands lose share to private labels when times are tight. They regain customers when economic conditions improve. So while they may be an essential part of a company's marketing arsenal and a key measure of its value, the years ahead are sure to see many brands go to the wall, and many distributors promoting their own names rather than the products they sell.

The brands that survive and grow will be those whose owners understand that brand value comes not from glitzy promotions, but from innovation and the daily grind to perfect the execution of strategy. For it's what the customer doesn't see that captures and keeps her.

Philip Morris cut the price of Marlboro because discount cigarettes had grabbed 41 per cent of the American market. But by fighting back on many fronts, the firm quickly drove off the attackers and pushed sales and profits to new highs.

In the same way, Coke and Pepsi dealt with a threat from Cott Corporation's no-name cola drinks. And in many other categories, brand-name manufacturers regained lost sales and made their names worth more than ever. Every day's business pages carry stories about firms that have shed weight and shaped up.

Probably no company is more dedicated to its brands than Procter & Gamble. But even this consumer-goods giant had to confront reality. While juggling its marketing budget, it shut 30 plants and sent 13 000 workers home.[24] 'We must slim down to stay competitive,' said chairman Edwin L. Artzt. 'Our competitors are getting leaner and quicker, and we are simply going to have to run faster to stay ahead.'[25]

The lessons are clear: drive up value, drive down your costs. It's as easy as that. And as tough.

Underpinned by this logic, a brand name can have enormous value. Without it, no amount of promotion will ever be enough.

Changing gears

Adapting to the new customer is not just a matter of launching new products and services. Both consumer-goods and business-to-business marketers have to reinvent every aspect of the way they sell.

More and more vendors complain that the buying process has slowed down and become more complex and costly. Customers shop around, compare prices, and haggle for better deals. Corporate buyers call for multiple quotes, demand tons of information, expect detailed and glitzy presentations, and involve widening circles of people in the purchase decision.

South African government departments demand details of suppliers' affirmative action campaigns. Visible commitment to 'transformation' and the empowerment of small and micro-enterprises is a deciding factor. Friends in high places may be essential to open doors. Sales people have to be professional, patient, and well-connected.

At the other end of the scale, many consumers want to simplify their lives. Pressed for time, they see shopping as a chore. Selling to them hinges on how easy you can make it. The more help you can offer, the better.

Distribution methods must be tailored to new ways of shopping. Everything from life assurance to computers is already sold through direct response programmes. Banking transactions occur at ATMs, over the phone, or on the Internet. Groceries sell through wholesale clubs, delis, and spaza shops.

For some companies this means costly rentals in high-traffic shopping malls; for others it means big investments in technology; yet others must reinvent the art of personal salesmanship.

Technology changes everything

There are already thousands of electronic malls and speciality shops on the World Wide Web. Companies use the Internet to send customers information on their new products and to provide after-sales support, to sample and distribute new software, and to speed up and cut the cost of administrative tasks.

Whether you want to get free recipes from *Gourmet* magazine; order books, clothing, or CD's; or book a hotel or an airline seat, it's all possible on the Internet. And new technologies will make selling and buying even easier, faster, and cheaper in the future.

Amazon.com, the world's first on-line bookstore, threatens the entrenched business model to which other booksellers are committed.

When Microsoft launched its Explorer browser in 1996 – one of the biggest product launches of all time – the only way you could get it for many months was *free*, off the Internet. You couldn't buy it from a regular retailer. (Netscape tried to keep selling its browser, but when its market share evaporated it, too, had to resort to give-away marketing.)

After years of declining sales, the publishers of *Encyclopaedia Britannica* announced in 1997 that printed copies of the book set would be unavailable in the future. It has since become available on CD and an Internet connection lets you download regular updates.

In his latest book *The Circle of Innovation*, Tom Peters invites readers to access his website (tompeters@businessedge.net) and share ideas. In his trademark staccato style, he snarls:

> You've heard of the 'global village'.
> I say village is too big.
> Try 'global block'.
> Better yet, try 'global mall'.[26]

But this is just the start.

Listen to George Forrester Colony, president of Forrester Research in Cambridge, Massachusetts, on how you might buy a Domino's Pizza, or personal hygiene products sometime in the future:

> *Domino's might give you a little machine with two buttons: pizza with cheese, pizza with pepperoni. You throw it on top of your refrigerator and you come home late at night. You're so lazy you won't even make a phone call – you press one button! There's a cellular modem connected by cellular digital packet data, a new standard for sending data over cell lines to the cellular data network, back to Domino's. Fifteen minutes later, there's a pizza.*
>
> *Another thing I think may happen is the 'trash scan' idea. Suppose Procter & Gamble gives you a box you put in your trash can. When you throw products away, the Procter & Gamble box will scan the labels of those products and record that information. The next day, Federal Express brings you a box with toothpaste and shaving cream.*[27]

And here's Nicholas Negroponte, head of the Media Lab at Massachusetts Institute of Technology, on how shoppers might use 'smart agents' to find the products and services they want:

Today, marketers reverse-engineer a consumer's choice to infer why a decision was made. Advertisers cluster such demographics to further guess whether I might be inclined to purchase one soap flake versus another. Tomorrow, this will change. We can opt to tell a computer agent what we want, when we want it, and, therefore, how to build a model of us – the collective reasoning of the past, present, and future (as far as we know it). Such agents could screen and filter information and anonymously let the digital marketplace know that we are looking for something.

Two kinds of agents will exist in that scenario: one will stay at home (on your wrist, in your pocket, in your radio) and one will live on the Net, surfing on your behalf, carrying messages back and forth. To some degree, the homebodies will be hermetically sealed. They will read bit streams about products and services broadcast in abundance through wired and wireless channels. They will scoop off subsets of information of personal interest – an act as simple as grabbing a stock quote for you, and as complicated as determining your interest in a segment of a talk show. These agents will be all ears.[28]

Needed: new business models

In this climate it's essential to get under your customer's skin, to learn what drives her, and to change your business in whatever way is necessary to cement a long-term, win-win relationship.

Of course this means urgent attention to the behaviour of your front-line people: sales, clerical, credit control, deliveries, service and repairs, and so on. But real performance demands that you re-design your total business model: from its structure and the way communications flow to information systems and technology; from policies and procedures to your management style and your overall business philosophy.

If listening to the customer was important yesterday, it will be even more important in the future. And technology will make it far easier.

It has become commonplace for journalists and letter writers to invite dialogue by publishing their e-mail addresses with their names. Radio stations call for comment from their listeners; TV broadcasters solicit news tips and ideas from their talk show hosts. Manufacturers encourage users of their products to 'chat' about functionality, design, quality, and service.

This new transparency and accessibility makes companies increasingly vulnerable to customers' whims. So expect customer service to become ever more important. And prepare your company to foster radically new relationships with your customers.

Advances in IT offer many advantages that yesterday's manager could only dream about – or couldn't even imagine. Here are four of them:

1. **Disintermediation.** When you get rid of middlemen, you cut the costs and complexity they bring with them. You also eliminate the filtering barriers that they erect between you and your customers. And you greatly improve your responsiveness to both customer needs and competitor actions.

   As Michael Dell points out: '... if I've got 11 days of inventory and my competitor has 80, and Intel comes out with a new 450 megahertz chip, that means I'm going to get to market 69 days sooner.'[29] It also means much lower inventory levels, less storage space – and thus less risk.

   Disintermediation can have a profound impact on customer relationships. 'Close to the customer' has become a cliché; technology makes it a reality.

   'In the electronic world,' says Frances Cairncross in her bookThe *Death of Distance*, 'people leave a lot of tracks.'[30] The more you learn about what, why, how, and when they buy, the better you can serve them and the greater your chances of locking them into a long-term, profitable relationship.

   Momentum Life uses information technology to make it easy for clients to check the status of their insurance policies. Each enquiry to its Pretoria call centre is logged and adds to its knowledge about its clients. The more familiar they get with Momentum, the less reliant they – and the company – are on intermediaries who may not be around in the future.

2. **Outsourcing.** Pressure on costs, focus on core competencies, and easy access to swarms of suppliers are some of the factors causing companies to outsource more and more of their activities. But just as tasks can be outsourced to suppliers, so they can also be outsourced to *customers*.

   Industrial Age companies delivered 'complete' products and services to their customers. Now, customers are learning to take over many value-creating activities – and Information Age companies make it easy.

   Not long ago, shopping for a car meant a visit to a showroom and an encounter with a salesman. Now, the McCarthy Group lets you check stock and prices in its various dealers via the Internet. Microsoft's CarPoint site goes further with 360-degree SurroundSound views of the interior of various vehicles. Goodbye pushy or ignorant salesmen!

   Amazon.com encourages book lovers to post their own reviews on its site – so they become part of the sales team. Software companies enable you to dial up and solve your own problems. Mercantile Lisbon Bank offers more than 40 on-line products in its Bank@bility suite.

3. **Communication.** An old adage says, 'The more you tell, the more you sell.' David Ogilvy, the famous advertising man, found that long copy outsold short copy in almost every product category. Direct marketing experts know this to be true. In spite of the evidence, however, marketers are influenced by people who say, 'I never read long ads!' And they sell themselves short by trying to cram a complicated pitch into a few memorable words or an eye-catching picture.

As any Internet user knows, it's tempting to 'drill down' through a Web site in search of new layers of information. You can start with a simple message, then pull more and more information onto your desktop. 'Hypertext' lets you skip easily from page to page, to customize the material you get. It's little wonder that Net junkies spend so much time at their computer screens.

IT systems facilitate communication by making two-way exchanges easy. Companies that exploit the new technologies best have discovered the power of involvement and listening. They go out of their way to ask customers for opinions, suggestions, and complaints.

4. **Surprise.** People shop because they must, but they also shop for fun. They love the unexpected. Thanks to technology, companies don't have to rely on their front-line people to invent new sales pitches on the run; the process can now be easily 'industrialized'.*

   Firms that use the Internet best constantly ring the changes in their Web pages. They offer special deals, include guests on their sites, provide links to other interesting sites, bundle advice with their product offerings, and call for contest entries.

   Banks use their ATMs to conduct promotional activities. Pharmacies hype various products on the touch-screens of in-store kiosks. Once, juke boxes let customers pick the hits they wanted to hear; now, you can compile your own selection of songs and load them onto CD.

Technology makes totally new business models possible. It offers an almost infinite number of ways to cut concept-to-cash time, reduce inventories, speed up product delivery, conduct financial transactions, and bond with customers.

Sharing ideas has never been as easy as it is today. Reaching new markets gets cheaper by the day. The possibilities are awesome.

But while you test new tools, don't forget the human factor. People make companies tick. Served *by* technology, they can make magic. As servants *of* technology, they shrivel and die.

A framework for strategists

The four factors underpinning the jobs crisis also provide a framework for thinking about your company's competitiveness. The most aggressive companies worldwide are changing to embrace these issues. Are you doing the same?

- Are you exploiting technologies that will let you radically improve the value you offer your customers, while at the same time cutting the cost of doing it?
- Are you a 'lean producer' – doing twice as much, twice as fast, with half the resources, at half the cost?

* This powerful concept was described by former Harvard Business School marketing professor Ted Levitt, in an article called 'The Industrialization of Marketing' (*Harvard Business Review*, September–October 1976).

- Have you reviewed how you deliver that value, to eliminate unnecessary processes and outsource 'non-core' inputs.
- Do you hire the best people wherever in the world they are?

Clearly, if you pursue these strategies you'll need fewer people with different skills. That in turn, means fewer people who can afford to be customers. This is one of the painful paradoxes of business in a global economy, and a reason to take seriously the warning of economist Robert Heilbroner that 'whereas socialism may have lost, it is not so clear that capitalism has won'.[31]

Henry Ford paid his workers well, because he wanted them to be able to afford to buy his cars. But in a 'post-Fordist' era, job growth will be slow and most new jobs will be in the low-paying service sector.[32] Disposable incomes will be squeezed. Social pressures will grow.

South African companies cannot ignore their social responsibility to create jobs. If unemployment is not dramatically reduced, this country will become an increasingly hostile environment for business. But no firm will stay in business for long if it isn't competitive. So executives will have to take tough decisions about the number and types of people they employ, what they expect of them, and how they manage them.

Changes in the workscape have only just begun. It takes real vision to see what advances technology will make possible in the future, and guts to act on the insights. But one thing is clear: no executive, no politician, and no worker can ignore what's happening.

Endnotes

1. Thomas H. Davenport and Laurence Prusak, *Working Knowledge*, Boston: Harvard Business School Press, 1998.
2. Michael Dertouzos, *What Will Be*, New York: HarperEdge, 1997.
3. Joan Magretta, 'The power of virtual integration: an interview with Dell Computer's Michael Dell', *Harvard Business Review*, March-April 1998.
4. 'Joblessness may be 30% or 50% – it all depends on the definition', The *Sunday Independent*, April 7, 1996.
5. Simon Barber, 'Unemployment the mother of all crises, IMF tells SA', *Business Day*, March 26, 1996.
6. Ray Marshall, 'The global jobs crisis', *Foreign Policy*, Fall 1995, Number 100.
7. ASEA Annual Report, 1994.
8. 'Airlines going global to trim costs', *International Herald Tribune*, April 9, 1995.
9. 'Toyota: it's back on track', *Business Week*, April 4, 1994.
10. 'Japan is back', *Business Week*, February 19, 1996.
11. 'Clothier's CEO shows who's Boss', *International Herald Tribune*, August 16, 1994.
12. 'Siemens shapes up', *Business Week*, May 1, 1995.
13. 'Integrating the East, reinventing the West are one and the same', *Wall Street Journal Europe*, June 30–July 1, 1995.
14. James P. Womack, Daniel T. Jones, and Daniel Roos, *The Machine That Changed The World*, Rawson Associates: New York, 1990.

15. John A. Quelch and David Harding, 'Brands versus private labels: fighting to win', *Harvard Business Review*, January–February 1996.
16. 'Still smokin'', *The Economist*, March 11, 1995.
17. 'Brands on the run', *Business Week*, April 19, 1993.
18. David A. Aaker, *Building Strong Brands*, New York: The Free Press, 1996.
19. Tesco Annual Report 1995.
20. 'Sainsbury sees future in U.S., but its own brands need push', *Wall Street Journal Europe*, May 15, 1995.
21. *Business Week*, April 19, 1993.
22. Quelch and Harding, op. cit.
23. Will Hamilton, 'Brands must change channels', *Marketing Week*, February 16, 1996.
24. 'No cheer for Procter & Gamble', *Newsweek*, July 26, 1993.
25. 'Amid record profits, companies continue to lay off employees', *Wall Street Journal Europe*, May 8, 1995.
26. Tom Peters, *The Circle of Innovation*, New York: Alfred A. Knopf, Inc, 1997.
27. David Buerger, 'Power pundit', *Wired*, March 1995.
28. Nicholas Negroponte, '000 000 111–Double agents', *Wired*, March 1995.
29. Magretta, 1998.
30. Frances Cairncross, *The Death of Distance*, Boston: The Harvard Business School Press, 1997.
31. Robert Heilbroner, *Visions Of The Future*, New York: The New York Public Library and Oxford University Press, 1995.
32. Stewart Lansley, *After The Gold Rush*, Century Business Books: London, 1994.

5

The QWERTY Trap

My view is you perpetuate success by continuing to run scared, not by looking back at what made you great, but looking forward at what is going to make you ungreat, so that you are constantly focusing on the challenges that keep you humble, hungry and nimble.

— Lou Gerstner, chairman and CEO, IBM[1]

If we want not just to survive but to flourish, we must choose the daring, creative route of corporate renewal: fundamental, systemic change.

— George Fisher, chairman and CEO,
Eastman Kodak Company[2]

... it is nearly impossible to build a cogent case for diverting resources from known customer needs in established markets to markets and customers that seem insignificant or do not yet exist.

— Joseph Bower and Clayton Christensen,
Harvard Business Review[3]

The message is consistent: make a difference or die.

And don't think you can get away with small improvements or marginally better promises. If you want to occupy profitable market space, *radical differences* must be your goal.

I often ask executives in seminars, conferences, or business school classes, 'How many of you work in companies that have undergone some radical change in the past 12 months?' Typically, no more than ten per cent raise their hands. Then I ask about changes in the past six months, six weeks, or six days, and the hands drop. Clearly, the rate of change outside most firms is much faster than the rate of change inside!

This is no time for business as usual. More of the same is suicide. Yesterday's rulebooks are being torn up and new ones are being written. Yesterday's high ground is tomorrow's hole in the ground. Unless firms act – and act fast and radically – the end *is* in sight!

Managers fail not because they make the wrong decisions, say Joseph Bower and Clayton Christensen of the Harvard Business School, 'but because they make the right decisions for circumstances that are about to become history'.[4]

Every company now faces more opportunities than it can cope with. But most need very different strategies than they've used so far. They'd do well to remember that one definition of insanity is 'doing the same thing over and over, and expecting different results'.

In a recent strategy workshop, one senior executive argued: 'Mine is a mature industry. Nothing has changed for years. I don't see any need to start rocking the boat now.'

He hasn't noticed, but the boat is rocking already. And it's full of holes!

Yesterday's best

The typewriter keyboard we all curse was designed in 1873 to slow down early typists, as their fingers moved too fast for their clunky machines. It would make perfect sense to redesign it so that today's users could exploit the speed of computers and word processors. But we're locked in. There are just too many old-style keyboards around. Too many people have spent a long time learning to use them. The cost of change would be huge all round. It would take an extremely brave marketer to launch a really user-friendly keyboard.

Like the QWERTY keyboard, many *strategies* were designed for a different time. They neither exploit today's opportunities nor prepare organizations for the future.

New technology allows companies to do extraordinary things, but old systems and practices make them boring and vulnerable. Direct marketing techniques offer cost-effective ways to capture and keep customers, but companies continue to use mass media for advertising. Highly-educated workers offer the prospect of new levels of innovation and service, but employers hang onto those whose lack of skills is a major handicap.

Accepting the need for a new strategy is easier than making the switch. New costs are inevitable. Past investments are hard to write off. Ego and emotion tie you to the past. And when you do change, there's always a lag till you see the rewards.

Woks and chopsticks

To understand the central challenge facing every company, let me use a simple analogy (Figure 5.1):

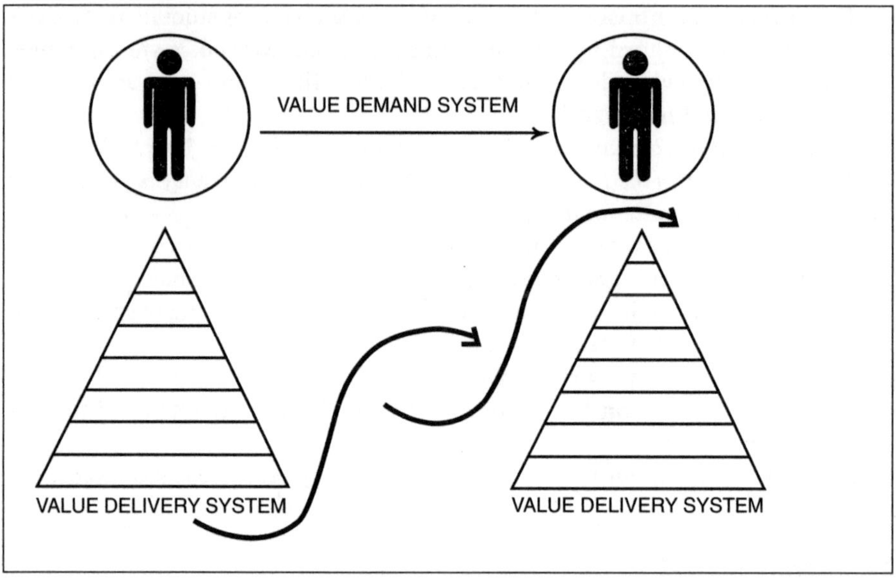

Figure 5.1: *Abandon the past to own the future*

Let's say you enjoy cooking, so you decide to open a restaurant. Like a good marketer, you ask customers what they like to eat, when and where they prefer to eat, how much they're prepared to pay, what service they expect, and so on. And you discover a market opportunity: many people say they enjoy Chinese food. Specifically, they want take-away fast food. So you build a value delivery system to satisfy them.

Everything you do – your location, decor, menu, prices, the way you serve food, the way you prepare it, the way you buy ingredients, your accounting system – is planned to satisfy specific customers. Your new organization is a textbook example of outside-in design.

Naturally, since your value delivery system is so precisely tailored, things go well for a while. Then sales start to slip. You investigate, and find that your customer has changed. Now she wants health food – lean cuisine, bran, fresh fruit and vegetables – not fried rice and noodles and meat. She also wants to sit down in comfortable surroundings, with table service and perhaps a glass of mineral water or white wine. And, of course, she wants to use a knife and fork; the novelty of chopsticks has worn off.

A new business opportunity stares you in the face. You're in the food business already, you reason, so why not expand? Astute marketers often exploit their reputations and investments through 'line extensions', so why not do the same?

You still have your trusty wok, plus a zillion chopsticks. You rent extra space next door, call shopfitters to fix up the place and put in some chairs and tables, and place orders for lettuce and bran muffins.

> You've hardly opened the door, when the first new customer walks in. He sits down and orders a fruit salad and a glass of Perrier. 'Certainly, sir,' you say, knowing that you have to make a good impression fast. And in no time at all you're back with his order ... together with a pair of chopsticks.
>
> 'Excuse me,' he says, looking puzzled. 'Could I please have a spoon?'
>
> 'Afraid not,' you say with a smile. 'Here, we only have chopsticks.'
>
> 'I can't eat fruit salad with chopsticks!' he says.
>
> 'Well, you'll just have to.'
>
> 'Look, if I wanted to eat with chopsticks, I would have gone to the Chinese place next door. Now will you please bring me a spoon.'

That relationship is doomed. You want to exploit your old business system for too long. You insist on doing some of the same old things for a brand new customer. You can't bring yourself to cut your ties with the past, and to create a new future from scratch; you've got a huge investment in chopsticks.

But sunk costs aren't the only barrier between you and your health food customer. That Chinese takeaway gave you your entrepreneurial start: you have a powerful emotional attachment to it. Your ego is tied to the old place. You love your wok.

Time to let go

The same problem faces virtually every organization in every industry. Successful companies suddenly find that a new breed of customer makes demands they're not prepared for. Aggressive new competitors steal customers away with breakthrough products and services. Just when managers think they've got the perfect strategy, someone comes along and challenges it. Just when they think they've got the rules of the game licked, an upstart arrives from nowhere and changes the game.

Want an example? Here's John C. Dvorak, writing in the August 1994 issue of *PC Magazine*:

> *It's hard to imagine that a solid industry like the vinyl-record industry would disappear almost overnight. I recall going to my local Tower Records one day, expecting to find the usual vinyl shop with some CDs scattered about. I walked in and was floored by the change – 100 percent CDs.*

Dvorak's experience is not unusual. It will become increasingly common as the pace of change continues to accelerate. America's Big Three carmakers missed the sudden shift to small cars. Microsoft didn't see the Internet explosion coming. The publishers of *Encyclopaedia Britannica* were slow to launch their product on CD, and even slower onto the Internet. Even the smartest managers do too little, too late.

Firms become trapped in the past by investments in plant and machinery, by specific skills that took years to hone, by distribution arrangements that were the envy of all, and by advertising campaigns that won many awards and which they still love with a passion. Companies that were most successful in the past usually have the toughest time escaping it.

But if you don't ditch that baggage, you'll sink with it. New times demand fresh thinking. What you need to consider is not how to preserve the past, but what you've learned from it that might be useful in the future. Ask yourself now:

- What does the future hold for your organization?
- What future do you want?
- What radical steps must you take to make it happen?
- What should tomorrow's value delivery system look like, and how can you create it?
- What resources do you have that could be useful tomorrow?
- What must you abandon?

Every strategy involves both technology – equipment, structures, systems – and people. Changing technology is in many ways easier than changing the people who underpin it. Yet more planning, money, and effort goes into changing things than changing minds and behaviour.

As you look ahead, remember my earlier warning: that building a flexible, adaptive organization is all-important. Be sure you consider your people early. Everything else is only there to help them discover and leverage their potential.

Forces shaping the business arena

The business arena is shaped by six forces:

1. Political/legal.
2. Economic.
3. Social.
4. Technological.
5. Competitor behaviour.
6. Customer behaviour.

These forces all impact on every organization. They also impact on each other, which complicates things. Managers must watch them *separately* and anticipate how they might *interact*. For when they collide, they cause unexpected trouble. And they throw up opportunities – which you'll miss if you're not alert.

Organizational life cycles occur because the environment changes while companies cling to the past (Figure 5.2). Entrepreneurs breathe life into an idea in a particular environment. But the world of 1920 was clearly different to that of 1970; and we can only imagine what 2020 will be like. Products and services that were winners when they came to market a decade ago are of little interest now; and today's best offerings will have few fans a decade hence.

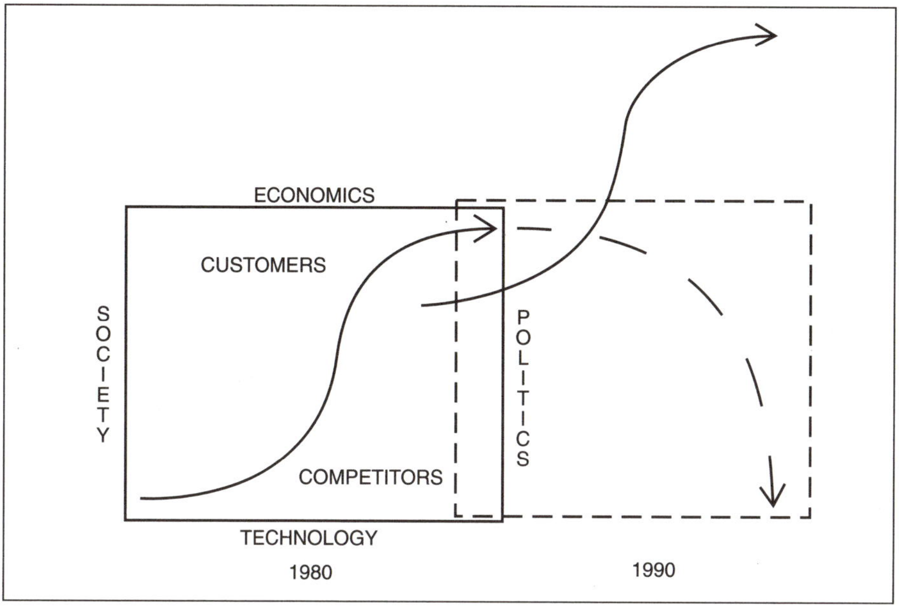

Figure 5.2: *When yesterday's best won't do*

What let you 'fit' back then is hardly useful now.

However, those 'good early days' have a magnetic pull. They can drag you down just when you think you've got it made. Without deliberate effort, they'll prevent your growth and ensure your decline and death.

Ironically, the most dangerous time for any firm is precisely when it's most successful. Because it's then that managers think they've got the answers; they think they've 'cracked the code', and that if they just keep repeating what worked in the past, their future will be assured.

Yesterday's knowledge

Every manager would like a crystal ball to know what lies ahead. But every forecasting method is flawed. Sudden discontinuities can turn your best guesses into the worst of nightmares. Surprises derail the best of plans.

All predictions are based on what we already know. Useful clues to the future lie in today's sales figures, headlines, and meeting reports. Many of the changes that will impact on your business tomorrow have already been triggered. Much of what is now under way will have consequences for months or years. Being alert to what has already happened helps you prepare for what might happen.

Knowledge of the past is easy to get (or should be). It's based on what actually happened. Although you can't extrapolate from it to know what will happen in the future, it is extremely valuable. It gives you clues. But it also has a short shelf life. What happened a minute ago probably tells you more about what'll happen next than something that happened a month ago. Though you can learn from history, recent history is more useful than the distant past.

Management information systems capture history and make it digestible. But many companies use it long after it has become stale. Listen to Steve Jobs, co-founder of Apple Computer:

> *If you knew what was going to happen in advance, every day, you could do amazing things. You could become insanely wealthy, influence the political process, et cetera. Well, it turns out that most people don't even know what happened yesterday in their own business. So, a lot of businesses are discovering they can take tremendous competitive advantage simply by finding out what happened yesterday as soon as possible.*[5]

Flooded by facts

The Information Age is characterized not just by explosive growth in the amount of information that now swirls around us, but also by technologies that make it accessible and useful. Companies need to be more alert than ever to what's happening around them. New hardware and software give them real-time sensitivity and enable them to crunch, interpret, and share information with great efficiency.

Video-conferencing equipment, cell phones, electronic mail, and 'groupware' products like Lotus Notes all enrich the organizational mind. The Internet dramatically expands a firm's 'neural' reach. Intranets and extranets facilitate conversations inside organizations and with customers and suppliers.

But the impact of technology on business is not all positive. A flood of easy-to-access information is both a plus and a minus. Having it helps you think; but too much of it wastes time and blocks thinking.

IT systems make it easy to check inventory, analyse yesterday's sales, track a competitor's market share, or measure work in progress. Specialists both inside and outside companies add copious amounts of information from a wide range of sources. Databanks bulge. In the past, executives began the day by reading the newspaper; now, they switch on their desktop computer.

But ask them what they *do* with all that information. Ask them what they last did differently as a result of it. Chances are, they don't use much of it, they don't use it often, and they don't use it well. Their most powerful competitive weapon is wasted.

As knowledge becomes more easily available, managers tend to rely on it more. Faced with almost any decision, they insist on 'getting the facts'. And this can embed the idea of incremental improvement in every process and procedure.

Like guided missiles, organizations use data-bites to adjust their course into the future. They capture a stream of information fragments, add them to what they already know, and then adjust course by a few degrees.

Radical change sounds exciting when you hear a business guru talk about it, but it would tear many companies apart. So in the real world, most change very slowly.

Using information well takes discipline. If you don't manage it, it manages you. There are only two reasons you need it: to know where you are and to think about where you're going. For the first, focus on a few key indicators in depth. The second demands a wider, shallower view.

As a manager, you have to anticipate the future. You have to act not just to occupy a comfortable space 'out there', but to shape tomorrow's business arena. You also have to take other people with you. While some rare leaders might get away with saying 'trust me', most of us have to offer some assurance that we know what we're about.

A stab in the dark

No matter how hard you peer into the future, you can't see it clearly. Events rarely unfold exactly as you expect them to. Even the most consistent trend line can suddenly change direction. A product that has been selling well suddenly dies. A swing in exchange rates knocks your costing for a loop. A dozy competitor snaps to life and starts a price war.

Strategy is based on assumptions, so planning usually begins with some sort of environmental scan. This activity is inevitably biased towards the past. Management looks back to look ahead.

This is natural, given that you can see yesterday's production reports or last month's sales figures. Current events are tangible. But tomorrow is a mystery. To talk about it is to speculate. And naturally, we feel better writing specific, measurable objectives and precise action plans, rather than guessing at something we know we'll get wrong.

Without a view of the future – and where we want to be in it – objectives and action plans make no sense. For example, if you plan to buy a house, it must meet certain needs; you also want to know it's a good investment. So you explore various suburbs, you check what's happened to prices in the area you like, and you gather information on development plans. At the same time, you think about your own finances – your ability to pay and whether this is the best way to invest. And you look ahead. Who will move in next door? Will you stay in this house after you retire? Are you buying to make a killing, so you can move elsewhere? What will your lifestyle be in ten or 15 years?

This major personal decision is based on a bunch of guesses. Some might be better than others, but they're all risky. Important as this investment is, you have to accept that you might be wrong.

Business decisions are no different. The brightest people misinterpret what's happening 'out there'. Everyone sees a different picture. People respond to the same facts in various ways.

Before the 1994 elections in South Africa, many projects were put on hold by executives who expected the worst. A few bold souls, on the other hand, went ahead with 'business as usual'. In fact, the day before the poll, I ran a strategy workshop with the top management of a motor manufacturer. For them, it was more important to debate how they'd grow in the future than to worry about what might go wrong.

Even the best managers respond inappropriately to what they see. They expect the economy to grow, but hedge their bets and hold back on capital investment or promotional spending. They project rising sales, but get their product mix wrong. They know they should push affirmative action faster, but won't take the difficult steps needed to make it happen.

Some moves look brilliant when they're made, and turn out that way. Some look idiotic – but confound the sceptics. The best results come when imagination, preparation, resources, execution, and luck conspire. One without the others rarely does it.

What's in the wind?

Hunters are stalked by uncertainty. When they toss dust into the air or hold up a finger to test the wind, they want to know what *is* so they'll be ready for what *may be*. They strive to narrow their margin for error, not close it; to lessen risk, not avoid it; to improve their chances of success, not guarantee it.

In the same way, managers need to detect 'weak signals', because the earlier they're aware of an issue, the more time they have to prepare. But Igor Ansoff, author of many authoritative books on strategy, points to a paradox: if you wait for enough information to make a decision you'll be 'increasingly surprised by crisis' but if you act on vague information you'll make bad decisions. The way out, he advises, is to plan and act as information comes in. Early on, you should aim to increase the strategic flexibility of your firm. Later, as information becomes more exact, you can become more specific.[6]

Another strategy expert, Russell Ackoff, says that knowledge of the future 'can be classified into three types: certainty, uncertainty, and ignorance; each requires a different kind of planning: commitment, contingency, and responsiveness'.[7] Managers must continually ask: 'What's happening right now that we must deal with?' 'What might happen that we must prepare for?' And, 'What might surprise us?'

The traditional SWOT (strengths, weaknesses, opportunities, threats) analysis is one way to 'hold your finger to the wind'. Recently, the use of scenarios has become a popular alternative. But while they may widen your perspective, they do little to set you on a safe course.

Place your bets!

During the 1980s, South Africa suffered from 'scenario fatigue'. A massive effort by Clem Sunter and his team at Anglo American thrilled the crowds with its high road/low road notions. Then came the Old Mutual/Nedcor effort, which focused on the possibility of kick-starting the economy through large-scale home building and electrification projects. The Mont Fleur Scenarios followed in 1991-92, with futures labelled 'The Ostrich' (government with its head in the sand, refusing to face reality); 'The Lame Duck' (transition too slow); 'Icarus' (a popularly elected government tries to do too much, too fast); and 'Flight of the Flamingos' (lots of birds that take time to take off, but then fly in a purposeful direction).

It's a moot question whether these efforts changed managers' operational strategies. I never sat in a meeting where managers picked either 'the high road' or 'the low road' as most likely. I heard few people talk about what to do if South Africa went one way or the other. Mostly, they sat tight and focused on next week.

I did, however, watch many 'scenario' presentations which were no more than lists of vague impressions, feelings, and even rumours. They got attention, but were so broad as to be virtually useless. The usual response to them was, 'Oh, shit!' rather than, 'Okay, if those are the external possibilities, here are our internal options.'

Survival is a powerful driver. Given a choice, managers focus on the present rather than the future. They can do something about today, but they're not sure about tomorrow. They're happier doing than speculating.

Unfortunately, though, managers must act now for then. They must commit themselves to one future or another. They cannot get away with doing nothing, for even that is a choice that will affect what happens later. Strategic management is about movement, not stasis.

The value of scenarios is that they open people's minds to a range of possibilities. They force us to face the fact that a preferred outcome may not materialize. But having seen the alternatives, what do you do?

There are five options. You can:

1. Bet on the most likely one.
2. Bet on the one for which your company can create the best strategy.
3. Hedge your bets, by creating a strategy that will work reasonably well under all the scenarios.
4. Stay flexible, so you can respond no matter what.
5. Try to influence which one happens.[8]

The bottom line is, you have to place a bet. You have to decide. And ultimately, you have to follow your choice by committing a critical mass of resources.

Certainty is an impossible goal. It's tempting to think that if you simply gather enough information, you'll be okay. But how much is enough? Which snippet will take you across the dangerous divide between opinion and truth? And how can you be sure that some unseen force won't change everything?

No amount of information gathering, of expert input, or of scenario-planning will eliminate uncertainty and its attendant risks. But if thinking about the future doesn't make it clearer, at least it lays out your options. At least it underscores the need to accept and prepare for many possibilities.

Strategic management is a continuous process of preparing for the future, navigating the rapids reasonably safely, learning as you go, and building new strengths for the next challenge.

Fear of what's to come

One reason people avoid thinking about the future is that they fear it. They expect to see problems and dangers ahead. And they don't like bad news.

A specific goal of the Anglo American scenario process was to show that there was a way out of South Africa's mess. The prospect of a high road was held out at a critical time. There's little doubt that Sunter and his colleagues* made an important contribution to change in this country.

The Old Mutual/Perm scenarios also helped. But again, the good news was much more acceptable than the bad. At a presentation by Bob Tucker, then head of the Permanent Building Society, the man next to me became extremely agitated by the seemingly intractable troubles that faced South Africa. But his mood changed when Tucker showed a way out: electrification and home building could kick-start the economy. Several people I spoke to afterwards were equally shocked-then-relieved. They liked the happy ending. What they most liked was that someone else would make it happen!

Research shows that as much as 90 per cent of the information we search for goes not to *change* our minds, but to *confirm* what we already think. We also seem to remember the confirming stuff much better.[9] While man is the most adaptable of all animals, we are also wired for failure. Our powerful mental circuitry, capable of expressing such a wondrous range of emotion, and of producing ideas that test the edges of imagination, has a dark side that condemns us to repeat the past.

Memories of tomorrow

The popularity of scenarios owes a lot to the efforts of the planning team at Royal Dutch/Shell, and particularly to the missionary zeal of its former head, Arie De Geus. He, in turn, was greatly influenced by the work of Swedish neuro-biologist David Ingvar.

According to Ingvar, part of our brain spends its time anticipating what lies ahead. These 'memories of the future' are sequentially organized and stored. As new information comes in, we compare it to this 'template', and we filter out anything that doesn't fit.[10]

There's an old saying that says we see what we want to see. But it seems we also see *what we prepare to see*. So it's essential that leaders prepare to see many possibilities, lest they close their minds too early and make themselves incapable of responding in real time.

One of the most important things any executive needs is peripheral vision – the ability to see emerging trends 'out of the corners of your eyes'. A narrow

* The scenarios were actually written by Michael O'Dowd and Bobby Godsell.

view of the world reveals only what's already well under way and visible to everyone. But you need more than that. A wider sweep gives you not only a more complete picture, but also an early warning of what's to come.

To cope with the future, you need to remove the blinkers of both yesterday and tomorrow. You need to peer into the distance as well as scan a wide horizon, consider multiple possibilities, and mentally practise many responses.

To think strategically is to 'rehearse the future'. The purpose of scenarios is not to predict the future, but to recognize that various futures are possible and to prepare for them.

Armies use war games to test battle strategies and let armed forces experience combat. Before Israeli commandos rescued 103 hostages from pro-Palestinian guerillas at Entebbe airport on July 3, 1976, they practised at a scale model of the airport built in the desert. Today, special forces use multimedia to familiarize themselves with targets. Pilots learn to fly in simulators which subject them to various weather conditions, test them in emergencies, and let them land at major airports without leaving home. NASA's astronauts spend years practising everything they'll do during space missions. Sports stars study videos of their competitors.

Strategic conversation lets you rehearse your business future. So here's another reason to manage it well and to involve all of your people in it. The earlier they're engaged, the better they understand that the future has many possible outcomes, and that your company needs to be ready for change.

When formal research doesn't help

While managers need data, facts, details, and conclusions, they also need attitudes, opinions, and feelings. The latest sales figures are essential. Surveys and focus groups help, and it's useful to get an economist's forecasts.

But for too many managers, 'getting the facts' falls into the realm of science rather than art. And even the most meticulous research can be very wrong.

- When Edwin Land invented his instant camera, Polaroid market researchers estimated that there might be a worldwide market for only 100,000 of the units.
- 'There wasn't a single solitary soul in IBM who grasped even a hundredth of the potential the computer had', said Thomas J. Watson Jr.[11] In 1943, he suggested that there was a worldwide market for five machines; in the 1950s, IBM marketers revised the number upward to 55.
- Sony chairman Akio Morita recalls an early trip to America like this: 'I took my little $29,95 radio to New York and made the rounds of possible retailers. Many of them were unimpressed. They said, "Why are you making such a tiny radio? Everybody in America wants big radios. We have big houses, plenty of room. Who needs these tiny things?" '[12]
- Coca-Cola changed its formula in 1985, after 400,000 consumer taste tests 'proved' that a new formula beat the old one – and Pepsi – hands down. But

the bold switch quickly became the most famous debacle in marketing history. After 79 days of consumer outrage, the original product was brought back as Coke Classic. (And year-on-year sales shot up at a record pace.)

To sit in an ivory tower and decide what to do next purely on the basis of some research report is to fool yourself. As Henry Mintzberg points out, 'no one ever found a diamond by flying over a forest'.[13] Sooner or later – and better soon than late! – you have to get out into the real world 'where the warm armpits are',[14] and sniff reality.

The search for 'Aha!'

Information is the stuff of which winning strategies are made. It's the decision-maker's raw material. But with the same information and the same technology available to almost everyone, you need something else to give you an edge.

No matter how much information you collect, or how well you do it, collection alone doesn't lead to successful strategy. Facts, figures, and opinions are only useful when they help you discover new meaning, and when they prompt you to do different things differently.

If you and your competitors all respond to emerging issues in the same way, none of you has an advantage. Even the 'best' and timeliest information has limited value until it yields insights.

Until you experience 'Aha!' and until you turn that fresh view of things into a unique way of doing things, you're no better off than anyone else. Information levels an industry's playing field. Insights and the ensuing ideas give you control of the commanding heights.

Information is the weapon that helps us make sensible decisions, and the tool with which we sell them. Insight, a product of information, gives us a unique view of the world and of what moves to make in it.

What's in your 'mental attic'?

The product of strategic thinking must be unique action. If thinking doesn't lead you from new ways of seeing to new ways of doing, it may be interesting and perhaps even entertaining, but it's not much use. Daydreaming is one way to pass the time, but it doesn't reshape the world.

Reflecting on the 'nature of the mind', artificial intelligence expert Marvin Minsky tells us that '… much of its power seems to stem from the messy ways its agents cross-connect'.[15] Essential for creativity, says legendary adman David Ogilvy, is a 'richly furnished mind'.[16]

You need a lot of 'junk' in your head to produce new ideas. Invention occurs when you dip into that cluttered resource and combine old bits and pieces, add to them, subtract from them, magnify them, 'minify' them, turn them upside down, and so on. To make connections, you need raw material.

Most managers complain that they suffer from information overload. Paper pours across their desks. They're wired to the world through PCs, networks, modems, and cellular phones. They're swamped by reports, attend endless meetings, pick up industry gossip in the corridors, and catch the news via radio, TV, and newspapers. Their worldviews are made up of a zillion snapshots, sound bites, headlines, and passing comments. They know a lot. Their potential to be creative is enormous.

However, much of what they know is within a narrow field. Too many people starve their brains of real stimulation. They read 'the office stuff', but skimp on the rest. Their reading list is narrow. They get *Inc.* or *Business Week* and pick up the odd copy of *Fortune* or the *Harvard Business Review*, and think that's enough. It isn't.

If you want to be creative, you have to be an 'information junkie'. If you want to be a compelling storyteller, you have to have things to say. If you want to inspire others to open their minds, you have to set the example – and flood them with facts, questions, challenges.

Creative space

Just as some people are more creative than others, so are some organizations more conducive to creativity than others. And just as individuals can be taught creativity, so can organizations become better contexts for creativity.

If work is conversation and leadership is storytelling, the workplace is a conversation pit. What does yours look like? What does it feel like? Closed doors and hushed corridors hardly stir the thinking juices.

Every advertising agency I've been into is an ideas factory. The walls are plastered not just with ads (or award certificates), but also with photos, press cuttings, cartoons, headlines, and funny quotes. People decorate their offices with toys, masks, and their kids' drawings. The hallways are noisy as hell. Pranks and practical jokes are normal. There's electricity in the air.

In contrast, their clients' offices and factories are sterile, stultifying places. People move quietly. They're deadly serious. They communicate 'through the right channels'. Meetings are ruled by agendas.

Breakthrough ideas come from unexpected quarters; the best ideas come most often when the context encourages them. Imagination is the most valuable corporate resource – and the most wasted!

Kinds of change

As you monitor your environment, it's essential that you know what kind of change you're seeing.

Some changes are *cyclical:* they come and go, ebb and flow, swing this way or that. These changes are temporary; you can often sit them out and wait for things to 'get back to normal'. They include such important factors as interest, inflation, and exchange rates; the gold price; and rainfall.

A second type of change – *structural* change – is often harder to deal with. It's permanent. Once it's occurred, things are never the same again. Examples are the switch from white rule to black rule in South Africa; the declining importance of gold in this economy; the influx of people from rural to urban areas; and the globalization of markets (Figure 5.3).

Cyclical changes occur all around us all the time. Structural changes may come more irregularly, but when they do their impact is enormous. They can turn a business on its head literally overnight.

The danger to companies is that they confuse structural change with cyclical change. They assume that a new technology, a competitor's new product, a demographic shift, or a change in the structure of their industry is just a passing blip. 'Don't panic,' they tell themselves. 'We can ride this storm. Things will settle down.'

In fact, things might have changed forever. And by missing this fact, companies will surely do too little, too late. Even if they respond aggressively, they might do entirely the wrong things.

The flip side is also true. If you think a change is structural when in fact it's cyclical, you're likely to over-react. You might throw resources into massive changes, when doing nothing would be wiser.

As Intel chairman Andy Grove says, it's vital to separate 'signals' from 'noise'.[17] It's also important to see the signals for what they really mean. A lot of what's happening around you is attention-grabbing, interesting – and probably just a distraction. You can't do anything about a lot of it, nor should you try.

Effective leaders know that at any time there are just a few things they have to respond to. So they avoid laundry lists of issues, and cut straight to the quick. They also know when to charge and when to 'chill out'.

What's driving the change?

Merely noticing a change, and classifying it as cyclical or structural, is not enough. You need deeper insights.

Say you're watching the economy. The obvious questions are:

- How fast will it grow – or is a slowdown in sight?
- What's the likely direction of interest and exchange rates, and inflation?
- How durable are the changes?
- What does it all *mean* to your organization?
- How should you respond?
- When should you act?

How do you *know* where the economy is headed? What are the signs to look out for?

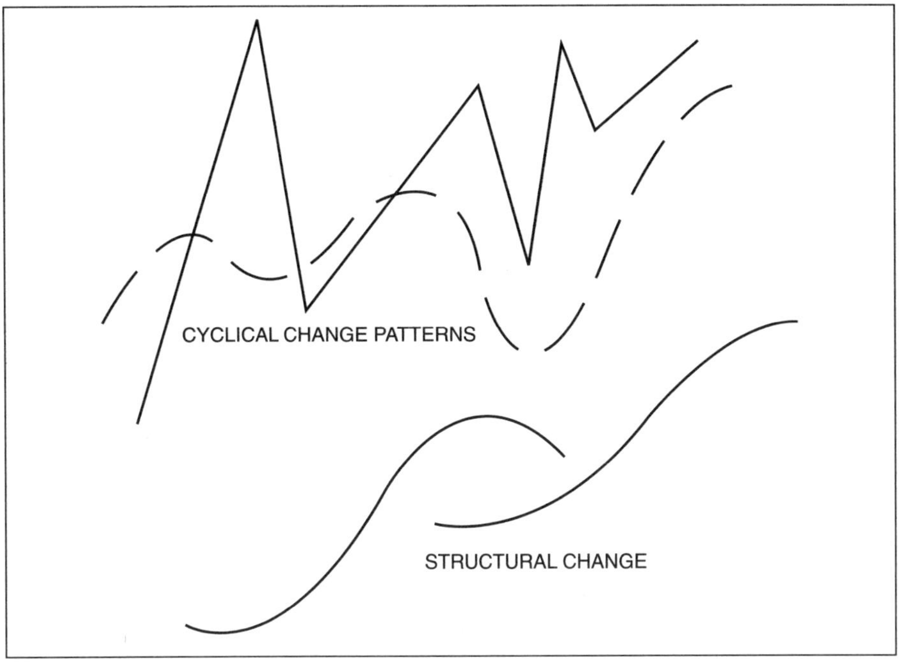

Figure 5.3: *What will cause your discontinuity?*

Begin with obvious indicators like capital expenditure plans, consumer spending, imports and exports, inflation and interest rates, and taxes. Watch key sectors like tourism – and possibilities in eco-tourism and archaeo-tourism, sports events, conferences. Consider factors that might drive the gold price up or down. Listen to weather forecasters, to gain a sense of how agriculture will fare. And look at these issues from a global perspective.

Then, to really understand what lies ahead, dig down to see what underpins the trends. What's driving them? How are those drivers likely to affect the future?

What new forces will be set in motion when economic currents 'collide' with other changes such as political instability, Aids, or crime? What will be the effect of new technology such as electric detonators for the mining industry, high-speed commuter trains, or network computers?

The economic news that makes headlines may be critical to your business. What's causing it may matter even more. Strategists need wide-angle lenses to see what's coming. They also need to do their homework and look beyond the obvious to get to the real issues.

Imagine the unimaginable

Organizational life encourages people to fine-tune what is, rather than to invent what isn't. Measurement and reward systems use yesterday's performance as a starting point. Most strategic plans include objectives based on past performance: 'Increase market share by three per cent', 'increase turnover by ten per cent', or 'reduce downtime by four per cent'.

Typically, strategic reviews begin with a look at what happened last year, then follow with a view of future prospects. Seldom do I hear executives say, 'Let's ignore where we are for a while. Let's imagine how people might live in 2010. Let's think about the three or four biggest opportunities they'll offer us. And let's talk about what we might do to own the market.'

It's hard to see a different future from where you stand today. Minor improvements look adequate. But by imagining that you already are in a future place, then looking back at where you are now, you gain a sense of just how radically you must change.

Some people do this naturally – they're always asking 'what if' questions. But in business the process has to be more deliberate. Those questions must be asked often, and of everyone.

A 'quantum leap' approach obviously causes unease and can chew up plenty of money. There's also the risk that you'll get so far ahead of the market that you can't exploit your discoveries.

But that's probably the worst that can happen. And anyway, you might be able to 'bank' your ideas till customers catch up. So best be bold and push the envelope.

The future will be owned by visionaries. Those executives and organizations with the clearest picture of tomorrow, and with the imagination and the balls to start reinventing themselves now, will gain the edge. All others will pay dearly for waiting.

From quantum leaps to small improvements

In most organizations, the budget is the roadmap. When the numbers are okay, it's business as usual. But when there are deviations, the red flag goes up.

The first sign of trouble is usually a slump in sales or profits. Some managers respond by trying to regain market share or increase margins. But in my experience most turn reflexively to their costs.

Faced with the need to change, companies tend to move down a predictable path:

STEP 1: Do the same things cheaper. (Cut costs.)
STEP 2: Do the same things better. (Fine-tune current processes – the *kaizen* approach.)
STEP 3: Do different things. (Change direction – quantum leaps.)

When costs get out of kilter, you obviously have to trim the fat. You should also constantly seek new ways to wring more revenue from your assets. But sooner or later, you'll find yourself doing the wrong things cheaper or better. Sooner or later, small improvements will become very expensive and won't matter. Sooner or later, you have to change direction.

Too often, the differences between companies are too slight to make a difference. Too much time and attention goes into activities that will have, at best, a marginal impact. 'If you have to measure carefully to see any difference at all,' says Nicholas Negroponte, director of the MIT Media Lab, 'maybe we are not working on things that matter enough.'[18]

Doing different things is always risky and usually expensive. The payoff isn't clear till after the event. If you jump the wrong way, recovery may be impossible. It's not surprising, then, that executives often fail to jump at all. Nor can they be blamed for seeking as much assurance as possible that they're moving the right way.

But remember the old saying: *you can't cross a chasm in two jumps*. When you have to get to the other side, you have to go for it.

Competition now is a race not just to *create*, but rather to constantly *redefine* value. So while continuous improvement has to be a goal in every part of every organization, continuous *invention* is even more important.

It's not enough to beaver away at 'small wins'. Quantum leaps are essential. You have to do radically different things, in radically different ways, to capture customers' attention. You have to surprise them constantly to hold their affections. So while you pursue incremental, step-by-step change, you should aim even more aggressively for the quantum leap that will put you out front, where you can 'ambush' customers. Your intention should be to seize as much control over the future as possible by getting there faster than the competition, and by dictating both the game and the rules.

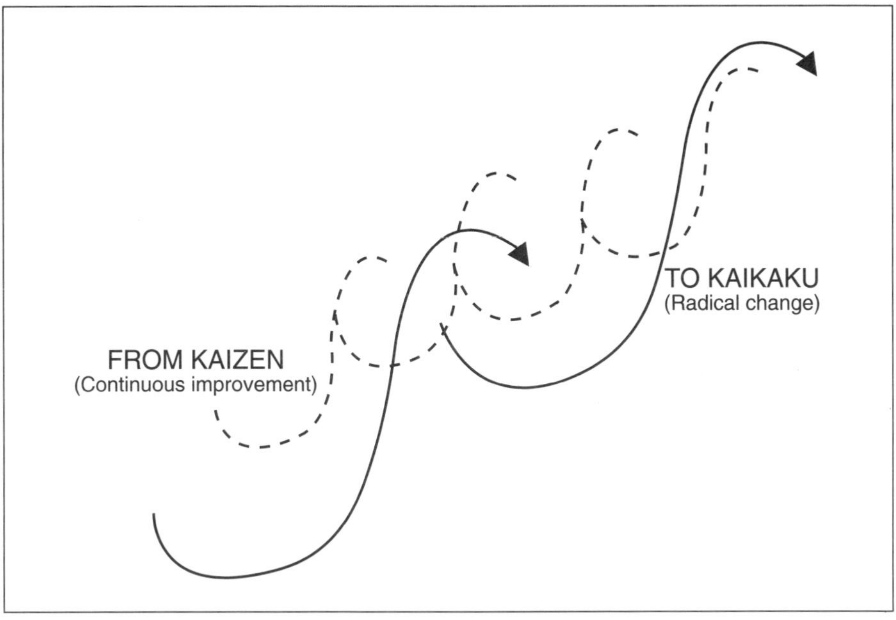

Figure 5.4: *From kaizen to kaikaku*

Companies have life cycles because they spend too much time on fine-tuning and too little making the bold moves that will launch them into the future. The mind-set that served them well in their early years becomes a deadly handicap in later life.

Continuous improvement (what the Japanese call *kaizen*) has become an obsession in many companies. It is a core factor in TQM and productivity programmes. But while it should be a way of life, it isn't the answer to life. In times of turbulence and surprise, bold change (*kaikaku*) is essential (Figure 5.4).

These two different views of change are lenses through which you view strategy. If you set out to make many small improvements to what you're doing, chances are you'll see only small possibilities. But begin with the expectation of *radical* shifts, and not only do you create the possibility of seeing big opportunities, but also the likelihood of small ones.

When you're brave, you win both ways.

A radical mindset gives you many options.

Endnotes

1. 'Big Blue-eyed boy makes good', *Financial Times*, April 22/23, 1995.
2. George M.C. Fisher, 'Corporate renewal and workplace anxiety', *Agility & Global Competition*, Vol.1, No.3, 1997.
3. Joseph L. Bower and Clayton M. Christensen, 'Disruptive technologies: catching the wave', *Harvard Business Review*, January–February 1995.
4. Bower and Christensen, 1995.
5. 'Waking up the new economy', *Fortune*, June 27, 1994.
6. H. Igor Ansoff, *Implanting Strategic Management*, New York: Prentice-Hall, 1984.
7. Russell L. Ackoff, *A Concept of Corporate Planning*, New York: Wiley-Interscience, 1970.
8. Michael E. Porter, *Competitive Advantage*, New York: The Free Press, 1985.
9. Spyros Makridakis, *Forecasting, Planning, and Strategy for the 21st Century*, New York: The Free Press, 1990.
10. Arie De Geus, *The Living Company*, Boston: Harvard Business School Press, 1997.
11. Thomas J. Watson Jr. and Peter Petre, *Father, Son & Co.*, New York: Bantam Books, 1990.
12. Akio Morita with Edwin M. Reingold and Mitsuko Shimomura, *Made In Japan*, New York: HarperCollins, 1994.
13. Henry Mintzberg, *The Rise and Fall of Strategic Planning*, New York: The Free Press, 1994.
14. Theodore Levitt, *Thinking About Management*, New York: The Free Press, 1991.
15. Marvin Minsky, *The Society of Mind*, New York: Touchstone/Simon & Schuster, 1985.
16. David Ogilvy, *Confessions Of An Advertising Man*, Great Britain: Longmans Green & Co. Ltd, 1963.
17. Andrew S. Grove, 'Navigating Strategic Inflection Points', *Business Strategy Review*, Volume 8, Issue 3, 1997.
18. Nicholas Negroponte, *Being Digital*, New York: Alfred A. Knopf, 1995.

2

THE STATE OF STRATEGY

6

False Gods and Flaky Ideas

... novelty seeking seems to be displacing truth seeking in much of the research on management.

— Frederick G. Hilmer and Lex Donaldson, *Management Redeemed*[1]

Beware of glib talkers with books. The fact that someone can stack up case after case in which a practice seemed to work is no guarantee it will work for you.

— James O'Shea and Charles Madigan, *Dangerous Company*[2]

The fundamentals don't change. They really don't.

— Richard G. Hamermesh, *Fad-Free Management*[3]

After decades of research into business strategy, how is it that, with all the brainpower at work in companies around the world:

- Almost half of the firms that are first into a market don't survive?
- More than nine out of ten new products fail in less than two years?
- Customers keep complaining and shopping around, even though so many organizations claim to be committed to excellence, world class performance, or hyper-growth? (American corporations – and probably most others in other countries – lose half their customers every five years?)
- From 1983–1993, the average *Fortune* 500 industrial company saw an annual change in revenues of –0,3 per cent?
- Some of the most consistent profit-makers are 'elderly' companies in dull and mature industries?
- Most change projects – reengineering, quality, productivity, customer service, you name it – don't deliver the expected results?*

* These conclusions come from a wide range of studies; many will be referred to later.

Why is it that so many exciting start-ups, often staffed by smart MBA graduates and backed by rich venture capitalists, fizzle so fast?

Why is it that so many people in so many organizations never reach their potential?

Why is it that profits are so mercurial, especially in 'hot' new industries?

How is it that, even though everyone seems to know what's needed to win, one or two companies break free of the pack and streak away to success?

You might well ask.

There are literally millions of experienced managers on the planet. Business schools churn out new talent. Bookstores report booming sales of business books. A flood of management newsletters, journals, and audio and videotapes provide information, insights, and advice.

Enough people participate in courses and seminars on any given day to populate a fair-sized city. As you read this, it's likely that tens of thousands of people are being 'infotained' by management gurus at corporate conferences. Many more are sharing ideas with their colleagues in phone calls and meetings. And who knows how many are caught in traffic, jogging in a park, or gazing into space while they apply their minds to beating the competition?

Incredible, isn't it! All that brainpower, and so little progress along the path of business performance! Still so many executives searching desperately for The Answer! So much time, energy, and money going into the quest for The Edge!

But why are we so surprised? Aren't managers a market? And doesn't it pay to promise them the earth?

Obsessed with change

'Change' has suddenly shot to the top of most corporate agendas. Most firms I work with have suddenly woken up and decided that 'world class' should be their goal. Under that umbrella, they're committed to many programmes. A favourite is 'customer care'. Yet here's an example of how hard it is to move from talk to action.

The need is obvious. It's easy to work out what must change. Yet while senior people are sure they've improved, their customers often can't see the difference and staff at all levels brush off the efforts as wishful thinking. (According to Frederick Reichheld, more than 90 per cent of customers say they're satisfied or very satisfied, yet only 30–40 per cent buy again from the same supplier.)[4]

Asked what they need to do to make their firms world class, most executives have a pat answer: 'Change the culture.' The problem, as they see it, is 'to get people's attitudes right'. This leads them to buzzwords and packaged interventions that are well worn and often quite useless.

Even today, the magic word – excellence – appears on posters and pocket cards, and somewhere in most mission statements. In their search for solutions, executives are seduced by slogans. Faced with the challenge of shaping up fast in a chaotic environment, they try value-sharing, cross-functional teams, replacing managers with leaders, and crafting their 'strategic intent'. Benchmarking and reengineering are on every to-do list.

Experts are hauled in to improve productivity, quality, or customer service, or to help cut costs or cycle time. People who don't get the message or buy the new religion are sent away on management development, or 'sensitizing' programmes.

Potentially, most of these interventions do have value. In practice, most don't work.

Are they important?

Absolutely.

Are firms putting enough time, energy, and money into them?

In many cases, *more than enough.*

Are they getting the results they want?

The evidence says no.

Too many failures

'Over the past decade,' wrote professor John Kotter in a recent issue of the *Harvard Business Review*, 'I have watched more than 100 companies try to remake themselves into significantly better competitors ... A few of these corporate change efforts have been very successful. A few have been utter failures. Most fall somewhere in between, with a distinct tilt toward the lower end of the scale.'[5]

A growing list of studies supports Kotter's findings:

- A 1993 study at Harvard Business School asked managers at almost 100 companies about the effect of 21 different change programmes, and 'found 75% of them to be unhappy with the results in their organizations'.[6]
- A survey by Arthur D. Little of change projects at 250 companies showed that three-quarters of them hadn't reached their goals. This, despite the fact that their boards planned and communicated their objectives 'adequately'.[7]
- Reengineering is hugely popular, but *The Economist* reports that as many as 85 per cent of reengineering efforts fail. In a study of 497 big companies in America and 124 in Europe, 69 per cent of the U.S. firms and 75 per cent of the European sample were busy with reengineering projects. Of those aiming for more market share, less than half got it.[8]
- The American Management Association reports that only 34 per cent of firms that had downsized saw any productivity improvement, and only 45 per cent saw profits rise.[9]
- Of 1,468 restructured companies surveyed by the Society for Human Resource Management in the U.S., more than half said productivity either stayed the same or fell after staff cuts.[10]
- Massachusetts Institute of Technology professor Paul Osterman says that nearly 80 per cent of companies have tried quality circles, TQM, teams, or a combination. Yet results have been mixed.[11]

- A study of 531 mostly big American companies showed that more than two-thirds had started TQM programmes, but only 41 per cent said their efforts had been very effective.[12]
- A survey of more than 300 American electronics companies showed that while 73 per cent were busy with TQM programmes, 63 per cent had 'failed to improve quality defects by even as much as 10%'.[13]

The Trail of Hope

Like most managers, you're probably wrestling with many challenges. You have to do *something* – and you have little time.

But where do you start? Which 'magic bullet' will save you? And what comes *first* – after all, you can't do everything?

Do you:

- Change your company's culture?
- Redesign your 'corporate architecture'?
- Rethink your technology strategy?
- Improve customer service?
- Attack quality and productivity?
- Try to create a 'learning organization' (or a virtual or 'agile' organization)?
- Enter into strategic alliances?

Should you be flattening, your organization? What 'core competencies' do you need? Will a 'generic strategy' work for you? What about empowerment, self-managing teams, 'customer intimacy', 'systems thinking' – or perhaps even newer ideas like a 'balanced scorecard', 'managing in the marketspace', 'co-opetition', or 'business ecosystems'?

Every executive worth her salt 'knows' that these are sure-fire ways to gain competitive advantage. But are they really? Are there other ways to win?

What about something more radical – a bash at *ubuntu*, for example? Or what about searching for the soul of your firm, learning about leadership from Star Trek, or tapping into the wisdom of wolves?*

Most companies suffer from 'interventionitis'. Too many new programmes are started in too many places. Each operates in isolation. Each has its own goals and champions (Figure 6.1).

As competition increases, companies skip from one fad to another in a fruitless – and costly – search for the ultimate answer. Programmes are started with great fanfare, then abandoned in frustration. New 'solutions' clash with old ones.

Because these programmes aren't integrated they cause trouble and raise costs. Instead of focusing energy they spray it all over the place, causing chaos and confusion. Instead of leveraging resources they waste them.

---

* Believe it or not, this is the stuff of book titles!

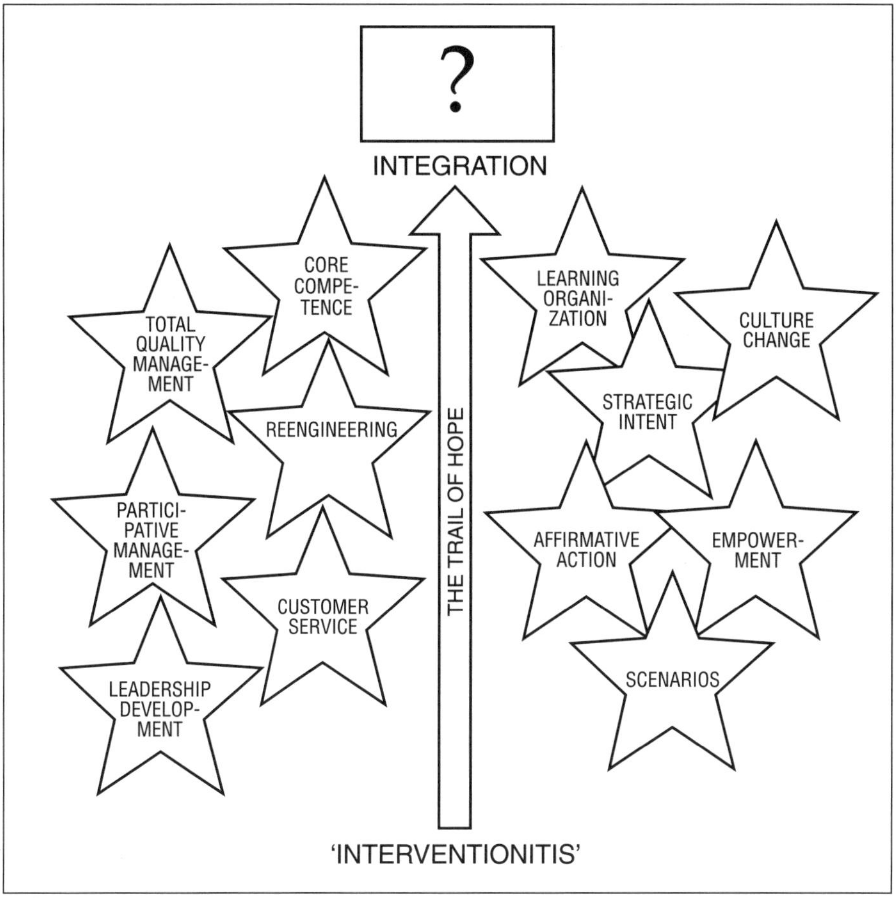

Figure 6.1: *The trail of hope*

Result: each new effort adds to the BOHICA effect ('Bend over, here it comes again!'). Trust and commitment are killed. People become demoralized and cynical, and future change becomes ever more difficult.

No quick fixes

In 1881, Frederick Winslow Taylor began to show managers that they could apply 'scientific' management to improve human output. In the 1960s, experience curves, learning curves, and the Boston Consulting Group's Strategy Matrix with its 'stars', 'cash cows', 'dogs', and 'question marks' found a ready audience – and still have avid fans – because they seemed to take care of messy problems through precise analysis and structured thinking.

Then there were 'T-groups', 'Theory X and Theory Y', 'process consultation', and 'organizational development' (OD). And more recently, we've been bombarded by nifty notions like MBO (management buyout), TQM, 'One Minute Management', 'skunk works', 'intrapreneurship', 'time-based competition', 'lean manufacturing', and 'empowerment'.

Stern Stewart's powerful approach to financial measurement and incentives – 'free cash flow', economic value added (EVA®)*, and market value added (MVA) – suggests a neat cause-effect answer to many complex management questions. The notion of reengineering companies around processes similarly makes 'soft' issues into 'hard' ones.

Corporate walls are covered with 'house of quality' posters; managers are obsessed with 'envisioning' their future; 'intellectual capital' is the new asset everyone wants.

It is always tempting to suggest simple formulas for business performance. Faced with new threats and ambiguities and a crushing workload, executives need relief. The advice industry – academics, business publishers, consultants, trainers, speakers – offer plenty of it. There's profit in platitudes.

Someone, somewhere, has a solution for every problem. Every new fad is a seminar idea. It's all good comforting stuff, because the manager's world is a risky and uncomfortable place. Easy answers make no sense, but they sure are attractive.

The rise and fall of 'Japanese management'

Of all the nostrums that have captured management attention in recent years, none comes close to 'Japanese management'.

During the 1970s and 1980s, the awesome advance of 'Japan Inc.' struck fear into the hearts of western investors, executives, and workers. There were dire predictions of Japan not only overtaking America as the world's largest economy but, far worse, of driving the U.S. to ruin early in the new century.

Best-selling author Michael Crichton exploited this anxiety in his 1992 novel *Rising Sun*, which later was made into a movie featuring Sean Connery. Says one of his American characters:

Our industries have fallen behind the rest of the world. Our workers are less educated than workers in other countries. Our investors demand short-term gain and cripple our industries' ability to plan for the future. And as a result, our standard of living is declining rapidly. The outlook for our children is bleak.[14]

Managers in the West responded to the threat by aping the Japanese. They snapped up books like *The Art of Japanese Management*, *Theory Z*, *Kaizen*, and *The Book of Five Rings*, and eagerly attended courses and seminars on quality circles, workplace participation, and 'Zen and the art of leadership'. They wrote company songs, and encouraged workers to do callisthenics together before each shift.

But the onslaught continued.

Japanese carmakers seemed unstoppable. First they took the small car market, then they went for the high end with models like Toyota's Lexus, Nissan's

* EVA is a registered trademark of Stern Stewart in the United States, Canada, Mexico, France, Australia and the United Kingdom.

Infiniti, and the Honda Accura. The same thing happened in industries ranging from TV sets to machine tools, from cameras to medical equipment.

Paranoia about Japan reached fever pitch when Sony bought Columbia Pictures for $4,9 billion in 1989, and Matsushita paid $6,59 billion for MCA, another Hollywood film company, two years later. Attacking the car business was one thing; attacking the entertainment industry – an American original if ever there was one – was the ultimate insult. Nor did it help when many companies that symbolized western might – IBM, GM, and Kodak among them – started reporting record losses.

But the Japanese economy ran into trouble in the 1990s. Property and stock prices slumped. And as financial problems raged across Asia in late 1997, westerners suddenly lost all interest in the models they'd watched so avidly and for so long.

The notion of 'Japanese management' is a relic of the past. But was there ever such a thing? And if so, what might it have embraced?

Academics promoted the idea, books were written about it, managers scrambled to 'do' it. But long before the infatuation with Japanese words like *kanban* (just-in-time), *kaizen* (continuous improvement), and *ringi* (consensus) had worn off, it became clear that a lot of what Japanese managers were doing was plain common sense with catchy labels.

What's more, even while managers in the West were trying desperately to use 'Japanese' approaches to planning, decision making, and career advancement, Japanese companies were trying to abandon many of them in favour of western practices.[15]

Today, the hot word around Japanese companies is *risotura*, or restructuring – the very word that obsesses the West. It's not unusual to hear of executives being brought in from Europe or America to make the tough changes. And once again, western ideas are in demand.

Facing reality

In 1995, Sony introduced a new stock-option package for directors. It was the first time a Japanese company had adopted such a reward system to improve financial performance, as few are under pressure to boost stock prices.[16]

The same week, Toyota appointed Hiroshi Okuda, described by the *Wall Street Journal* as a 'ruthless cost-cutter', as president. The world's most efficient car-maker was losing market share in Japan and facing tougher competition abroad. Okuda said he'd appoint more young managers (in a company where it could take 35 years to reach a top job), change the paternalistic family culture, and speed up overseas production; he also called for a study on closing domestic plants.[17]

Lifetime employment, which never involved more than about a quarter of Japanese workers, is a dying practice. 'Salarymen' can no longer rely on their companies for career security; promotion depends increasingly on merit, not on years of service. If non-performers once could expect to be shuffled into face-saving posts, now they get shoved right out.

Many years passed before anyone acknowledged that while some causes of Japan's success were cultural, and some had to do with relations between the Japanese government and business, that was just part of the story.

Conveniently overlooked was the fact that General Douglas MacArthur had set the stage for business-labour relations in the post-World War II Japanese constitution, that the Japanese government had clamped down on unions to get rid of left-wing membership, and that Japan is a homogeneous society in which there's great respect for authority and a deeply held belief in the value of social cohesion.

But there was more. American management experts such as Deming, Juran, Schewart, and Drucker got more avid attention from Japanese managers than from those back home. The world economy improved for everyone from 1945 through the 1960s. And for a long time Japanese companies enjoyed access to cheap and patient capital.

Perhaps most important of all, though, was the pathetic fact that western companies had taken things too easy for too long.

Not all of Japan's success was won because its managers were especially smart: a large dollop came because managers elsewhere were simply slow to adjust to new competitive realities.

Today, 'Japanese management' is hardly mentioned. The practices that drew attention to it for perhaps two decades – participative management, cross-functional teams, continuous improvement, target costing, fast cycle times, benchmarking, just-in-time deliveries, mass-customization, building invisible assets – have been universally embraced. But no one anywhere thinks that there's some other magic formula to learn from.

A lesson for South African managers

Local companies are under great pressure to shape up in a hurry. Executives are suckers for quick-fix solutions. But they should tread warily.

Many major companies are busy with big change projects. Some will definitely see improved results. But a lot have bought nothing but frustration. Having started boldly down the transformation road, they find themselves stuck. The wheels spin.

Much of what is touted as 'new' or 'revolutionary' in the field of management thinking is neither new nor revolutionary. A lot of what's dished up is just a glib rehash of well-worn ideas.

Too often, yesterday's tired concepts are given a face-lift, then glamorized, publicized, and merchandized to a market hungry for solutions. They become what Thomas Robertson, professor of marketing at the London Business School, calls a 'Holy Grail'.

It's not surprising, he notes, that the most common response to the need for change is 'lots of rhetoric and very little committed action ... firms wittingly or unwittingly resort to jargon based on the holy grail, often with a total absence of substance. Graffiti is written on corporate walls, in company newsletters and annual reports, and appears in corporate advertising.'[18]

Only a few years ago, Albert 'The Lion' Koopman fascinated South African audiences with tales of how he transformed Cashbuild. They loved it when he talked of rolling around on the floor to make a point to his workers; of driving a combi until they said he deserved a better car; and of celebrations that involved slaughtering an ox.

Around the same time, Nissan introduced 'green areas' in its Rosslyn factory. Executives from other companies rushed to the plant to watch workers meet in these spaces before and after shifts. They went back to their own organizations enthused by the idea of involving production line people in scheduling tasks, identifying problems, and resolving safety issues.

More recently, '*ubuntu*' has become the hot topic. Human resources people talk about it as if it were the answer to every corporate ill. The word appears everywhere. It's a favourite theme in conference programmes.

However, most of the people touting 'new' insights with a local flavour are simply re-branding old ideas. They're repeating what management experts have advised from as far back as Frederick Taylor.*

Anxious though managers may be to drive their companies' growth, and appealing as the idea of an 'African management paradigm' may be, this is no time to reinvent the wheel.

We know what works. Now, we must put that knowledge to work.

Local culture must be taken into account in any organization, anywhere in the world. This has to happen here, as the workforce becomes more diverse. But at the same time, business needs to look to the best management practices and adopt these as rapidly as possible.

What goes wrong?

What causes the sad performance of so many well-meant change efforts? Why do programmes fail after so much money, time, and energy are poured into them? What can managers do to make the difference that they must?

Here are ten key reasons goals aren't met:

1. **Change agents fall in love with notions that sound sexy but have no substance.** They're suckers for the latest 'package'. They too readily accept that if they do A, B will follow. Causes and results are too readily linked.

* Peter Drucker effectively debunked the view that Taylor saw humans as machines. In his book Post-capitalist Society (London: Buttorworth-Heinmann, 1993), he wrote: 'Taylor's motivation was not efficiency. It was not the creation of profits for the owners. To his very death he maintained that the major beneficiary of the fruits of productivity had to be the worker and not the owner. His main motivation was the creation of a society in which owners and workers, capitalists and proletarians had a common interest in productivity and could build a relationship of harmony on the application of knowledge to work.'

2. **They attack the process from the wrong end.** More often than not, they start off with the notion that they have to change their company's culture to make it more competitive. But culture is a means to an end, not the ultimate goal.

3. **They over-complicate things.** To appear responsible or professional, they chart processes in minute detail. This often means that Step 3 can't be taken before Steps 1 and 2, whereas doing things in any order might be better than doing them according to plan.

4. **They get busy with specifics, but ignore the context in which the changes must occur.** Training people to be team players is useless if the team doesn't have a clear purpose. Talking about customer service is useless if the CEO isn't seen to be passionate about customers. Sharing values is easier than living them.

5. **Organizational arrangements pull in different directions.** The reward system pays people to maintain the status quo rather than change. The organization's structure keeps power in the wrong places, and blocks communication. Old policies and redundant systems block new practices and processes. Obsolete equipment gets in the way of new technology.

6. **The wrong people are put in charge of the process.** Because change always involves people, and because line managers have 'real work' to do, the management of change is usually delegated to someone from Human Resources, or to a nominated 'champion'. But no matter how competent or well intentioned these people might be they're not taken completely seriously. They have limited clout.

7. **Too much time is allowed for results.** Conventional wisdom says that change takes time. But when deadlines are too far out, it's easy to worry about painting the factory rather than launching a revolutionary product. Current problems come first; 'strategic' issues can wait.

8. **'Real work' comes first.** Faced with taking urgent action to fix an immediate problem, or doing something that will bring longer-term results, guess which way most people swing? Change projects tend to take on a life of their own, 'parallel' to ongoing work. They never get woven into the fabric of the organization's life. This means they are attended to when there's time – which there never is.

9. **There's not enough money.** Some changes can be made for free. Many cost a lot. People may need training, new technology may be necessary, old facilities may have to be shut down. Heavy investment might also be required during the shift from one opportunity to another. And sales may slump during the switchover.

10. **The effort is abandoned too early.** Either people lose interest and turn to something new, or they abandon their efforts to change, and 'get back to

work'. And the need for short-term results always blurs managers' view of what they should aim for in the long run.

Of course, there are many other factors that get in the way of successful change. But these are the ones that recur most often.

New tools needed

As we head towards the Millennium, companies everywhere are faced with the need for radical change. Yet their thinking tools were designed for a different time.

Many managers base their strategies on concepts that are obsolete. They strategize in ways that ensure they don't reach their goals.

There are many approaches to business success. Some are based on sound research, while others are a figment of someone's imagination. Often, they are based on false assumptions – or on assumptions that no longer hold. Too often the 'audit trail' from cause to effect is unclear. Theories that might once have had value are no longer valid.

There's big money in management concepts. There's every reason for them to be heavily hyped. And there's dismay when they don't deliver the expected results.

But why should they?

Popular models and frameworks describe just a small part of the manager's world. A lot of them are based on very small studies: samples of six, ten, or maybe even 20 companies. Bigger than that is unwieldy and would take forever.

The findings are neatly packaged and sent to market. And that's where things go wrong.

There's no clear way to link various ideas – Concept A with Concept B – or to deal with the mess of the real world. And almost always, implementation is problematic.

Conventional approaches to business improvement fail for many reasons. To create a new kind of strategy, you need a new way to do it.

On the one hand, you need to face up to the realities of business: how things actually work. On the other, you need new thinking tools.

Endnotes

1. Frederick G. Hilmer and Lex Donaldson, *Management Redeemed*, New York: The Free Press, 1996.
2. James O'Shea and Charles Madigan, *Dangerous Company*, New York: Times Business, 1997
3. Richard G. Hamermesh, *Fad-Free Management*, Santa Monica: Knowledge Exchange, 1996.
4. Frederick F. Reichheld, 'Learning from customer defections', *Harvard Business Review*, March–April 1996.
5. John P. Kotter, 'Leading change: Why transformation efforts fail', *Harvard Business Review*, March–April 1995.

6. Nitin Nohria and James D. Berkley, 'Whatever happened to the take-charge manager?' *Harvard Business Review*, January–February 1994.
7. 'A level playing field', *The Observer/Business*, July 24, 1994.
8. 'Reengineering reviewed', *The Economist*, July 2, 1994.
9. 'Getting beyond downsizing', *Fortune*, January 10, 1994.
10. 'Cost cutting: how to do it right', *Fortune*, April 9, 1990.
11. 'The new world of work', *Business Week*, October 17, 1994.
12. 'Study delves into causes of failures in downsizing', *Wall Street Journal Europe*, October 5, 1993.
13. Robert H. Schaffer and Harvey A. Thomson, 'Successful change programs begin with results', *Harvard Business Review*, January–February 1992.
14. Michael Crichton, *Rising Sun*, New York: Random Century, 1992.
15. 'Demystifying Japanese management practices', *Harvard Business Review*, November–December 1984.
16. 'Sony offers stock options to board, in unusual move', *Wall Street Journal Europe*, August 11–12, 1995.
17. 'Zealous cost-cutter named to head Toyota: is an industry shake-up on the way?' *Wall Street Journal Europe*, August 11–12, 1995.
18. Thomas S. Robertson, 'Corporate Graffiti', *Business Strategy Review*, Spring 1995.

7

From Theory to Reality

The genius of a good manager lies in his ability to manage effectively a system he does not understand completely.

— Russell Ackoff, *Creating the Corporate Future*[1]

If you aren't comfortable with complexity and ambiguity, you aren't going to do well around here.

— Ralph Larsen, chairman and CEO, Johnson & Johnson[2]

By purging our organizations of what is ambiguous, we risk losing our sense of what is possible.

— Richard K. Lester, Michael J. Piore, and Kamal M. Malek, *Harvard Business Review*[3]

Business researchers and writers like to pretend that they can unravel the 'audit trail' that reveals what a firm did in the past to produce its current results. They like to reduce complex processes to catchy ideas for an anxious market. But the reasons for a firm's success can be hard to fathom.

Many management fads and 'revelations' simply don't work. Too many of them offer an incomplete picture. For example, ask:

- Has Pick 'n Pay done well because Raymond Ackerman positioned himself as the consumer's friend? Or is it because his buyers are extremely tough and adept at squeezing good terms from suppliers? Or because he uses customers' cash for longer than his competitors? Or because his property department ties up the best locations? Or because he was first to install scanners at checkouts, so has been able to tightly control his stock? Or because he has always looked after his people? Or … ?

- Is Bidvest a favourite with investors because of chief executive Brian Joffe's leadership skills? Or is it due to the skills of his colleagues? Did the Group strike it lucky in buying companies just as cyclical factors improved their prospects? Have they been especially good at striking deals ... or at running the companies they acquire? Does their focus on basic industries give them a special advantage? Are they simply reaping the rewards of customer relationships built before their time?
- Is Nando's a big hit because of its 'taste of Portugal'? Or is the real secret the fact that fast food fans were simply tired of deep-fried chicken and wanted a healthier option? Or could it be that Robbie Brozen and his team are marketing opportunists, who get a lot of publicity from newsworthy events? Do they have unique buying skills? Are they better at stock control than other players? What about their locations or the look of their stores? Or was Nando's able to build critical mass faster than others because the company had strong financial backing?

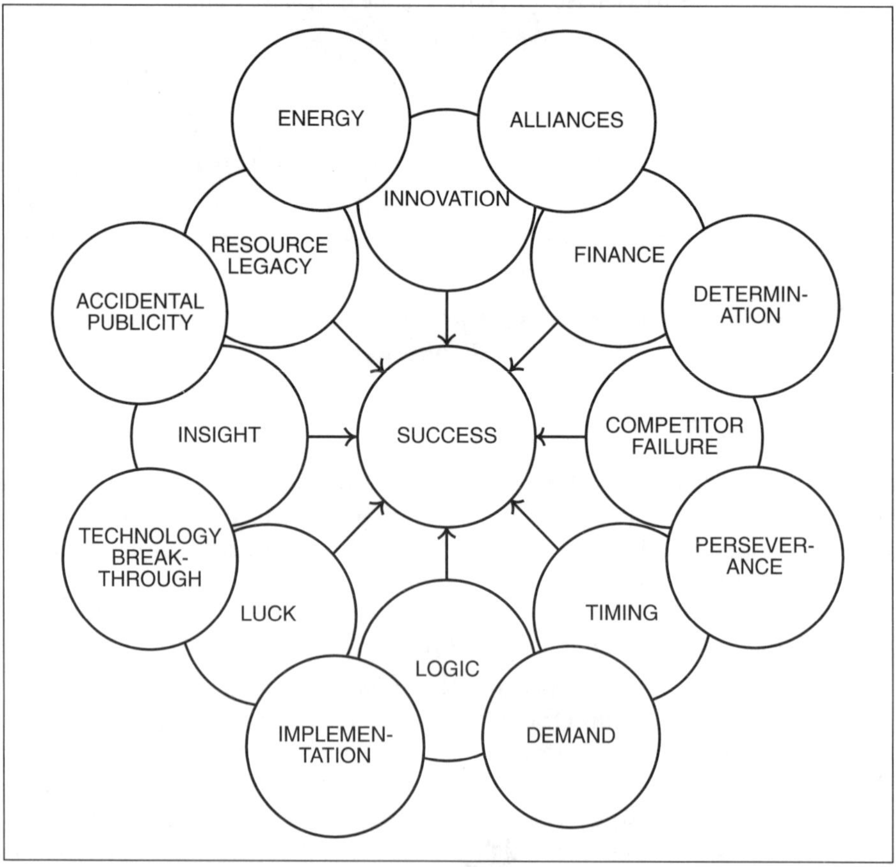

Figure 7.1: *Causes of corporate success*

The answer in each case is, it's all of those things and more. Corporate results are a product of many factors, only some of which you may see. Powerful leadership is an obvious one; others are less clear but no less important (Figure 7.1).

To suggest that a handful of factors separates winning firms from losers is nonsense. Handy checklists always leave something out. Guiding a business through turbulent times is not as easy as A-B-C. The real edge always comes from a 'bundle' of activities, from collaboration, from synthesis.

It isn't smart to look for a silver bullet that will save you in the new business arena. A 'graffiti response' is more likely to make you sound foolish than give you an edge. Besides, following the same fads as everyone else goes against the essence of strategy – which is to be *different,* not the same.

Unexpected successes

Many of today's best-known companies were born by accident. Many great product or service breakthroughs were unplanned and unexpected.

- When Bill Hewlett and David Packard founded their business in 1937, they had no real idea what to make. These were some of their ideas: a clock drive for a telescope; a shock device that would help people lose weight; an automatic urinal flusher; a foul-line signal for bowling alleys.[4]
- Rubbermaid was started in 1932 when James Caldwell, a Massachusetts inventor, started selling rubber dustpans door-to-door. Retailers said they wouldn't sell for $1 when the metal type sold for 39 cents. After Caldwell added a drain-board mat, a soap dish, and a sink plug to his range of rubber products, he was persuaded to join Wooster Rubber Co., which was founded in 1920 to make toy balloons.[5] Rubbermaid was voted No.1 in *Fortune*'s Corporate Reputations survey in both 1994 and 1995.[6]
- One day in 1943, Edwin Land's three-year-old daughter asked him why she couldn't immediately see the photo he'd taken of her. In less than an hour, he'd thought up the idea of the instant photography system.
- Computer researchers are developing a concept called 'smart agenting' to profile customers and search the infosphere for goods, services, and information to meet their specific needs and wants. Says Barry Diller, chairman of QVC: 'I stumbled upon smart agenting the same way I came upon QVC – as an unintended consequence of playing with the different technologies.'[7]
- Retired Merck CEO, Roy Vagelos describes a drug breakthrough this way: 'Early on, I was working with the endocrinology group, which had a number of projects in progress. It was clear that the group had to focus its efforts, and discussions about how to achieve that focus went on for a while. One day in the midst of all this, I picked up a journal on my desk and saw a study by a group at Cornell University describing a rare congenital problem … I walked down the hall carrying that journal, and the head of the chemistry section in the endocrinology group was walking out of his office with the same journal. We met in the hall, and I said, "This is it." He said, "This is it." '[8]

A great little book called *How The Cadillac Got Its Fins* strips away myths about many corporate success stories:

- Apple Computer founders Steve Wozniak and Steve Jobs got their start building 'blue boxes' which let users make free long-distance phone calls and tune into secret government communications networks. In 1975, Wozniak designed a computer, and Jobs persuaded him they should sell it as a kit for club members and other hobbyists. One club member owned three electronics stores, and he ordered 50 completely assembled Apple I computers. The two Steves raised $25,000 in credit and started production in Jobs' parents' garage. Their first computers were bare circuit boards without cabinets, keyboards, disc drives, or software. Then came the Apple II – an instant hit.
- When Sony engineers produced a tiny tape recorder with built-in microphone and loudspeaker, journalists loved it. But the 'Pressman' was a mono machine, and radio interviewers wanted stereo. So the engineers developed a small stereo player – but they couldn't fit a recording mechanism into it. One day, Masaru Ibuka, the company's honorary chairman, saw the product and remembered a small set of headphones he'd seen in another lab. He took the idea to Akio Morita, who told the engineers to go ahead with development. The marketing department thought it would be a sure money-loser. Launched as the Soundabout in America, and the Stowaway in England in 1979, the little machine sold slowly. But then sales took off, and a market was created that every other major manufacturer had to go for.
- Bennett Cohen and Jerry Greenfield were two fat kids who met in a seventh-grade gym class. They tried various jobs after college, then decided to go to Vermont and start a food business. 'We were both big into eating,' said Greenfield. They thought about making bagels, but the equipment was too expensive. So they signed up for a five-dollar correspondence course in ice-cream making. By the early 1980s, a *Time* magazine cover story proclaimed their product 'the best ice-cream in the world'.
- In the early 1950s, the McDonald brothers created the first fast food restaurant around an assembly line process called the Speedy Service System. A few years later, an entrepreneur named Ray Kroc started franchising McDonald's outlets. When a Pittsburgh franchise holder suggested a double-decker burger with special sauce and trimmings, Kroc refused. He finally relented in 1967, on condition that the product was tested only in one out-of-the-way store. Within a year, it was on sale across the country.
- Marlboro cigarettes were launched in 1924 – for women. There was a red band around the filter to hide lipstick stains: 'Beauty Tips to Keep the Paper from Your Lips.' Two decades later, Philip Morris decided to aim the brand at a new market niche: men afraid of lung cancer. Chicago ad man Leo Burnett suggested that cowboys should be used in the advertising. Research said that was probably not wise, given that there were only 3,000 cowboys in America. But the campaign worked; within a year Marlboro was the fourth biggest brand in the country. Today, it's the biggest in the world.[9]

The chances of being successful over the long haul are not great. They diminish as the pace of change accelerates and turbulence rises.

Executives get rich and famous by getting more things roughly right, more of the time. They deliver in good times and bad. This is partly due to judgement and ability, and largely because they try more things, more often. By allowing for failure, they set themselves up for success.

'Street smarts'

Corporate results are a product of many factors, only some of which are manageable. Powerful leadership is an obvious one; others are less clear but no less important.

Much business success hinges on instinct and leaps of faith. Important decisions must often be made before all the facts are in. Managers seldom have 'enough' information.

Faced with the need to act, street-wise executives can't always explain why they opt for a particular course; all they can say is, 'I just know it's right.' Somehow they've made connections in their heads that make them reasonably sure. Experience, information, and vision combine to provide a picture of what they must do.

Paradoxically, while organizations today have access to more and more information and increasingly sophisticated decision-making tools, it doesn't get easier to make the *best* decision.

Many crucial choices are based on hunch, hope, gut feel, and just plain bloody-mindedness. Moves that make no sense at all are floated as 'trial balloons', funded, lobbied for, and lied about. To everyone's surprise – including their lunatic sponsors' – they often pay off.

On the other hand, ideas that look absolutely brilliant are often starved of support, badly sold, savaged by critics, or conveniently left to 'go away'.

No amount of research and preparation guarantees that a strategy will work. Nor does all the energy, cunning, or political clout an executive might muster. Businesses come and go because they are human institutions, and human beings work magic – and get things horribly wrong.

Get lucky!

Accident, surprise, and luck all play a role in life. Opportunities and problems that you cannot imagine right now are sure to pop up 'out of nowhere', and take you off in new directions. The next phone call can change your destiny.

Luck is a crucial ingredient in almost every organization's fortunes. When it comes, it adds impetus to all the sensible things 'professional' managers do. It opens doors, unleashes new technologies, and connects companies and customers. Yet which executive is trained to look for luck? Who likes to admit that a big project worked out because 'we got lucky'?

Business schools still teach planning, organizing, and controlling. 'Take charge' attitudes are widely admired. Even today, many companies like to think they can determine the future in minute detail. (Why else do they produce those fat plans?)

As a leader, your task is not to provide certainty, but to exploit uncertainty. Not to arrange the future, but to anticipate it. Not to limit possibilities, but to create them.

Of course, you want to reduce the need for luck. But you do need to position your organization in the way of it.

A joke reinforces the point:

> An elderly man is on his knees in a casino. 'God,' he says, 'please let me win the jackpot. I need the money. Please help me.'
>
> Next night, people see him there again. 'God, I need that money,' he says. 'Work with me. Make me lucky tonight.'
>
> Third night, the same thing. Then suddenly a voice from above: 'Jim, work with *me*. Put some money in the damned machine!'

The lesson is clear: you have to be in the game if you want to win. If you don't turn up and take a risk, you won't get rich.

But unlike gambling, where a 'flutter' may give you the jackpot, business success is measured by its consistency. A 'win some, lose some' approach will get you nowhere. You have to deliver year after year.

To do that, you have to be in the right game. You have to understand your opposition. You have to play skilfully and hard.

Luck undoubtedly helps; but strategy and spirit bring it your way.

Everything a business does is a stepping stone towards its future. Limited resources must be applied where they will bring maximum rewards. Every investment of time, money, energy, or whatever, takes you a step along one path or another. If the direction is wrong, the investment is wrong. If it doesn't make your company better off, and position it to move even further ahead in the future, you shouldn't do it.

Forget about sustainable advantages

'Sustainable advantage' is the strategist's mantra. The idea is to find something – access to raw materials, a unique product/brand, technology, a lock on distribution, or whatever – that will provide an edge over competitors which can be defended over time.

But in the knowledge society, it's hard to stay out front. Today, as Marshall McLuhan anticipated, 'the message travels faster than the messenger'.

We live, say the information experts, in 'communicopia', in a 'telecosm', in the 'digiverse'.[10] We all know the same things at pretty much the same time. CNN and Sky News have shrunk the world. We all tap into the same global information networks, read the same journals, go to the same conferences.

Satellite dishes dot the landscape like flowers. Every month, millions of people sign up to surf the Internet.

As South African townships are electrified, people who now listen to the radio will start to watch TV. Cellular phone numbers are given to people, not places, freeing us to talk on the move.

By 2010 the world's 'wired' population will grow from 750 million to about three billion users. New technology will cut the cost of a one-hour trans-Atlantic call to about three cents. The 'information superhighway' already exists, and it's made the world a smaller place.

Secrets are hard to keep.

The knowledge component of products is rising, and information flashes around the planet literally at the speed of light. There are already thousands of on-line-only scientific journals, and growing numbers of print publications are now available on the Internet.

Patents are hard to protect, and when they expire, generic products flourish. Design has become a major selling point – and it's easy to copy. Intellectual piracy is big business

Competitors within industries share huge amounts of information. Enemies band together in strategic alliances to share development costs, learn about distribution, or find synergies between their strengths. Products and services can be quickly reverse-engineered.

Almost any advantage you create is quickly seen, analysed, copied, improved upon, and nullified. Today's breakthrough becomes the 'entry fee' for playing a particular game. Today's edge become tomorrow's handicap.

The challenge is to compete successfully despite most advantages being unsustainable.

Keep moving

The evidence is overwhelming: strategy has a short shelf-life. While it might be possible in a few industries to create a long-term plan, more and more firms are being forced to duck, weave, and bob as they fight for the future.

- 'Strategic concepts such as fit, sustainable advantage, barriers to entry, long-range planning, the use of financial goals to control strategy implementation, and SWOT analysis all fall apart when the dynamics of competition are considered,' warns Richard D'Aveni in his book *Hypercompetition*. 'The new code of conduct is an active strategy of disrupting the status quo to create a series of unsustainable advantages.'[11]
- Writing in the *Journal of Business Strategy*, Heinz chairman and CEO Tony O'Reilly says, 'Being first certainly does not ensure that one will last. The very success of the category one creates, in fact, inevitably inspires determined competitors. Heinz has answered these challenges through constant rebirth – a renewal of technology, procurement, pricing, oversight – anything that inhibits company growth.'[12]

- Or listen to James Collins and Jerry Porras, who spent six years studying 18 very successful American companies. 'Over time,' they say in their book *Built To Last*, 'cultural norms must change; strategy must change; product lines must change; goals must change; competencies must change; administrative policies must change; reward systems must change.'[13] In other words, *everything* must change!
- 'Fame is a fleeting thing,' says Gary Tooker, CEO of Motorola. 'When the alarm clock rings tomorrow morning, you'd better get up and understand that your customers expect more from you than they did the day before. You'd better find ways to be better.'[14]

All this leaves most strategic plans in the bin. It makes the architecture of many organizations obsolete. It makes their best practices potential liabilities.

You can't deny the message. No company can assume that its 'world class' performance will keep it out front. No company will survive on its 'legacy' skills, its reputation, or its passion for continuous improvement.

No company can settle for anything less than constant *revolution*. The world is simply too dangerous today. Competition evolves too fast. And it comes from places you don't expect.

Yesterday's formulas

If strategists are to think differently about their companies and how they compete, they must begin by thinking differently about strategy itself. It makes no sense to use old weapons in a new war.

GE's famous nine-cell matrix, Ansoff's 'critical issues' matrix, and Porter's 'generic strategies' may all have a place in your thinking, but before you use these or any other famous concepts, be sure you know why you're using them. Be sure what you expect from them. There are any number of models and frameworks available, and if you follow the creators' instructions and apply yourself diligently you may get some value from almost all of them.

But face the facts: *yesterday's dynamite formulas may be today's surest route to disaster*. They are based on assumptions which may not apply today. Their simplicity is problematic in a messy world. In attempting to neatly lay out options for managers – and the few basic moves open to them and their competitors – they sacrifice possibilities.

They do not account for the creativity, surprise, or irrational behaviour which people bring to everyday life. They assume predictability. They rely on everyone playing by the rules and being perfectly sensible. And they depend on executives being able to make clear choices: Direction A *or* Direction B ... this move *or* that ... Step 1 *then* Step 2.

Blind adherence to any concept is dangerous. To deny the ability of human beings to make almost infinite choices, to embrace paradox and to succeed by doing the 'wrong' things, is folly. Also, it's crazy to assume that your enemy sees the world like you do, has the same resources, and will act the same way.

The fallacy of one right way

In the early 1980s, Porter attracted a great deal of attention with his concept of 'generic strategies'. Applying the cool logic of an industrial economist, he suggested that there are essentially two ways to compete:

- Cost leadership
- Differentiation.

Low-cost producers are relentless in their efforts to drive costs below those of competitors. Differentiators (Mercedes-Benz, Moët et Chandon champagne, Mont Blanc writing instruments, Louis Vuitton luggage, or Gucci clothing) offer perceived added-value and usually charge a premium price for it.

Competitors in both groups have a further decision to make: which market sector to aim at. Mass marketers sell to 'everyone'. Focusers concentrate on a particular market or sell a narrow product line.

The cost/differentiation choice mandates managers to follow mutually exclusive paths. As Porter points out, 'Effectively implementing any of these generic strategies usually requires total commitment and supporting organizational arrangements that are diluted if there is more than one primary target.'[15]

In other words, each approach requires a specific type of value delivery system. The more precisely you tailor your organizational arrangements to the needs of your customer, and to the strategy you intend pursuing, the better. 'No frills' needs one kind of business system, 'bells and whistles' another.

In similar vein, Michael Treacy and Fred Wiersema argue in their book *The Discipline of Market Leaders*, that customers fall into three categories: one group seeks value in product performance or uniqueness; a second values service and advice; and a third shops for the lowest total cost.

Market leaders, say these authors, design their 'operating model' to satisfy one of these targets. They excel at one of three disciplines – 'operational excellence' (middle-of-the market products, best prices, least inconvenience); 'product leadership' (cutting-edge technology, best design and functionality); or 'customer intimacy' (personal care, flexibility, support) – while maintaining 'reasonable standards' in the other two areas.[16]

Another influential concept is core competence. 'Only if the company is conceived of as a hierarchy of core competencies, core products, and market-focused units will it be fit to fight,' wrote Gary Hamel and G.K. Prahalad in the May-June 1990 issue of the *Harvard Business Review*. Their thinking underpins many reengineering projects. Hardly an annual report appears without some mention of the company's commitment to its competencies.

These formulas are based on clear logic. But while many companies subscribe to them, few make them work. And those that try hard may find themselves in trouble. Here's why:

1. Competitors are unlikely to behave predictably or rationally.
2. Though 'strategy-as-positioning' demands hard choices, the will to choose is often absent.
3. The choices you make today will be wrong for tomorrow.

Consider why these are problems.

1. **Unreliable competitors.** As I mentioned earlier, conventional wisdom holds that the essence of strategy is to position yourself where your enemy is not. So competitor analysis is an important activity in most organizations. Lots of effort goes into pinpointing where competitors are now, and where they're likely to move to. Fortunes are spent on tracking their sales, talking to their customers and suppliers, measuring their advertising expenditure. Spies are sent to their annual general meetings. 'Mystery shoppers' buy their goods.

   True, some companies do act in obvious ways. You can see their next move coming. Mergers, acquisitions, spin-offs, or divestments do tell you something about their intentions. Their choice of technology does suggest where they're headed. Yesterday's training programmes do lock them into certain behaviours. Today's distribution strategy will probably be in place for some time.

   If competitor behaviour were perfectly predictable, life would be easier. But you can no more read a competitor's mind than you can read the mind of your wife or best friend. The world is a messy and dangerous place. And competitors are canny, creative, unpredictable – and even irrational.

   You expect them to do A and they do B. You confidently predict that they won't be around in a year or two (IBM, Chrysler), and they come back stronger than ever. They make a move that you think is permanent, and then switch without warning.

   So here's another one of those infuriating paradoxes: competitor intelligence is vital; but to rely on it is downright dumb.

2. **Neat concept, no commitment.** The second problem is that while strategy always demands hard choices, the will to choose is often absent.

   Almost every management team I know talks about being 'the low cost producer'. But it hasn't occurred to most of them that there can only be one low-cost producer in an industry. Nor are they dedicated to owning that position. Decisions to get there are often made in plush boardrooms or in strategy retreats at exotic locations. Executives talk tough about slashing head-count, downgrading company cars, or instructing middle managers to fly economy, but they dodge cuts that affect their own comfort and status. Important symbolic savings – dismantle the corporate structure, sell the head office building, get rid of the art collection, cancel the golf day – are not allowed to become issues.

   The same lack of clear commitment shows in other ways.

   For example, while cost leadership is trumpeted as a goal, so is differentiation. But usually it's on a superficial level. Marketing meetings focus on questions of 'image'. Managers love watching commercials that win awards at the Cannes film festival, and sigh with envy when competitors win Loeries, but won't risk their own money on way-out ideas. Even more fundamentally, they don't invest enough in R&D to produce different products. Neither do they build organizations that will continually 'surprise and delight' customers.

The result is that these firms can't deliver a clear promise through a focused operating model – as Treacy and Wiersema recommend they should do. They become fairly good at many things, so they never progress beyond also-ran status. They wind up stuck in the middle – exactly the trap Porter warns against. Simply put, they're amateurs in a professional game with high stakes.

Which brings us to a third problem.

3. **Focus and flexibility.** You have to place a bet to win. If you don't pursue one strategy for some time, you'll neither build the capabilities it needs nor will you learn enough to discover its true value. Half-hearted competitors are seldom a threat for long.

   However, commitment to one product line, one technology, one market segment, or one positioning strategy shuts out others. By choosing what you will do, you also choose what you won't do. Doing the sensible thing – dedicating yourself to one direction – can be the kiss of death.

   Caterpillar once dominated the earthmoving equipment business, but lost market share when it concentrated too much on quality and too little on price.

   Texas Instruments was the cost leader in computer chip production until competitors with better technology overtook it and nullified its cost advantage.

   Digital Equipment Corp. ran into trouble when its engineers became obsessed with quality and reluctant to give customers novel products at acceptable prices.[17]

   These examples and many others show the risks and contradictions inherent in the pursuit of a narrow set of core competencies. 'The right answer' has a dark side: 'core rigidity' is always a possibility.[18] As Harvard professor Pankaj Ghemawat reminds us, commitment 'is a constraint that must be reckoned with, *not a recipe for success*'[19] (my italic).

   But if single-mindedness is dangerous, trying to take advantage of every opportunity is even more so. While it makes sense to have a Plan B in the bottom drawer in case Plan A goes wrong, the danger is that the very presence of a back-up plan will cause attention to wander and resolve to weaken. And if there's also a Plan C, D, and E, it's even harder to stay on course.

   So here we see the need for both commitment and flexibility in strategy. Judgement must be informed not only by a keen sense of external changes, but also by internal capabilities, needs, values, and principles.

   You have to be single-minded … and open-minded!

Brilliant at the wrong things

Executives who strategize around their core competencies often haven't given enough thought to what they're doing. Like other popular management ideas, this one is open to any number of interpretations.

There's no rigorous discipline for identifying competencies, so almost any skill or technology fits the bill. The competence label is too readily fixed to things that made a firm famous, but no longer matter. And all too often, companies choose exactly the same competencies as their competitors.

One company I worked with listed 'the ability to build relationships with customers' as their No. 1 competence. Another saw 'owning the entire value chain' as its key to success, when managers openly admitted that to be the reason for consistently poor results!

In the short term, you might gain an edge by doing a few things exceptionally well, but will such a strategy let you win over the long haul? Should you invest even more heavily to develop those competencies? What can you safely stop doing? What happens when others build or buy similar strengths?

What if your reputation for making fine buggy whips suddenly doesn't matter because someone invents the car?

What if you stake your future on producing the ultimate record player, and suddenly CDs appear?

What if customers stop visiting the shops you serve so well, and start buying through TV shopping channels, by mail or phone, or via the Internet?

What happens when the brand you've built at such cost is attacked by no-name brands? Or when the customer who loved your Chinese food becomes a health food freak?

Competencies obviously matter. But as Abell points out, it's not enough merely to have a resource or a competence; competitive advantage rests on having *superior* resources and competencies.[21]

What you *do* must count. You must do it better than anyone else. And most importantly, you must be able to preserve and defend your special skill over time.

It makes sense, but ...

Before you grasp at the latest strategy formula, check that it's supported by current realities.

Aggressive competitors move fast. Concepts of strategy – not just strategies – are rapidly outmoded. And when academics, consultants, and other observers try to reduce a firm's strategy to a model or a few simple steps, they often put their own conclusions before the facts. 'Company X is successful because it does so-and-so,' they say, when it actually behaves quite differently.

For example, Treacy and Wiersema cite mail order specialist Dell Computer as masters of operational excellence. But when they describe the strategy, we see something else.

Dell's strategy, they say, has been to integrate its logistics with those of suppliers; develop slick, user-friendly systems and a low-cost culture; and sell by mail to avoid third-party distribution costs. This way, 'Dell undercut Compaq and other PC makers in price while providing high quality products and services.'[22]

So there's the real secret: low prices, high quality, *and* great service!

To be fair, Treacy and Wiersema do say that while market leaders are best in one of the three disciplines they must also be pretty good in the other two. But Dell has blown a hole in that theory.

While the firm might have been founded on the single-minded notion of operational excellence, it has clearly advanced. Competitors have invaded its turf. Dell has had to adopt their tactics and beat them at their own game.

According to *Business Week*, mail order is today 'the preferred method of the best PC customers – experienced PC clients and knowledgeable consumers looking for the most cutting-edge (and expensive) models'. Dell might have been the pioneer in this marketing method, but it's not alone. If home users once were Dell's target market, now big *corporate* customers account for more than 50 per cent of sales.

Dell switched to the new Pentium chip ahead of many competitors who might have claimed title to 'product leadership'.[23] It also beat them in the race to pre-install Windows 95. And Dell computers consistently rank at the top of technology reviews in computer magazines.

Now consider the company's performance in terms of 'customer intimacy'. Ads for Dell Dimension systems promise a 'next-business-day-at-your-desk service guarantee'. Dell's help desks offer unbeatable support. And customer surveys rate Dell tops.

In a recent *Harvard Business Review* interview, Michael Dell explained how his firm builds customer relationships:

> *Boeing, for example, has 100,000 Dell PCs, and we have 30 people that live at Boeing, and if you look at the things we're doing for them or for other customers, we don't look like a supplier, we look more like Boeing's PC department.*[24]

As with so many other successful companies, there's far more to Dell's success than meets the eye. Dell's focus on low costs is no longer its only advantage; many other players do the same and perhaps even better. So Dell's managers must continue to add value *and* cut costs – and do it faster than Compaq, Gateway, Hewlett-Packard, and others who are racing along the same path.

And so it is with any number of other companies in every industry. Just when you think you've pinned down what makes them go ... *vroom!* ... they're gone! Competitiveness cannot come from a static notion of strategy. It's a never-ending race to learn, to change, and to turn what 'everyone knows' right on its head.

Where's the real advantage?

Once, a long time ago (in cyber-time, that is) you could find neat answers to complex strategic questions. Now it's not so easy. Just watch what's happening in the cut-throat PC industry. And consider the implications for firms in other industries – and for your own firm.

In 1996, Dell started selling computers via the Internet. Barely a year later, sales were up to $4 million *a day*. Compaq had to follow the strategy. So does everyone else.

Imagine trying to stick with a different business model. You'd be in worse trouble by the minute.

For one thing, customers are learning to buy in different ways. They're discovering that it's far more convenient and pleasant to shop from their homes or offices than to visit a store. Even having a sales person call is less of an attraction than it was; they take time and may not be able to answer every question. As more customers see the benefits of on-line shopping, they'll go that way in droves.

Secondly, Internet marketing shifts responsibility for a lot of work from sales staff to customers – in effect, outsourcing it. But it's so easy for customers that they don't mind. In fact, they enjoy the control they have over the process, as they select what information they need and choose the options they want. They can query, configure, and customize to their heart's content. And no matter how long they take, or how much they want to know, or how picky they get with their order, the cost of satisfying them doesn't go up!

The third issue is that of critical mass. By its very nature, conventional channels limit distribution – and therefore sales. There's only so much shelf space in so many stores. There's a limit to how fast people can get in and out of a shop. But the Internet applies no such constraints.

Critical mass means clout. The 800-pound gorilla in the PC market has the advantage of buying power. So – best component prices and terms, best deliveries, and most promotional support.

Direct selling allows make-to-order production. This cuts factory and inventory costs. It also lets producers switch quickly to upgrade their products.

When PC prices fell to under $1,000 in 1997, sales took off. The industry's 'centre of gravity' shifted suddenly, as 200mhz or 233mhz Pentium machines became affordable to a wide audience. The question now is, how low can prices go? And what kind of business model will be needed in the future?

The PC industry is dominated by a few big players: Compaq, Dell, IBM, Hewlett Packard. Those in the middle are being squeezed out. Brand names are obviously important. But building a brand costs big bucks, so firms that sell the most have the edge. For players in the game, this is a virtuous cycle; for those who want to break in, it's a vicious cycle.

What all this shows is that what we know about strategy may not matter any more. What you see not only lags behind reality, but often has little to do with it.

So how should you compete? What can you do to shape a strategy that will give you an edge – and let you hold it over time?

Given the complexity of the environment and the shock of the changes that are coming at us, it's little wonder that many managers are stuck for what to do next. Some seem to think that if they do nothing, their problems will simply go away. Others are searching frantically for 'the mother of all strategies'.

In fact, we do know what to do. Yet most companies don't do what they should, or they don't pay enough attention to the how.

The most dangerous course is to wait for better times or search for perfect answers. Not to think, not to act, is unforgivable.

Endnotes

1. Russell L. Ackoff, *Creating The Corporate Future*, New York: John Wiley & Sons, 1981.
2. 'Dusting the opposition', *The Economist*, April 29, 1995.
3. Richard K. Lester, Michael J. Piore, and Kamal M. Malek, 'Interpretive management: what general managers can learn from design', *Harvard Business Review*, March–April 1998.
4. Andrew E. Serwer, 'Lessons from America's fastest-growing companies', *Fortune*, August 8,1994.
5. 'Small-town values make a big firm', *International Herald Tribune*, April 6, 1995.
6. 'Corporate reputations', *Fortune*, March 6, 1995.
7. Barry Diller, 'Don't repackage-redefine!' *Wired*, February 1995.
8. 'Medicine, management, and mergers: an interview with Merck's P. Roy Vagelos', Nancy A. Nichols, *Harvard Business Review*, November–December 1994.
9. Jack Mingo, *How The Cadillac Got Its Fins*, New York: HarperBusiness, 1994.
10. 'America's television industry: incest is best', *The Economist*, April 17, 1993.
11. Richard A. D'Aveni, *Hypercompetition*, New York: The Free Press, 1994.
12. Anthony J.F. O'Reilly, '125 Years at the Heinz Table', *Journal of Business Strategy*, May/June, 1995, Volume 16, No.3.
13. James C. Collins and Jerry I. Porras, *Built To Last*, New York: HarperBusiness, 1994.
14. 'Keeping Motorola on a roll', *Fortune*, April 18, 1994.
15. Michael E. Porter, *Competitive Strategy*, New York: The Free Press 1980.
16. Michael Treacy and Fred Wiersma, *The Discipline of Market Leaders*, Reading, Massechusetts: Addison-Wesley, 1995.
17. Danny Miller, 'The generic strategy gap', *The Journal of Business Strategy*, January/February 1992.
18. H. Kent Bowen, Kim B. Clark, Charles A. Holoway, Steven C. Wheelwright, *The Perpetual Enterprise Machine*, New York: Oxford University Press, 1994.
19. Pankaj Ghemewat, *Commitment: The Dynamic of Strategy*, New York: The Free Press, 1991.
20. Abell, 1993.
21. Treacy and Wiersma, 1995.
22. 'The computer is in the mail (really)', *Business Week*, January 23, 1995.
23. Joan Magretta, March–April 1998.

8

Planning's Past and its Purpose

... clinically framed and contractually based relationships do not inspire the extraordinary effort and sustained commitment required to deliver consistently superior performance.

— Christopher A. Bartlett and Sumantra Goshal, *Harvard Business Review*[1]

We want to achieve management by motivation and goals instead of by instruction and directives.

— Percy Barnevik, chairman ABB[2]

Countless companies in all industries, young or old, mature or booming, are finally learning the limits of strategy and concentrating on tactics and execution.

— Amar Bide, *Harvard Business Review*[3]

Andy Grove, chairman of Intel and *Time*'s 'Man of the year' in 1997, is well known for his view that 'only the paranoid survive'. He has written extensively about the need for companies to understand their environments, to keep looking over their shoulders, and to anticipate the future.

In a recent interview with the *Financial Times*, Grove described Intel's attitude to long-term investment. 'You would have a hard time finding other investors willing to do what we do,' he said. 'We invest $5 billion a year in factories to build a product that is non-existent for a non-existent market. That is the stuff of junk bonds!'

He then acknowledged that forecasting economic and market trends was not Intel's strength.[4] And as the record shows, the world's fourth most valuable company has made some costly mis-steps. Andy Grove is apparently as human as any of us. He calls things just as wrong.

His problem is every manager's problem: you have to lay bets when you haven't got all the facts. So how do you reduce the risk?

The answer, most managers think, is through better planning. More specifically, in producing better *plans*. And this is where their problems begin.

Corporate charades

Strategy is serious, right? So managers should take it seriously, right?

Well, maybe they do, but something's wrong. Look at what happens in the real world:

- Not long ago, the top eight executives from a major corporation gathered in a conference room in a remote game lodge, to talk about their company's future. The setting was businesslike: tables arranged in a U-shape; an overhead projector, a screen, and two flip charts at the front of the room; coloured felt pens, writing pads, and name cards. Serious tools for a serious discussion.

  'Perhaps we should begin by reviewing our vision,' said the CEO. 'We worked on it last year, and we need to be sure it's still on target.'

  There was a deathly hush. His co-directors looked bewildered.

  'Well, come on,' said the CEO. 'Is our vision still right?'

  More uncertain stares. Then one man plucked up his courage and said, 'Maybe it would be a good idea if you reminded us exactly what it said.'

  Fortunately for the CEO, last year's strategic plan lay on the desk in front of him. For the truth was, he couldn't remember the vision either!
- The managing director of another company called me in to help sharpen his firm's strategic planning process. While he was briefing me, I mentioned that all too often the product of planning was a thick document that did nothing to change a company's behaviour. He chuckled and led me into a small room next to his office, where a huge cardboard box was stuffed with plans. 'That's last year's lot,' he said. 'I still haven't looked at them. But now we have to redo them.'
- I told these stories to a group of 50 general managers. They laughed like hell. Then one explained: 'We've learned to short-circuit the planning process. We used to go through the hard slog of updating our strategies every year, but then we realized that the whole pile landed on the MD's desk at once, and he had absolutely no chance of looking at them. So now we just change the date on the cover, and when we get together for our annual strategy review, we stand up and tell him what he wants to hear.'

Encouraged mediocrity

These examples mirror what I see day after day in the most successful companies everywhere.

Strategic planning is regarded as an important task in most large companies, and many small ones. Senior people devote a lot of their costly time to it. It 'happens' at a particular time in the year. Economists or socio-political experts are called in to do kick-off presentations. Documents must be turned in by a certain date. Perhaps there's a meeting or retreat at which managers show and discuss their efforts.

Some companies expect everyone to follow an agreed format. Managers know what indicators count. Secretaries all use the same page layout. When you review the results you know that Section 1 will cover assumptions, the SWOT analysis will start on Page 20, and departmental tactics will follow divisional goals.

Other firms let managers do their own thing. Everyone has a different view of what to cover, what matters, and how to present themselves. They tackle the task in different ways. Some are inevitably more thorough, more logical, or more creative than others. The results are a mish-mash of formats and styles.

Often at the final presentation meetings, executives stand up with slides or overheads and say things that don't add up, can't be defended, and won't change anything. (And with computer technology, they can really go to town on the graphics and special effects!) They trot out last year's numbers, bump them up by a safe percentage for the year ahead (inflation or less), and brag about their new customer care programme.

There may be some mention of hassles with the trade union, or an explanation of why the last sales forecast was so wrong. Clichés from *In Search Of Excellence* or references to being the low-cost producer or the service leader are common. Some mention of reengineering or flattening the structure seems to be mandatory. Then the presenters sit down to applause from their colleagues.

There's more ritual than rigour in these charades. Despite the straight faces, they fool no one.

The purpose of strategic debate is to improve a company's competitiveness. Yet it's seldom as rewarding as it should be.

Too often, the conversation lacks rigour, direction, or purpose. Too much time is wasted on circular, ambiguous debates, and too little goes into rigorous thinking. Too much time is spent on tactical rather than strategic issues. There are too many buzzwords, too many vague theories, too many glib assumptions. Time is given to presentations with no point, conversations without conclusion, and detail without decisions.

What's needed, of course, is a more disciplined, tougher process. Strategy discussions should be robust. Strategy presentations should be tests. People who make them shouldn't be allowed to waste others' time. They should know that they're under the spotlight, that their views are on trial, and that their performance affects their careers.

Strategy is shaped by the conversations that leaders encourage and allow. If they don't grasp this, and if they don't actively manage the process, they set the stage for mediocrity.

They also miss a major opportunity.

No guarantees

Heading for a conference centre to talk strategy is no guarantee that a company will improve its performance. Strategic planning usually does less than expected to ease the pain of managing in the real world. Most of the planning models managers use are well-worn and badly used; rather than provoke fresh thinking, they too often keep dysfunctional behaviours alive.

There are two basic reasons.

First, there's the fact that most managers don't have a clear idea of what 'success' means, or a clear concept of what causes it.

Challenged to define success, they are seldom as sure as GE's Jack Welch, who told his top people that any business that wasn't No. 1 or No. 2 in its industry would be fixed, closed, or sold. They aren't as clear as Richard Branson, the flamboyant British entrepreneur, who aims to knock Pepsi out of second place in the world soft drinks business in ten years, and to challenge Coke for top spot.[5] Nor do they spell it out like the Microsoft executive who told the *Financial Times*, 'My job is to get a fair share of the software applications market, and to me, that's 100 per cent.'[6]

The fact is, they are not sure whether success means profits, market share, or something else.

And when it comes to *how* to succeed, they grasp at straws. One day they talk service, then it's reengineering or value chain analysis. You can tell who the keen readers are, because they toss out terms like competencies or customer intimacy, or boast about building a learning organization. They can go on for hours about intellectual capital, the wisdom of teams, and balanced scorecards.

I spend a lot of time listening to busy people arguing over a single word in a vision or mission statement, when none of them can explain why that statement is needed in the first place. I hear too many managers ascribe specific results to the wrong causes. I see them try to sell their colleagues on a particular course of action when their underlying assumptions are full of holes. I can hardly recall a team that was confident of its planning process, and could justify it.

The second reason things come unstuck is that for all their talk of five or ten-year visions – and their admiration for Konusuke Matsushita's 250-year view* – most managers look about five minutes ahead. Immediate problems get most attention.

IMD professor Derek Abell, author of *Managing With Dual Strategies*, notes that 'while planning for today requires organization, planning for tomorrow quite often requires reorganization'.[7] Dealing with an urgent matter is often easier than making changes for the long haul.

Executives with a short-term orientation focus on fine-tuning the current business rather than inventing new ones. Incremental improvement is more pressing than quantum leaps. Problems get more attention than opportunities. Fixing weaknesses is higher on the agenda than exploiting strengths.

* He spelled it out in 1923.

Not surprisingly, these executives lock themselves into a self-fulfilling prophecy: managing from moment to moment, they rely on data from the past ... which tells them what worked or went wrong ... which tells them what to fix ... which commits resources to urgent matters ... which draws attention away from longer-term issues.

Henry Mintzberg puts it like this in his book *The Rise and Fall of Strategic Planning*:

> *... conventional planning tends to be a conservative process, sometimes encouraging behavior that undermines both creativity and strategic thinking. It can be inflexible, breeding resistance to major strategic change and discouraging truly novel ideas in favor of extrapolation of the status quo or marginal adaptation, ultimately, therefore, focusing attention on the short term rather than the long term.*[8]

What the boss doesn't hear

When I ask groups of managers if the strategic planning process deserves the time it gets, they always say yes. The people in charge of planning (whose jobs, in some cases, depend on it) defend it especially strongly.

'Our success has been largely due to our planning discipline', one 'champion' told me proudly. Said another: 'We couldn't operate without our plan. It's the most useful thing we do.'

But when I ask managers in private what they think, they all too often just shake their heads. If just a fraction of the pressure that caused them to toe the line went into some radical thinking and determined action, the results would be immediate and impressive.

Typical views:

'A total waste of time.'

'The wrong people talking about the wrong things in fantastic places.'

'A very expensive way of distracting us from what really counts.'

Or, as one man put it: 'It's like pissing down your leg. It makes you feel nice and warm, but the results are terrible.'

Despite the weight given to strategic planning, few firms know how to make it meaningful and fewer still use it to provoke radical change. If virtually every manager talks about strategy, and most are involved quite regularly in creating plans, very few can say how the activity pays off. All too often, it provides no more than a picture of the past. Mostly, it's an exercise in futility, a time-consuming chore that ultimately influences behaviour much less than anyone admits.

Why companies plan

A lot of planning, says professor James Brian Quinn of the Amos Tuck School of Business, is like 'a ritual rain dance; it has no effect on the weather that follows, but those who engage in it think it does'.[9]

If that's the case, why keep doing it? What causes powerful and intelligent business leaders to spend time and money on an activity whose outcome is suspect?

Ask them, and their reasons are perfectly rational:

1. **To manage risks.** Many investments have a long lead-time. Huge sums must be committed years – even decades – before any payoff can be expected. Managers must make assumptions about a world they cannot see, and persuade their backers that going for the ride is worth the risk. Planning makes the process systematic.
2. **To identify and exploit current strengths.** Most firms grow by building on their current capabilities and resources. Past investments are a springboard for the future. Managers need to enhance or develop existing advantages. The strategic planning process helps identify leverage points.
3. **To minimize or eliminate weaknesses.** No company can do everything well; they all have chinks in their armour. Hopefully, strategic planning will reveal weak areas and show how a firm compares to its competitors. Managers can then take remedial action.
4. **To highlight opportunities.** Any executive worth her salt knows it's essential to keep searching for new customers, for new products and services, and for new ways of promoting and delivering them. Planning includes environmental scanning, which shows the gaps.
5. **To be warned early of possible threats.** The world is a dangerous and surprising place. The firm that stumbles blindly forward is likely to be caught off guard. Managers need some way to sense likely dangers, so they can develop ways to respond.
6. **To align and coordinate activities.** Without a plan, the organization's left hand is unlikely to know what the right hand is doing. Planning helps get everyone pulling in the same direction and helps integrate activities.

Not surprisingly, most of the justification for planning is taken care of by the familiar SWOT analysis (strengths, weaknesses, opportunities, threats). It's a key aspect in most strategic planning sessions. In fact, many teams see it as the most important thing they do.

Nor is it surprising that participants come away from these meetings wondering why they're not satisfied. Or that they write the same stuff on their flip charts year after year. Or that most major changes that they do make are a reaction to external events, rather than a result of proactive thinking.

The gap between theory and practice exists for several reasons.

First, the goals of the planning process are usually badly defined. Managers find it hard to be precise when they're asked ahead of a retreat: 'What will make this meeting a success?' or 'What must we achieve?' So a debate which is supposed to yield specific objectives and action plans is itself vague and directionless.

Second, planning is usually attached to budgeting – and is almost always less important. Companies are driven by 'the numbers'. Talking strategy seems a sensible first step.

The outcome of strategic planning is neither here nor there; the budget, on the other hand, is a matter of life or death. Present a strategy with holes in it, and who cares? Screw up the budget, though, and you're history!

This gives rise to the third problem, which is that strategic planning – and thus strategic thinking – is mostly an intermittent, calendar-driven activity. It happens outside of 'real work'.

Life presents a constant stream of challenges. Managers have to deal with them in real time. But maybe once a year they take a break, head for a resort in the mountains or the bush, or near a beach, and talk strategy.

Their new plans sound great in a workshop, and even better if there's lots of hype around the occasion. But all good things come to an end, and Murphy's Law pretty well guarantees that the shit will hit the fan while the bosses are thinking big thoughts. So within moments of getting home, they have to put their good intentions on the back burner and deal with immediate hassles.

The result is that while planning may lead managers to feel that they're truly future oriented, it is unconnected to reality. It often does little to build on an organization's strengths, minimize its weaknesses, seize opportunities, or cope with threats. What's more, since most people never see a company's plan, the effort does little to focus or prioritize their efforts, less to align them, and nothing to inspire them.

Other objectives

While the above objectives are the ones managers most readily mention, there are others which they seldom recognize or speak about. These have more to do with a manager's self-image, with power and personal worth, than with taking a company to a new place.

1. **Certainty.** Afloat in a sea of uncertainty, managers feel an intense need to make the future predictable. They know it's impossible, but they at least want to narrow the range of 'maybe's'. They like to think, 'If I do so-and-so, such-and-such will happen.'

2. **Comfort.** Often when managers have been through a planning process – whether a long formal exercise or a brief getaway – the best they can say is, 'Well, at least we've done it.' Nothing changes, but they feel they've gone through the motions. If anyone asks, 'Do you have a strategy?' they can whip it out and show they've done what managers are supposed to do.

3. **Control.** Executives have many demanding constituencies. They're under pressure from stakeholders such as employees, bankers, investors, and suppliers to look as if they're in control and can create a particular future. A 'take-charge' manner is widely admired.

4. **Reliability.** The last thing any organization needs is unreliable people. They soak up management time and attention, and their omissions and errors cost money. Reliability is an especially important trait in anyone aspiring to a position of power. A track record of 'delivering the goods' is a valuable asset, and a strong selling point on any CV. Men and women who deliver are rewarded and promoted.
5. **Rationality.** An essential aspect of an executive's image is that he or she makes decisions carefully, sensibly, and on the basis of solid information. I've yet to meet anyone in a high position who admits to shooting from the hip. Managers boast about their 'no surprises' approach to business. They are proud that they make decisions only 'when all the facts are in'. Entrepreneurship is a sexy idea – especially in hide-bound bureaucracies where no one has any intention of changing anything, and opportunities are threats to be avoided at all costs.
6. **Tidiness.** The notion of 'a place for everything, and everything in its place' is attractive. Executives are generally uncomfortable with ambiguity. The logic of strategic plans, a definite planning/budgeting cycle, and a neatly bound plan all remove doubt and uncertainty.

The trouble is, these objectives are illusory. Business is inherently uncertain, risky, and surprising. Life is messy; organizational life especially so. The fact that a plan describes in detail how things should work out is no guarantee that they will.

Chris Argyris has written at length about the difference between our 'espoused theories of action' and our 'theories-in-use'. Most theories-in-use, he says, are driven by four needs: to maintain control; to win, not lose; to suppress negative feelings; and to be rational. Their purpose is 'to avoid vulnerability, risk, embarrassment, and the appearance of incompetence'. But, he warns, they have an unforeseen and harmful side effect: they block learning.[10]

Strategy is not a straight-line process. Your ability to make effective decisions is directly related to your willingness to expose yourself to new information, ideas, challenges, and conflict – and to criticism, pain, and even danger.

Growth does not come cheap.

Executives who work from a paradigm of control unwittingly defeat themselves. Your ability to achieve great things in an organization is entirely dependent on the willingness of others to support you. You can't go it alone. You can't turn their imagination and spirit on and off like a tap, or command their loyalty. If they don't volunteer, you lose.

Myths revisited

'Strategy is the king of business disciplines,' writes Richard Pascale in *Managing on the Edge*, 'because, at its best, it causes us to question the fundamental premises on which all else rests.'[11] Maybe so. But 'all else' doesn't necessarily include 'the fundamental premises' on which our *strategic thinking* rests.

Like everything else, strategy has its own sacred cows. Managers 'know' things about business. But close observation of what actually happens tells us that it's time to challenge our thinking.

Here are some realities:

1. **Very few companies are successful for one or even just a few reasons.** There's always more to long-term growth, profits, etc., than may be evident at first glance. The best executives are able to leverage one early advantage – access to raw materials, a technology breakthrough, a special customer relationship – by wrapping it in others. Instead of relying on one advantage, they think in terms of 'layers of advantage'.

   Strategy builds strength over time. The foundation may be in 'visible assets' such as buildings or equipment. But as fast as possible these must be replaced or reinforced by 'invisible assets' such as skills, understanding, relationships, imagination, creativity, flexibility, responsiveness, perseverance, confidence.

2. **Managing the simplest business is a complex process.** Effective leaders seem almost to revel in that complexity. Whatever they have to do, they 'just do it' – as the famous Nike slogan advises. This keeps them moving ahead. But it also causes them to waste time on problems that would go away if left alone, or to take on tasks they should leave to others.

   Their followers, on the other hand, spend a lot of time rationalizing why things shouldn't be done, or seeking the easiest way out. This way, they avoid doing many 'wrong' things – but they also fail to do many right things, or do them too late.

3. **Most business processes are far too complex.** Instead of making life easier, they make it much harder. Executives accept the need for simplicity, but beaver away at confusing themselves and the people around them.

   They also like to think that their companies and the industries they compete in are unique and special, so 'off-the-shelf' ideas won't help them. They insist on the need to start every new project from scratch, and waste huge amounts of time and money reinventing the wheel.

   Another trap is the illusion that 'we're a big company' (so our problems are big, too, and will take forever to fix) when, in fact, they're quite small. A lot of my time in strategy meetings goes into holding up a mirror for managers, to give them a reality check. Often, when they see themselves in context, and see their firms as they really are, there's an audible sigh of relief. Issues that appeared unmanageable suddenly shrink to a do-able size. Insurmountable problems become achievable challenges. Confidence replaces helplessness.

   Management isn't rocket science – though sometimes it might seem like it. I remind executives that there are just four ways to improve operating profits: sell more units, sell them at a higher price, sell them faster, and cut costs. One of my favourite accounting books is called *Buy Low, Sell High, Collect Early, Pay Late*, a title that says it all.[12]

   Conclusion: Keep things in perspective. Keep them simple. Cut through the clutter and try to find the real issue you must deal with. Spend more time thinking through the few factors that will deliver the best results for your company.

4. **Top executives often hold an inaccurate view of what's happening in their organizations.** Though some practice 'management by walking around' (MBWA) with great enthusiasm, most don't get around nearly as much as they should. Information reaches them through many filters, and messages are carelessly distorted or deliberately changed to suit the ends of the messengers.

   Being human, senior people see the world the way they want it to be. They draw conclusions which satisfy their existing values and beliefs. What they think – and hope – is happening may not be the way things really are at all.

   Often they get carried away by their own deep understanding of the need for a particular intervention – TQM, customer service, 'empowerment' – or by the hype they've drummed up around it. They assume that because they circulated an article out of the *Harvard Business Review*, their colleagues are as turned on as they are. Or they think that because they made a speech, produced a video or a beautiful brochure, or handed out prizes at a glitzy company dinner, that everyone got the message, and embraced it.

   Paradoxically, too, as Argyris points out, an organization's best communicators may turn out to be its worst enemies. They are so good at making a point that the truth of what they say isn't challenged.

5. **The factors that seem to cause particular results are often not the ones that really make the difference.** When sales go up, for example, managers boast about their brilliant new ad campaign; in fact, the real trigger might have been something else entirely – price cuts, more effort by the sales force, keener distributors, or a weak showing by competitors. Or they give credit for the latest productivity improvement to a new training package, when maybe there are new supervisors in the factory or the trade union has decided to play ball for a while.

   Sustained superior performance is not a one-dimensional matter. As we've seen, it hinges on many things. Few companies become overnight successes. Winning over the long haul is more complex than most of us like to admit, and further, any intervention must be seen in its total context.

   If you don't know what resources give what results, you'll blow time and money. Also, there's a good chance that your people will be critical of the effort – and of you – and they won't support it. Then, when you come along with your next great initiative, they'll cry, 'Here we go again!' and your credibility will suffer.

Planning's fall from grace

During the 1960s and '70s, strategic planning was a function few major companies would do without. Planning departments grew bigger and bigger. Planners became incredibly powerful. But as the environment became more turbulent and the pace of change accelerated, executives found to their cost that plans often hurt more than helped. Worldwide, office shelves are weighed down by planning documents that are ignored or forgotten.

'Strategic planning fell into disfavor,' says creative thinking guru Edward de Bono, 'when the future refused to play the role assigned to it by the planners. The sheer unpredictability of the future, the rapid rate of change, the instability and positive feedback loops in nonlinear systems made a nonsense of planning. At best, there had to be a sort of rolling strategic plan with reassessments every week.'[13]

According to a recent article in *Fortune*, even though 3M has been one of America's ten most admired corporations ten times in 11 years, it has no strategy. Said 3M CEO DeSimone: 'We're going to do two principal things: be very innovative and satisfy our customers. We don't have one core; we have lots of cores – sticky stuff, optical and safety stuff, medical stuff, etc.'

Asked how executives know if a business fits, vice-chairman Ron Mitsch said, 'That's a good question. None of us is foresightful enough to decide that, because our people might find some way to make whatever they're doing work.'

Another top man observed that '3M fundamentally is a collection of a lot of stuff'.[14] The company has been known to boast: 'We consider a coherent sentence to be an acceptable draft for a new product plan.'[15]

Forecasters' failures

According to 'random walk' theorists, planning is just a bad form of guesswork. In 1966 *Forbes* magazine picked 20 stocks by throwing darts at the investment page of *The Wall Street Journal*. Fifteen years later their portfolio was up 239 per cent, while the Standard & Poor's 500 had gained a mere 35 per cent.[16]

The Wall Street Journal itself regularly entertains its readers by pitting investment pros in a race with a 'monkey'. A story in the issue of January 17, 1995 tells how: 'A portfolio of four stocks picked at random last June – as if by a monkey throwing darts at the newspaper – has scored exactly the same return over the past six months as a portfolio of four stocks picked by a team of European investment professionals.' As the challenge continued, the paper reported that 'the accurate ape has just won another round'(July 18) ... and 'the champion chimp beat all comers in the most recent round' (September 19).

In 1984, *The Economist* sent a questionnaire to four ex-finance ministers of OECD countries, four chairmen of multinational companies, four Oxford University students, and four London dustmen. They were asked to make three predictions: what would happen to inflation over the next decade, what would the exchange rate of the pound against the dollar be, and when would Singapore's GDP per person pass Australia's? The dustmen tied with the businessmen. The finance ministers came last![17]

Want more?

A 1986 study by Andrew Meltzer, a professor at Carnegie Mellon University, looked at 20 years of economic forecasts. On average, even the smartest of forecasters couldn't tell at the start of a particular quarter whether the economy would grow or slow in that quarter.[18]

As a leader in the *Financial Times* notes: 'Economists have plenty to say about the forces behind the economic headlines, but rarely can they accurately predict the news in advance. Time and again, the world asks them to gaze into their crystal balls and, time and again, they oblige with ever-more precise, but mistaken, estimates of future events.'[19]

What about 'the vision thing'?

Executives in love with the idea of determinism would do well to study the Honda case. As Pascale reports, there is a gulf between accepted wisdom and reality. Here's a summary of the story as seen from two perspectives[20]:

What the outsider saw	What the insider did
A study commissioned for the British Government concluded that Honda's management had planned their attack on the U.K. and U.S. markets in minute detail. Their strategy was thought out in advance and executed in deliberate fashion.	Conversations with Honda executives who led the charge revealed that they had no strategy. All they had was a sales target. Their success was largely due to dogged determination and sheer good luck.

This story offers two valuable lessons. First, the observers saw what they expected to see. They made the facts fit their preconceived view. Second, if success IS possible without strategy, strategy is not a precondition for success.

Since the early 1980s, vision has been a central topic in discussions about strategy. But in 1993 – at the height of its popularity – several prominent global business leaders poured scorn on it.

- 'The last thing we need right now is a vision,' said Lou Gerstner shortly after he was appointed chairman of IBM. This was a startling view, given his track record as a successful McKinsey consultant and boss of American Express and R.J. Reynolds. IBM staff and investors were not impressed. Industry analysts said it was a sure sign this outsider would fail to fix the company.
- Said Chrysler chairman Robert Eaton, the man driving one of the most remarkable turnarounds of the 1990s: 'Internally, we don't use the word vision. I believe in quantifiable short-term results – things we can all relate to – as opposed to some esoteric thing no one can quantify.'[21]
- Microsoft's Bill Gates, obviously a long-term thinker, offered the blunt view that 'being a visionary is trivial'.[22]

- And then there was Ricardo Semler, head of Sao Paulo-based manufacturer Semco S/A, and author of the best-selling book *Maverick*, who said, 'I think that strategic planning and vision are often barriers to success ... Thinking about the future is a useful, necessary exercise, but translating such conjecture into "Strategic Planning" is worse than useless. It's an actual barrier to survival. Strategic planning leads us to make things happen that fly full in the face of reality and opportunity.'[23]

Many executives interpreted these views to mean that having a vision – and, by implication, a strategy – was 'a bad thing'. Others latched onto the 'chaos' fad, or were so swamped by urgent problems that it was easy to argue, 'You can't plan anymore.' Somewhere in most companies there's a sign that says: 'When you're up to your ass in crocodiles ...'

All of which brings us to inevitable questions:

- If you can't see the future, is there any point planning for it?
- Does strategic planning have a place in the modern company?
- Is there a strategic planning method that works?
- Do the familiar approaches have merit, and if not, what must you change?
- Is there any point in using terms like 'vision' and 'mission', and should you still do a SWOT analysis?
- When you've got a plan, how do you make it work?

Face facts. Planning is largely guesswork. But, as Woody Allen said of old age, 'It's better than the alternative.' And as Henry Mintzberg points out, 'Too much planning may lead us to chaos, but so too would too little, and more directly.'[24]

Paradoxically, the more unpredictable the environment, the more effort managers should put into preparing for it. In fact, strategizing is more important today than ever. But for the exercise to be meaningful, we need to re-think our thinking tools – and get some new ones. We need to change how we do it. And above all, we need to change who does it.

The challenge, says Gary Hamel, 'is not one of prediction, it is one of imagination. There is not one future; there are as many potential futures as companies. But any company that can't imagine the future is unlikely to be around to enjoy it.'[25]

The issue, then, is not *precision*; it's *direction*. Reality allows no more than that.

Breakthroughs and botch-ups

Peter Drucker, Warren Bennis, and many others have said that it's more important to 'do the right things' than to 'do things right'. 'Leaders,' we are told, 'do the right things' while managers 'do things right'.

But if a key task of leaders is to pick a direction, there's no way of knowing whether the best leaders more often than not choose the best direction.

Perhaps their real contribution is their willingness to settle on *any* direction, from the wide array possible, and to go at it with a vengeance. Single-mindedness, and the ability to 'bring people along', are what count in many cases.

Of course, there are plenty of examples where 'brilliant' leaders made 'breakthrough' decisions that altered a company's fortunes. Alfred Sloan's re-organization of General Motors in the 1920s is one example. Edwin Land's invention of instant photography altered forever our expectations of cameras and film. Roberto Goizueta's decisions first to launch 'new' Coke, then to bring back 'old' Coke altered forever the Coca-Cola Company's paradigms.

It's every executive's dream to hit on the big-bang idea that leaves competitors gasping. But given the unpredictable nature of life, and given the human strengths and weaknesses that breath life into every organization, leadership – and strategy – has to be more than a quest for certainty. And for every story of a truly inspired decision, there are dozens where the choice turned out to be daft, or the results disappointing. The best of companies screw up a lot.

Our search for 'one right way' always leads to strategies that are 'wrong'. Every strategy is sub-optimal. In hindsight, we will always see things we could have done that would have made us better off.

The best we can aim for is to settle on a direction that we will pursue whole-heartedly. Every company's best chance of success lies in the commitment and energy with which its people pursue a particular goal.

Focus on the big picture

'What about detailed plans?' you ask. 'Don't you need those to avoid a whole lot of unnecessary work and expense?'

In some cases, yes. Plans might be helpful, for example, in persuading some stakeholders that management has thought things through, and has a rational point of view. Feasibility studies are necessary ahead of new projects.

But too often, executives are lured into a process that sounds right but has unanticipated consequences. Too often, planning is an excuse for doing nothing or for putting off hard decisions. Too often, managers get so bogged down in small details that they fail to focus on the big picture. And as Malcolm Forbes, the late founder and chairman of *Forbes*, once said, while 'it is right that executives should draw up a perfect plan on paper ... it is all wrong for them to expect their paper plans to work out to perfection in this imperfect world'.[26]

Peggy Noonan, speechwriter for former U.S. president Ronald Reagan, provides a useful context for strategists:

> *Life, like politics, is an interesting mess. It's hard to call. A smart man I know, a businessman, once told me, as he spoke of a painful personal trial, that the important thing to remember when you have a problem is that reality isn't a painting. It isn't a static and unchanging canvas on the wall of a museum. Life is dynamic, the mural is full of movement – the wind blows, a central character leaves the frame, an unexpected group walks onto the canvas, leaves fall.*

> *As you consider your problems and their solutions, don't fix on the static picture,' he said. 'Just keep watching the movement, and figure out what it means. Opportunity, changed circumstances. And maybe tomorrow you'll be in the picture.*[27]

There's no rule that says business plans have to be written down. There's no rule that says they have to be precise or cover every eventuality. Many highly effective executives have only the vaguest notion of where they want to go, then fill in the details as they progress. What they do instinctively, more managers should perhaps do deliberately. The time that's invested in trying to be precise about the future – in attempting to replace assumptions with certainties – would be better spent in moving forward.

Thinking about the way ahead has many purposes, just one of which is to help you see the best path. No matter how carefully you peer into the future, you'll wind up at best with a grainy picture of it. But that's just fine.

Strategists spend too much time trying to 'defy gravity' by creating plans that consider every risk, cover every eventuality, and prescribe every action for years ahead. Instead of living life as it is, they try to create an ideal; instead of doing what's possible, they try to bend reality to their own ends.

'What can we do when things are hard to describe?' asks artificial intelligence expert Marvin Minsky. 'We start by sketching out the roughest shapes to serve as scaffolds for the rest; it doesn't matter very much if some of these forms turn out partially wrong. Next, draw details to give these skeletons more lifelike flesh. Last, in the final filling-in, discard whichever first ideas no longer fit.'[28]

Says Intel CEO Andy Grove: 'It is impossible for us to have formal management systems that keep track of every commitment and action that has to be taken in the rapidly changing environment we live in. Instead, there is an implicit understanding that if we nod our head in a discussion, we are going to do it.'[29]

Another technology leader, Edward McCracken, CEO of Silicon Graphics, concurs with Grove. 'In our industry,' he says, 'very often we don't have time to think. You have to do all your homework, but then you have to go with your intuition without letting your mind get in the way.'[30]

And you have to go mighty fast to keep up with companies like Intel or Silicon Graphics. Or with MCI, whose chairman, Bert Roberts Jr., summed up his strategy like this: 'We run like mad and then we change direction.'[31]

These realities are leading to new ways of thinking about strategy and leadership. When radical strategies are the only ones that will work, yesterday's best practices make no sense.

It's a matter of choice

Strategy is about making choices. The first choice is which customer to aim for. Next, you have to decide how to do it. (So you also have to decide whom to *ignore* and what *not* to do.)

'Strategy,' says Harvard's Michael Porter, 'is about setting yourself apart from the competition. It's not just a matter of being better at what you do – it's a matter of being different at what you do.' But it's not 'good enough just to be different. You've got to be different in ways that involve trade-offs with other ways of being different.'[32]

You have to be willing to make tough trade-offs, to abandon old – and perhaps even *proven* – ways, and to sacrifice some opportunities so you can concentrate on others. Focus matters.

However, strategy is not only about business design. It's also about the way you act on your choices. It's about the energy, imagination, and determination that drive you along your chosen path. It's about the speed with which you advance, improve, and change direction. It's about the aggression with which you attack competitors. And it's about how you surprise them with new blows from unexpected directions.

In a widely-acclaimed *Harvard Business Review* article called 'What is Strategy?' Porter describes how Southwest Airlines beats the competition. The key, he says, is that 'Southwest has staked out a unique and valuable strategic position based on a tailored set of activities'.[33]

But there's more to this astonishing success story. Listen to Kevin and Jackie Freiberg, authors of *Nuts!*, an authorized biography of Southwest. These two consultants spent a great deal of time inside the organization, talking to many people from CEO Herb Kelleher down. One conclusion:

> *In an industry where every carrier has access to the same kind of equipment, Southwest's real competitive advantage is the spirit of its people. This is why we think it will be very difficult to replicate Southwest Airlines in its entirety. Those who come close will have focused more on what Southwest has done to unleash the human spirit than on its techniques for turning airplanes quickly.*[34]

So who's right – Porter or the Freibergs? The answer, of course, is both of them. Southwest *chose* a specific market niche and it *operates* in unique ways. It's strategy obviously works. But the magic ingredient is not positioning but attitude.

In the same way, you have to decide which customer is 'right' for your business. You have to customize your business model – what Porter calls your 'activity system' – to satisfy that customer. But you have to do more. You have to develop a unique corporate character to deliver on your intentions.

Strategy is only partly an intellectual activity. More and more, in a crowded marketplace, it turns out to be not just a matter of information and purpose, but also of imagination, inspiration, organization, opportunism, and – yes – *perspiration!*

'Whole-brain' thinking

The planning process that most firms use is specifically designed to encourage logical, rational, step-by-step thinking. You might call this 'left-brain strategy', given that brain researchers tell us that this type of thinking is usually done by the left side of the brain.

Left-brain thinking is 'sensible'. It draws a straight line from current facts to future acts. If asked, 'How did you come to this conclusion?' you can easily explain the path you followed. When you think in this mode, you take the facts apart, lay them end-to-end, and come to clear answers.

The right side of the brain handles creative, relational thinking: what you might call 'right-brain strategy'. What happens here is harder to describe. A feeling from over here might be linked to hard data from over there ... your mind wanders ... you wear your 'visionary' hat ... questions are more important than answers (Figure 8.1).

LEFT-BRAIN	RIGHT-BRAIN
PROCESSES PARTS LOGICAL RATIONAL LINEAR JUDGEMENTAL	PROCESSES WHOLES CREATIVE RELATIONAL EMOTIONAL INTUITIVE

Figure 8.1: *Left brain, right brain*

Whole-brain leadership engages both thinking modes. It builds on what you know and explores what you don't know. Logic and imagination mingle. Yesterday's sales statistics trigger one line of thought; letting your mind wander over a trip to the mountains or a favourite novel leads to others.

The model managers have traditionally used is essentially a 'funnelling' process. It takes you from the general to the specific, from a broad view of the world to narrow instructions about the next step (Figure 8.2).

But just because it's systematic, doesn't mean it's totally effective. 'The more steps in our argument,' says Bart Kosko, in his book *Fuzzy Thinking*, 'the fuzzier our argument. As we walk down the steps of inference, of Sherlock Holmes-style deduction, each step becomes less certain, less secure, less persuasive.'[35] This is all the more so when the environment changes fast and in unexpected ways. The logic that applied when you started to move may be irrelevant after just a few steps.

No matter how hard you try to defend your strategic plan, it will become obsolete. Five minutes after you sign it off, a competitor will cut prices, launch a new product, or switch distribution channels. Imagine what's possible over several weeks or months!

If you're not alert, you can lose your way before the ink is dry on your plan. The assumptions you begin with are like the foundations of a building; if

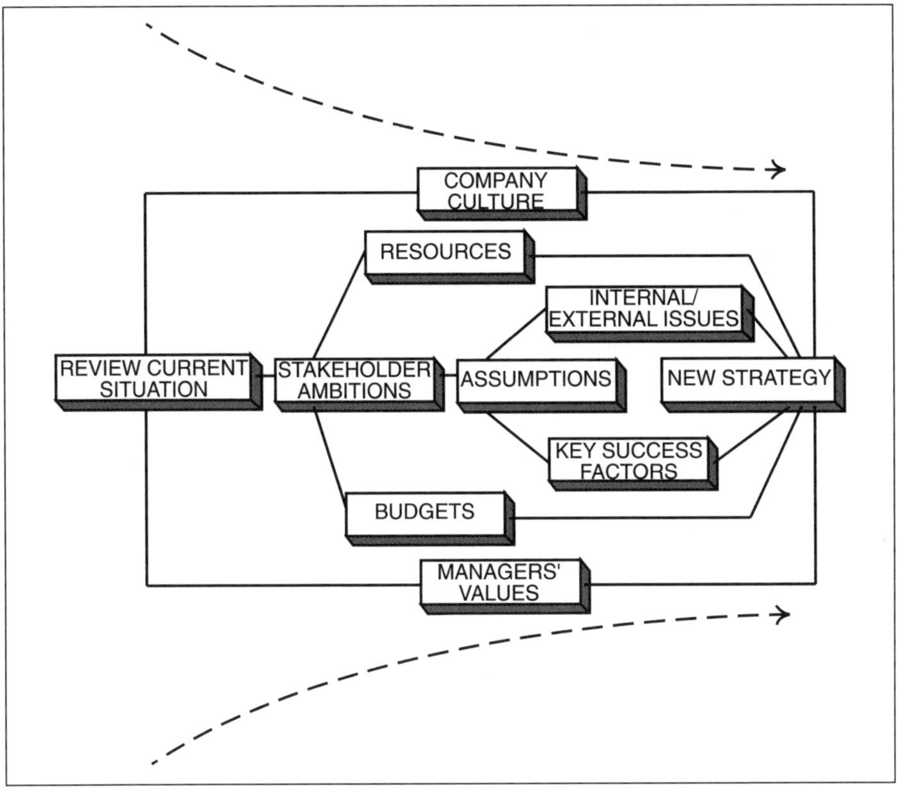

Figure 8.2: *Traditional planning process*

they're not solid, the whole thing will come tumbling down. But quicker than you imagine, those assumptions will change.

'Left-brained' strategic thinking takes us part of the way towards creating a strategy. But as Mintzberg reminds us: 'Systems do not think, and when they are used for more than the facilitation of human thinking, they can prevent thinking. Three decades of experience with strategic planning have taught us about the need to loosen up the process of strategy making rather than trying to seal it off by arbitrary formalization.'[36]

Planning is just the start

Strategic planning is not an optional extra. If you're not doing it now, you should be. On the other hand, if you are doing it now, don't stop.

This needs saying because many major firms are not committed to planning. In some cases it's tacked onto the budgeting process to show the board there's some thought behind the numbers. (Though whether the board cares or not is open to question. As one CEO told me: 'The buggers are all 70 years old, and when I've got to present to them after they've had a few drinks at lunch, I know they'll all be asleep. All they want to see is the number at the bottom. Does it go up or down?')

For other companies, strategy is a kind of 'impulse purchase' – like a new tie when you set out to buy a pair of jeans.

Often when I call clients I've worked with in the past, they say, 'Maybe it's time for another SWOT' or, 'Perhaps we should review our mission statement' or, 'We've got our budget meetings next month, so maybe we need to set some new objectives'. My telephone call or visit triggers the need. Otherwise it would be business as usual.

Many companies tackle strategic planning in a stop-start fashion. They go at it with a vengeance this year, then skip a year or two before having another bash.

Some see it as an opportunity for 'a bit of team building'. Guided by the notion that 'all work and no play makes Jack a dull boy', they make sure that between work sessions their people have lots of fun – plenty of food and booze, fancy dress events, beach games, sports, folk singers or magicians – to keep them happy.

And of course there are the few companies that make a mountain out of a molehill. They set up planning teams, appoint 'champions', read books and articles on strategy, chew up computer time, and churn out paper.

In one professional firm, the senior partner produced a plan that was tossed out by his colleagues. In the quest for 'consensus', a team was then created to find out what strategy should mean, and how they should 'do' it. People who knew nothing about strategy, and who should have been billing hours to clients, became students. The only result after weeks of work was an academic treatise full of long-winded definitions.

This company missed the point. When they set out to gain some control over the future, they thought the answer lay in producing a plan. In fact, it lies in creating the *capacity to survive in white water.*

It makes you think ...

Strategic planning is a thinking process with a bad name.

Strategically managed companies are likely to be more aware of their environment than those that simply forge blindly ahead. They're also more likely to be aware of why they do what they do. And by watching the impact of what they do, they're able to build on today's successes, and quickly change direction to avoid failure.

That's not to say that strategizing is a precise activity.

Strategy involves both analysis and synthesis, flights of creativity and hard-nosed thinking, off-the-wall ideas and thorough analysis. 'Even the best planning,' says Russell Ackoff, 'requires at least as much art as it does science.'[37] Its product must be both radical ideas and specific, down-to-earth objectives, action plans, budgets.

You and your colleagues can make strategic planning a nourishing, stimulating – and stretching – dialogue, or a toxic and wasteful interruption from real work. The way you view the process determines the results you can expect from it.

Strategizing may well confirm that what you're doing right now is exactly right. (Though if it does, challenge your conclusions fast!) More importantly, it should provoke radical change by:

1. Testing your assumptions about the world in the most rigorous way.
2. Generating fresh ideas about what to do.
3. Triggering new behaviour.
4. Empowering people to think and act strategically.

Before you get busy with your next plan, think about why you need to do it, what you can expect from the process, and how to go about it. And be guided at all times by the underlying precept of 'lean production': do twice as much, twice as fast, with half the resources, at half the cost.

Endnotes

1. Christopher A. Bartlett and Sumantra Ghoshal, 'Changing the role of top management: beyond strategy to purpose', *Harvard Business Review*, November–December 1994.
2. Manfred F.R. Kets De Vries, 'Charisma in action: the transformational abilities of Virgin's Richard Branson and ABB's Percy Barnevik', *Organizational Dynamics*, Winter 1998.
3. Amar Bhide, 'Hustle as strategy', *Harvard Business Review*, September–October 1986.
4. Louise Kehoe and Richard Lambert, 'That creepy feeling', *Financial Times*, March 6, 1998.
5. 'Virgin Cola aims worldwide', *Financial Times*, May 2, 1995.
6. 'Who's afraid of the big bad Microsoft?' *Financial Times*, May 8, 1995.
7. Abell, 1993.
8. Mintzberg, 1994.
9. James Brian Quinn, *Strategies for Change: Logical Incrementalism*, New York: Irwin, 1980.
10. Chris Argyris, 'Good communication that blocks learning', *Harvard Business Review*, July–August 1994.
11. Richard Tanner Pascale, *Managing on the Edge*, New York: Viking, 1990.
12. Dick Levin, *Buy Low, Sell High, Collect Early & Pay Late*, New York: Prentice-Hall, 1983 .
13. Edward de Bono, *Sur/petition*, New York: HarperCollins, 1992.
14. '3M Fights back' *Fortune*, February 5, 1996.
15. Sumantra Ghoshal and Henry Mintzberg, 'Diversifiction and diversifact', *California Management Review*, Vol. 37, No. 1, Fall 1994.
16. Makridakis, 1990.
17. 'Garbage in, garbage out', *The Economist*, June 3, 1995.
18. 'Where is this economy really heading?' *Fortune*, August 7, 1995.
19. 'Economics as futurology', *Financial Times*, 5 September, 1995.
20. Pascale, 1990.
21. 'Robert Eaton thinks 'vision' is overrated, and he's not alone', *Wall Street Journal Europe*, October 6, 1993.

22. *Wall Street Journal Europe*, October 6, 1993.
23. Ricardo Semler, 'Why my former employees still work for me', *Harvard Business Review*, January-February 1994.
24. Henry Mintzberg, *The Rise and Fall of Strategic Planning*, New York: The Free Press, 1994.
25. Gary Hamel, *The FT Handbook Of Management*, London: Pitman, 1995.
26. B.C. Forbes, *Forbes*, December 18, 1995.
27. Peggy Noonan, *Life, Liberty and the Pursuit of Happiness*, New York: Random House, 1994; reprinted in *Forbes*, April 25, 1994.
28. Marvin Minsky, *The Society of Mind*, New York: Touchstone/Simon & Schuster, 1985.
29. 'Corporate reputations', *Fortune*, March 6, 1995.
30. 'Leaders learn to heed the voice within', *Fortune*, August 22, 1994.
31. Tom Peters, 'The search for excellence continues', *Forbes ASAP*, December 2, 1996.
32. Michael E. Porter, 'Creating Tomorrow's Advantages', *Rethinking The Future*, London: Nicholas Brealey Publishing, 1997.
33. 'What Is Strategy?' Michael E. Porter, *Harvard Business Review*, November–December 1996.
34. Kevin Freiberg and Jackie Freiberg, *Nuts!*, New York: Bard Press Inc., 1996.
35. Kosko, 1993.
36. Henry Mintzberg, 'The fall and rise of strategic planning', *Harvard Business Review*, January-February 1994.
37. Ackoff, 1970.

3

REINVENTING STRATEGY

9

Lenses and Language

Everything that can be thought of at all can be thought of clearly. Everything that can be said can be said clearly.

— Ludwig Wittgenstein, British Philosopher (1889–1951)
Tractatus Logico-Philosophicus, 1922

It is a luxury to be understood.

— Ralph Waldo Emerson (1803–1882)

We must look at the lens through which we see the world, as well as at the world we see, and understand that the lens itself shapes how we interpret the world.

— Stephen R. Covey[1]

Strategy's time has come.

An editorial in the Spring 1997 *Sloan Management Review* begins, 'Strategy's hot again.'[2] At about the same time, *Business Week* comments, 'From "agile strategies" and "competitive gaming" to "core competencies" and "market migration analysis", today's most popular ideas focus on good, old-fashioned strategic planning.'[3]

Strategy is hot because after a decade or more of frantic attempts at total quality management, downsizing, reengineering, and whatever, executives have suddenly woken up to the fact that doing more of the same better, is futile.

It doesn't matter how well you make ox-wagons, or what bells and whistles yours have; the market is gone. You could make the best vinyl long-playing records in the world, but no one would buy them. You could try to launch a great new typewriter, then rapidly improve its quality, add new colours to your range, switch distribution channels, slash manufacturing costs, increase your adspend, or whatever. But don't bank on selling too many. PCs have killed your chances; network computers are just over the horizon.

This is an age of sudden, discontinuous change. The name of the game is not improvement, but *innovation*. Not fit, but *disruption*. Not sustainability, but *surprise*. Not strategic *planning*, but strategic *capacity-building*.

This is the age of *value creation* – and *value connections*.

Fine-tuning what you already do may allow you – at best – to hang on to some of yesterday's customers. It may give you a temporary advantage over some of your competitors. But sustaining any lead becomes increasingly costly as you play leapfrog with each other. And sooner or later someone is sure to come along with an offering that redefines value and puts you out of business.

So your choice is simple: either you disrupt the market or the market destroys you. Either change the game, re-write the rules, and launch an aggressive and surprising attack, or it'll be done to you.

Improvement may be the path of least resistance, but it's also the path of last resort. First comes strategy.

The search for snake oil

The question on every executive's mind is: how do you gain and hold an edge in a hostile marketplace? Providing the answer has become a mega-industry. But managers remain perplexed despite the efforts of academics, consultants, and professionals within organizations; despite the concepts and models which keep coming; and despite the hype as new insights hit the market.

- Clayton Christensen, an associate professor at the Harvard Business School, notes that 'strategic thinking is not a core managerial competence at most companies'.[4] But why should it be? There is so much confusion about strategy, and so many conflicting views about how to develop and implement it, that managers are bound to need help.
- 'The dirty little secret of the strategy industry,' writes Gary Hamel in *Fortune*, 'is that it doesn't have any theory of strategy creation.'[5]
- 'Why do some firms consistently out-perform others in the same line of business?' asks Jules Goddard, of the London Business School in Business Strategy Review. 'Is there a secret recipe? If so, what is it?' If we could answer these questions, he says, 'we would have the makings of a general theory of competitive strategy.'[6]

For all we know about business, there's apparently a lot we don't know. However, we *do* know what causes business success. We *do* know how to make organizations grow. But in our search for the *ultimate* answer, we overlook the *obvious* answers.

The first step in making any theory is to agree on language. Pilots can take off and land safely anywhere in the world because they use common terms. Physicians all know what 'myocardial infarct' means, and surgeons all know which instrument is a scalpel and which a pair of forceps. Engineers, architects, and other professionals all have their 'shorthand'. (While lawyers have their own language, they spend a lot of time arguing about what *other people* mean!)

Remarkably, though, management is a profession without a language. Managers name their tools as they choose. It's as if Tiger Woods were to reach into his golf bag, select a driver, and decide: 'This is a nine-iron.' Hardly the way to beat par.

A war of words

Strategy has become a semantic battlefield. Theories which were intended to help management navigate the future have instead confused them. The language is unclear. Concepts contradict each other.

Consider, for example, this 'definition' from Thomas Vollman, a professor at IMD, in his book *The Transformation Imperative*:

> *Strategic intent is the true mission, the operational corporate strategy, or whatever set of words one wishes to put on the driving force for the enterprise.*[7]

Or listen to David Collis and Cynthia Montgomery, both of the Harvard Business School:

> *... the discussion of corporate strategy necessarily begins with vision ... Crucial to the vision is a sense of purpose that can challenge and motivate employees ... Often visions also describe the ethical values a corporation will adhere to in the conduct of its business. Called a mission in some companies, this part of a vision usually reflects the code of behavior by which employees are governed.*[8]

In 1980, Benjamin Tregoe and John Zimmerman described the concept of the 'driving force' (products offered, market needs, technology, size/growth, etc.) as 'the key to strategic thinking'.[9]

In 1993, Michel Robert offered an almost identical list of driving forces (though he had ten to their nine), and also claimed to have invented the term 'strategic thinking'.[10]

In 1997, Clayton Christensen advised that the first step in developing strategy was to identify a firm's driving forces – but he described them as 'the economic, demographic, technological, or competitive factors in the company's environment that either constitute threats or create opportunities.'[11]

Two years after Gary Hamel and C.K. Prahalad published their seminal article, 'The core competence of the corporation', in the *Harvard Business Review* in 1990, George Stalk, Philip Evans, and Lawrence Shulman advocated 'Competing on capabilities' in the same journal. Immediately, a debate ensued about the merits of 'competence' vs. 'capabilities'. Which word meant what, and how did they differ? Then, to muddy the waters even more, Collis and Montgomery followed with a 1995 article titled 'Competing on resources: strategy in the 1990s'.

What is the busy executive to make of all this?

How does it help you make decisions and motivate your people?

And what is the value, you may ask, in terms such as 'vision', 'mission', 'strategic intent' – or most of the others that fly around workplaces – when their use seems so arbitrary?

Ways of seeing

The language of strategy – the terms you use when you talk strategy – is a lens through which you and your colleagues see the world. Your corporate conversation is a lever that helps you get things done.

Listen to Warren Bennis and Burt Nanus in their wonderful book *Leaders, The Strategies For Taking Charge*:

> *... all organizations depend on the existence of shared meanings and interpretations of reality, which facilitate coordinated action. The actions and symbols of leadership frame meaning. Leaders articulate and define what has previously remained implicit or unsaid; then they invent images, metaphors, and models that provide a focus for new attention.*[12]

For people to collaborate and to achieve great things together, they must talk to each other. What they say and how they say it determines what they will accomplish. But conversation is more than a means of communication. It is, says Harvard professor Chris Argyris, 'central to understanding reality and operating effectively within it. We perceive reality according to how it is prescribed in our language.'[13]

Business is awash with buzzwords. Many are based on flawed thinking, superficial research, or convenient stabs at what causes success. A lot are simply a re-hash of old ideas. Few are useful.

When members of a team use different concepts, or interpret concepts in different ways, communication is slowed or blocked. The time they waste decoding ideas and understanding one another could be better spent.

Executives would do well to heed the warning of Keith Bradley, a professor at the Open University Business School, that 'failure to appreciate that language is an important construct in knowledge can significantly damage initiatives to decant and package intellectual capital into company-owned structures'.[14]

By affecting communication, language affects relationships. It affects people's ability and inclination to cooperate with each other. It affects management's ability to build 'learning organizations'.

For any management term or concept to be useful, it must pass two tests:

1. Does using it help you *think* more clearly?
2. Does it help you *communicate* what you thought about?

If the answer's not 'yes' on both counts, you're on the wrong track. If you're unclear this early, things will surely get murkier and more confusing. That's something no executive can afford, given that this is the age of hostile competition – and this is just warm-up time.

Many views of reality

'We keep on trying to solve the problems of the Systems Age with our old Machine Age mentality,' says UCLA's Ian Mitroff. Only a new way of thinking will let companies ride the turbulence. What's needed 'is a far deeper appreciation of paradox and the absolutely vital role that assumptions play in treating all problems'.[15]

An old joke defines a pessimist as 'an optimist who knows the truth'. The question is: what is 'truth'? My version of reality is different to yours. We all see the world through different lenses. 'We think of "optimist" and "pessimist" as descriptions of people,' says futurist Peter Schwartz, 'but they are actually popular labels for well-known, radically different attitudes about the future.'[16]

An executive's decisions are influenced by her worldview. But there are many interpretations of the same situation:

> An 80-year-old man asks a doctor for a check-up. The doctor does all the tests, then calls the man in and says, 'You're in great health. For a man of your age, it's fantastic. But I'm intrigued. Why, at this age, did you want a medical?'
>
> The man gets embarrassed, but finally gives in. 'I'll tell you, but this has to be confidential because it's a very private matter. I've just met a 20-year old girl, the most gorgeous creature you've ever seen, and I'm going to make passionate love to her.'
>
> 'The doctor throws up his hands. That,' he says, 'could be very dangerous. You'd better be very careful.'
>
> 'Oh, I thought about it,' said the old man. 'I even felt a bit guilty for a while. But I figured, what the hell, if she dies, she dies!'

As we see in business school case study exercises, highly intelligent teams interpret information in radically different ways. Issues that one group sees as vital are ignored by another.

Team A: 'The problem here, is Smythson, the CEO.'
Team B: 'As we see it, the key question is how to get sales back on track.'
Team C: 'This company got into trouble when they cut back on research and development.'
Team D: 'Our expenses are too high.'

Because their starting points are different, each team tackles challenges differently. And their 'answers' almost always lead to one conclusion: there are as many possible strategies as there are strategists.

In the workplace, the situation is even more complicated. There, your team's 'theories of the business' can cause you all to see different problems, possibilities, and priorities. People from Finance understand the world one way; those

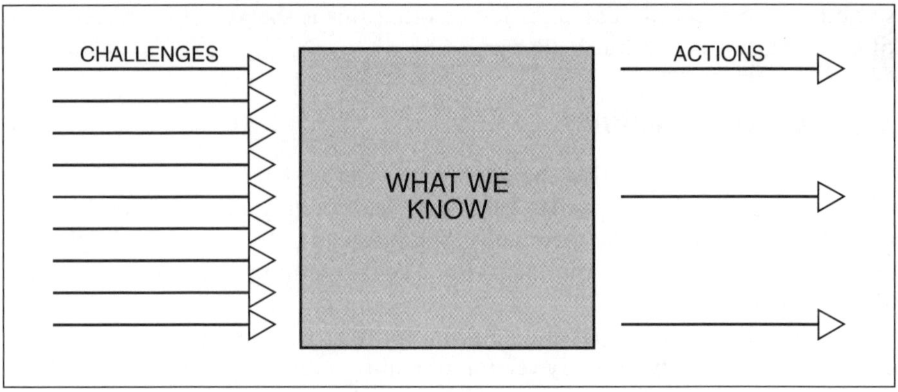

Figure 9.1: *The trap of 'what we know'*

from Marketing or R&D know it's otherwise. Power plays can lock individuals or factions into fighting irrationally for their point of view.

Your company's competitive potential is defined by 'what we know around here'. Your assumptions stand between your opportunities and your results (Figure 9.1).

'What we know' is a powerful filter that limits what you do. Tracy Goss, an expert on transformational leadership, calls it your 'winning strategy' because it's what got you where you are.[17] Edward De Bono calls it a 'logic bubble'. You might prefer 'paradigm', 'mental model', 'world view', or whatever. But recognize the problem. You – and your organization – are a product of the past.

'What we know' stands in the way of your future.

What is strategy?

What is strategy? What's the difference between strategic thinking, strategic planning, and strategic management?

Strategy is a *value-creating process*. It includes making choices, acting on them, and learning from what happens.

The starting point is to understand the world you operate in. Then, to shape your response through internal innovation and the alignment, mobilization, and accumulation of resources and capabilities.

Corporate strategy is largely about investment: which businesses to back, and how to manage the interest in them. Competitive strategy is about the moves a single company makes.

Strategy is a *decision-making process*. It involves choosing where and how you will compete. Ideally, it should let you compete in a different place from your competitors, in different ways. This uniqueness should give you an advantage over them for as long as possible.

Strategic thinking is the creative activity through which you design the future. To arrive at novel answers, you must travel a logical path: capture information → couple ideas → conjure up new insights → create new possibilities → make choices.

But it's not enough simply to make choices. 'Good' choices may quickly prove to be 'bad' if they are not well enacted. A 'sound' strategy is of no value when it's badly executed. The strategist is ultimately judged, not by his ability to chart a unique route to the future, but, rather, by measures like sales, market share, profits, or economic value added. Thus:

Choices + Action = Results

Strategic planning is usually understood to describe the deliberate and structured process by which managers define their firm's purpose, decide on the goals and actions that will get them there, and budget for the process.

Strategic management is the dynamic process by which managers create the future. It is the total stream of thought and action that takes them from where they are to where they want to be.

Strategic management is more than an intellectual exercise. It embraces activities such as innovation, improvement, and investments; human resources development; marketing; and, yes, even leadership. Factors such as resources, commitment, spirit, and perseverance all come into play.

The strategist's purpose

Business is a battle for resources – finance, ideas, components, labour, customers, etc. In a fast-changing world, companies need to either:

- See the future first, and do something about it, or
- Adapt quickly enough to the new realities.

Foresight – or the ability to *sense* what lies ahead – is a significant advantage. But while you may form quite a clear picture of tomorrow, surprise is the only certainty. Stuff happens. Things go wrong. Discontinuities will occur with little or no warning. So the strategy process should not only make firms more alert to what lies ahead, it should also prepare them to change direction when necessary.

To gain and hold a competitive edge, the strategist must:

- Identify the opportunities that offer a critical mass of results – i.e. choose where and how you'll compete.
- Win the support of a critical mass of stakeholders for current and future thrusts.

The product/market decision determines what you'll sell, to whom, and how. It defines, in other words, your competitive arena.

But merely knowing where you'll compete is not enough. You also have to choose *how*: which activities and resources will give you an edge over your competition. Then you have to execute your strategy with imagination, energy, and perseverance.

Every organization has numerous stakeholders who make up its 'ecosystem' and who can 'vote' for or against its success. Their support is essential. Some will shape your strategy; some will execute it; some will support it; some make it feasible.

The first task is one of *analysis*. The second has to do with *process*. By trying to keep them separate, companies create untold problems for themselves. Typically, a few senior people are charged with deciding on future moves. They then try to sell their 'plans' to others who were not privy to the debate. The result is usually resistance or ineffective implementation.

Many strategies that fail are in fact extremely sound. The problem is not the thought that goes into them, but the action – or lack of it – that follows. Ivory tower ideas simply don't travel. When inventors and the implementers are different people, communication is always a problem; what's more, you can't order people to buy your ideas, let alone take ownership of them.

In a fast-changing world, strategy quickly becomes obsolete. Without constant alertness and adjustments, it can lead a company down the wrong path. So companies must be both sensitive to changes around them and fast on their feet. Changing course may be as important as choosing a course.

Two views of strategy

Concepts of strategy fall roughly into two camps.

The first (the environmental view) assumes that any firm is a prisoner of its environment; that external forces determine what it can and cannot do. The most prominent advocate of this view is Michael Porter of the Harvard Business School. His large and influential body of work argues that firm profitability is determined by industry conditions; and that industry conditions are, in turn, affected by geographic location. In other words, some countries are better than others for some industries; and some industries are inherently more profitable than others.[18]

The second (the resource-based view) assumes that the real constraints are inside; that managers can overcome almost any external limitations by the application of imagination, knowledge, finance, or other assets. This school embraces ideas from Hiroyoki Itami *(Mobilizing Invisible Assets)*, Gary Hamel and C.K. Prahalad *(Competing For The Future)*, James Brian Quinn *(Intelligent Enterprise)*, Peter Senge *(The Fifth Discipline)*, and many others.[19]

In the 1960s, the emphasis was on achieving 'fit' between an organization and its environment; managers saw their challenge as being to match internal strengths and weaknesses to external opportunities and threats.

Building on this thinking, Michael Porter produced his concepts of 'generic strategy', 'the five forces analysis', and 'the competitive advantage of nations'. He argued that a firm had limited choices of strategy (cost or differentiation, and degree of market focus); that the profitability of a firm depended on conditions in its industry; and that industry performance was greatly influenced by geographic location.

But as turbulence and competition increased and profits slumped, managers sought alternatives. And to their rescue came consultants and academics with an old idea, (the resource-based view or RBV) in new clothing (core competence, competing on capabilities).

Champions of the RBV had a compelling story: Companies could not 'grow to greatness'. Reengineering, downsizing, and price cuts were not the only way to compete – and in fact would weaken rather than strengthen a company. Better to see 'strategy as stretch', and to use internal resources to achieve seemingly impossible results.

The timing of the re-launch of the RBV was perfect. The 1980s had been a decade of a 'search for excellence' which revived another old idea – the importance of people. Along the way, however, reengineering had done a lot to destroy the dream; people who had been assured they were 'our most important asset' suddenly found themselves on the street while bosses earned record pay.

The RBV restored the idea that people actually mattered. It also fitted in well with the IT revolution that made knowledge management a growing source of advantage.

It is tempting to believe that a company is hostage to its environment. There is some evidence that location is a key driver of performance: some places are better than others for some kinds of industry. But this isn't an iron-clad rule. Growing numbers of firms defy the constraints of their home bases to become global competitors.

What makes the difference? Why is it that some companies seem not to see the barriers that hold others back?

The answer begins, of course, with leadership. For in any organization it is the leader who shapes the context in which people think and act; who focuses their attention in a particular direction and on certain priorities; who ensures that they have the support they need; and who provides both the inspiration and the rewards they need to excel.

Performance levers

As we've seen, your industry map gives you a fine-grained view of the terrain in which you compete. Now let's look at why it doesn't entirely control your outcomes. Let's examine the factors that leaders use to create advantage despite what happens around them.

Seven factors influence how leaders produce results (Figure 9.2). Six of these have to do with *how* we think and act; only one – resources – is about *what* we have to work with. And even resources can be 'soft': skills, experience, reputation, and the like.

So here, once again, we see the importance of perspective and attitude. And once again here's an opportunity to check your company's competitive health – and to decide where to make changes.

1. **Organizational culture.** An organization's culture is a 'tape recording' of its past. This collective memory tells people what's possible and what's not;

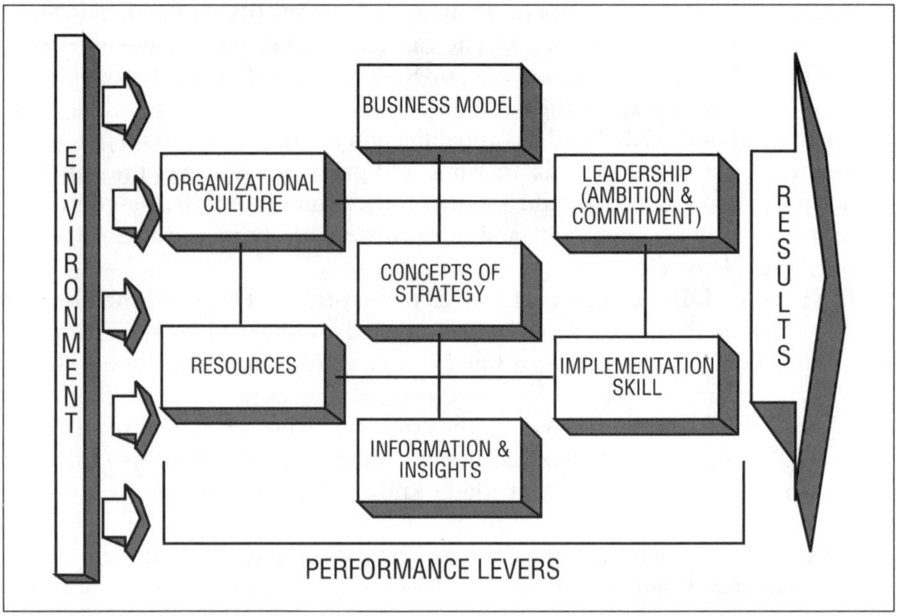

Figure 9.2: *Performance levers*

what behaviour is okay under various circumstances; and how to cope with a range of challenges. Culture can, of course, be immensely valuable; managers may be right to argue that 'our culture is our most important competitive weapon'. But they may also be wrong: those memories are products of a different time, and the moves that worked in earlier days may be totally inappropriate now. For all its fans, culture can kill! *(Question: does your corporate culture support your ambitions, or get in the way?)*

2. **Resources.** Firms set out with different weapons in their arsenals. Resources fall into two categories: assets (finance, plant and equipment, reputation, brands, experience) and capabilities (skills, systems). Having what you need is a great help. Not having it won't necessarily stop you doing what you want to. Human beings are incredibly resourceful; they have an awesome ability to overcome handicaps and disadvantages. *(Question: do you have the resources you need, or can you get them?)*

3. **Business model.** Every company is built around a model based on management's worldview. Different models work under different circumstances. What's best today can be quite inappropriate tomorrow. By constantly reviewing your business model and by changing it to suit new circumstances, you can disrupt competition and gain the advantage you want. *(Question: does your business model give you a real advantage.)*

4. **Concepts of strategy.** Though there are some well-known strategic thinking tools, every management team has its own favourites, and its own way

of interpreting and using them. All too often, even the members of a single team don't agree on the best way to create a strategy. When planning time comes around, they waste a lot of time trying to agree on what they're talking about and how to approach the process. If the team bases its thinking on, say, Porter's 'generic' strategies, it'll travel a particular path; the logic that there's a trade-off between cost and differentiation will suggest certain opportunities – but also close off others. The same happens when you conduct a SWOT analysis or write a vision statement. Concepts and models facilitate thinking by framing issues and provoking specific questions. But they're all over-simplifications. This very strength is a weakness. *(Question: are you using concepts of strategy that will let you win – or cause you to lose?)*

5. **Information and insights.** Put two management teams in the same place and show them the same opportunity, and they will each seek different information and have different insights about the situation. Some organizations are 'information rich' – their people are well-informed, there are few secrets, they openly discuss issues. Others are information-impoverished – they're not curious, little value is placed on learning about the world, there are lots of secrets. And then there's the matter of insights. Some firms actively encourage creative thinking and the development of fresh points of view, while others cling to the past. *(Question: how open and interested is your organization, and how creatively do you use information?)*
6. **Leadership (ambition and commitment).** Ambition can drive an individual to succeed against odds that stop others in their tracks. The world has largely been shaped by mavericks who refused to see – or couldn't see – the limitations that 'everyone knew' to be there. They went against the flow and changed things for everyone. Ambition is a powerful force. Couple it with commitment, and many things become possible. *(Question: how high are you aiming and how determined are you to reach your goals?)*
7. **Implementation skill.** A sound and imaginative strategy is obviously an advantage. Every management team should try to create one. But even the best strategy is worth little or nothing without effective, determined, spirited execution. How you do things is every bit as important as what you do. *(Question: how well do you pull things together, and get things done?)*

Endnotes

1. Stephen R. Covey, *The Seven Habits Of Highly Successful People*, New York: Simon & Schuster, 1989.
2. *Sloan Management Review*, Spring 1997.
3. 'Management theory-or fad of the month', *Business Week*, June 23, 1997.
4. Clayton M. Christensen, 'Making strategy: learning by doing', *Harvard Business Review*, November–December 1997.
5. Gary Hamel, 'Killer Competitors', *Fortune*, June 6, 1997.
6. Jules Goddard, 'The Architecture of Core Competence', *Business Strategy Review*, Volume 8, Number 1, 1997.

7. Thomas Vollman, *The Transformation Imperative*, Boston: The Harvard Business School Press, 1996.
8. David J. Collis and Cynthia Montgomery, *Corporate Strategy*, New York: McGraw-Hill, 1997.
9. Benjamin B. Tregoe and John W. Zimmerman, *Top Management Strategy*, New York: Simon and Schuster, 1980.
10. Michel Robert, *Strategy Pure & Simple*, New York: McGraw-Hill, 1993.
11. Clayton M. Christensen, 1997.
12. Warren Bennis and Burt Nanus in the book *Leaders, The Strategies For Taking Charge*, New York: Harper & Row, 1985.
13. Chris Argyris, *Knowledge For Action*, San Francisco: Jossey-Bass Publishers, 1993.
14. Keith Bradley, 'Intellectual Capital and the new wealth of nations', *Business Strategy Review*, Volume 8, No1, Spring 1997.
15. Ian Mitroff, *Break-Away Thinking*, New York: John Wiley & Sons, 1988.
16. Peter Schwartz, *The Art of the Long View*, New York: Currency Doubleday, 1991.
17. Tracy Goss, *The Last Word on Power*, New York: Currency Doubleday, 1996.
18. Michael E. Porter, *The Competitive Advantage of Nations*, New York: The Free Press, 1990.
19. Hiroyoki Itami, *Mobilizing Invisible Assets*, Boston: Harvard Business School Press, 1987; Gary Hamel and C.K. Prahalad, *Competing For The Future*, Boston: Harvard Business School Press, 1994; James Brian Quinn, *Intelligent Enterprise*, New York: The Free Press, 1992; Peter Senge, *The Fifth Discipline*, New York: Doubleday/ Currency, 1990.

10

The First Principles

There is nothing so practical as a good theory.

— Kurt Lewin

The break-through firm seeks profit leverage, first and foremost, through ways of enhancing value through quality while simultaneously reducing cost.

— James Heskett, Earl Sasser, and Christopher Hart, *Service Breakthroughs*[1]

The competitive environment of mass producers supports the generic strategies of cost leadership and product differentiation. Both of these strategies are based on the assumption that a firm can develop and sustain competitive advantages and, therefore, can avoid competition.

— Robin Cooper, *When Lean Enterprises Collide*[2]

Ironically, the most useful guide to competitiveness comes not from watching companies that have been successful for a long time, but from those that got into trouble and are making a comeback.

There are several reasons for this.

First, as we've seen, it's difficult if not impossible to pinpoint why companies succeed. Often, it's due less to smart thinking than to obscure historic reasons or a favourable environment. And a lot of companies succeed in spite of themselves.

Second, you could copy many things successful companies do – invest in R&D, train people, empower them, embark on a TQM process, boost your marketing spend, or whatever – and still go down the tubes.

Third, when companies are on a roll, they keep going. They develop momentum. Stakeholders stay loyal because of their 'sunk costs'; moving away is costly and difficult. So managers naturally give more time to housekeeping and incremental improvement than to rapid, radical change.

When companies slump, however, pressure builds for something to be done. It might take time, but sooner or later a sense of crisis is created. Managers charged with fixing sick organizations are under the microscope and the whip. Their every move is under scrutiny, and they're expected to deliver fast. 'The window that a new CEO has in a turnaround is shrinking,' says David Nadler, chairman of New York-based Delta Consulting Group. 'You used to have a couple of years.'[3] Now, change must be evident in months or even weeks.

Articles in the business press point to cost-cutting as the first and most important step in fixing sick firms. But savings alone don't lead to recovery. Frugality can kill.

So how do turnaround experts work?

When the corporate doctor calls

Searching for the secrets of corporate success, I turned from companies that were doing well to those that were in trouble. Across industries, executives charged with fixing sick companies used the same basic strategies.

- Since George Fisher took over as chairman of Kodak in December 1993, the company has sold almost all its non-photographic operations and concentrated its efforts on traditional film imaging and digital picture technology.[4]
- U.S. discounter K-Mart was the world's biggest retailer until Wal-Mart overtook it in 1990. But with profits skidding, CEO Joseph Antonini was pushed out and the firm was re-focused on its core business. Over 100 stores were closed, poorly-performing specialty stores were sold, and 6,000 people were laid off. Now, K-Mart is investing heavily in re-furbishing stores with potential.[5]
- After French banking group BNP was privatized, it had to get competitive fast. The company focused on 'the two core businesses of retail banking in France and international banking for large corporate clients'. Costs were cut and steps were taken to boost productivity and efficiency in the areas of administration, purchases, and information systems.[6]
- Reckless expansion during the 1980s led another French state-owned bank, Credit Lyonnais, to losses of $2,44 billion in 1994. Charged with fixing things as part of a government-backed rescue plan, new chairman Jean Peyrelevade outlined a new strategy: stop trying to act as a 'universal bank' with a complete menu of banking services, and focus instead on becoming a low-cost retailer of high-return savings and investment products in Europe. Also, exploit international opportunities with wholesale lines – project financing, aircraft financing, equity trading, and private banking – in which it had proven expertise. Cut 4,000 jobs and improve productivity by 20 per cent in four years. [7]
- Hit by rising pressure on health-care prices, Swiss-based Sandoz sold its chemicals division to focus on drugs and nutrition. This, said chairman

Marc Moret, would allow management 'to concentrate its energies, resources and creativity in priority areas'.[8]

- In the early 1990s, Schering, the Berlin-based pharmaceuticals company, chose to focus on high-opportunity niche markets. Its industrial chemicals, natural substances, and electroplating divisions were sold and the agrochemicals unit was shifted into a joint venture with Hoechst. Jobs were cut by 24 per cent, with more to go. Outside researchers were contracted to save new product development costs. Production facilities were modernized to supply customers more effectively.[9]
- After a planned merger with Renault collapsed, Volvo sold its food business and merged its beverages interests with those of Orkla, a Norwegian consumer products and chemicals group, in April 1995. Volvo planned to get rid of its beverage holdings entirely by the end of 1996 through a stock market listing. At the same time, it's investing aggressively in its core truck and car business.[10] This effectively reversed a drive to diversify which started in the 1980s.
- 'In 1994,' reports Zeneca chairman Sir Denys Henderson, 'we drove forward vigorously our strategy of focusing selectively on strengthening the three key businesses, divesting non-core activities and reducing costs wherever possible to ensure our long-term competitiveness ...'[11]
- When profits skidded, Goodyear Europe reversed its strategy of selling mainly to original-equipment customers, and re-focused on the more lucrative replacement-tire market. At the same time, the company cut its workforce by 12 per cent and closed half its distribution warehouses.[12]

Universal strategies

What those turnaround experts do is remarkably simple and consistent. They all apply the same three strategies (Figure 10.1):

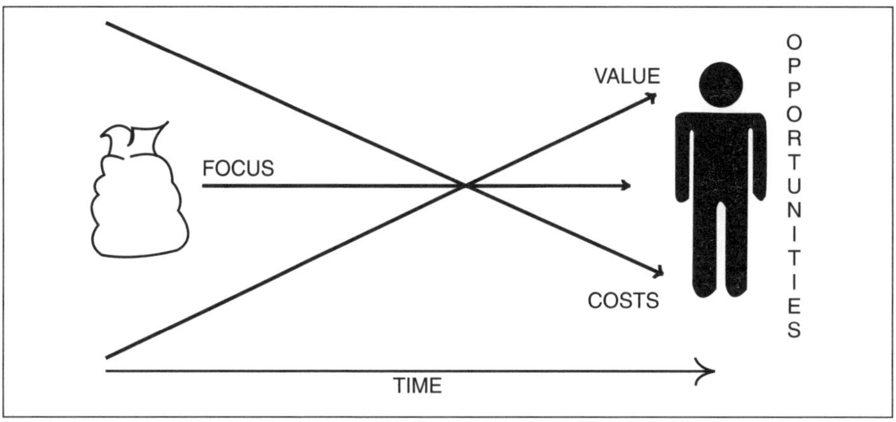

Figure 10.1: *First principles*

Strategy 1: **Focus.** With resources scarce and likely to get scarcer, they can't do everything or satisfy everyone. They have to apply the 80–20 rule – get maximum bang for their bucks. So they identify the customers, resources, and activities that will bring increased revenues, and they concentrate all their attention on these areas. This laser-like focus immediately cuts waste. Their firms stop doing the historic or merely interesting things that were dragging them down. Money and minds can be deployed where they'll make most difference. Freed-up capacity can be used to go back on the offensive.

Strategy 2: **Value.** To keep customers they've got, and to attract new ones, they aggressively seek new ways to add value to their offerings. It helps that they're focused, because they can get to know fewer 'right' customers much better.

Strategy 3: **Costs.** They cut costs to the bone – wages, debt, rent, interest, or whatever else doesn't fit with their new focus. This lowers their break-even point, so they can get by with less revenue. It also gives them the margin they need to fund their future. They can drop prices; invest in critical activities such as R&D, technology, training, or promotions; or simply pocket the savings.

Whether you sell baked beans or banking, sustained superior returns come from applying limited resources more effectively and efficiently than your competitors.

Although this is logically a sequential process, focus, value, and costs are clearly inter-dependent. Work on one brings results in the other two. Effective executives keep them all in mind as they work on each of them. When all three are seen as a 'holistic health' system, valuable spin-offs are inevitable.

Focus decisions are value drivers. When you make sound choices about where to aim your efforts, you can become expert in serving your chosen customers. You're likely to sense new needs faster than your competitors and thus to be able to redefine value with your customers.

But focus decisions are also *cost* drivers. By avoiding the 'spray and pray' trap that so many companies fall into, you automatically conserve resources. You can apply them where they'll make the most impact. This leverage, in turn, gives you further cost advantages.

Value decisions only make sense when you know which customer you want and what satisfaction that person seeks. If the customer is 'everyone', the best you can do is offer a product or service that more or less meets their needs. Some shoppers may buy from you some of the time, but you'll lose sales to competitors with a more tailored approach. By being clear and specific about the value you offer, you not only make long-term customer partnerships possible, you also avoid costly activities that customers don't really care about. Value decisions affect both focus and costs.

Cost decisions affect what, how, when, and where you sell, so they impact on both focus and value. They shape R&D efforts, personnel programmes, and promotional thrusts. They determine whether your firm will merely survive today or own tomorrow. Managers who slash costs without considering focus and value may improve results in the short term, but long-term they'll run into trouble.

The First Principles

Focus, value, and costs add up to the First Principles of Hostile Competition. Like the laws of physics, they are not negotiable. They apply to every organization in whatever industry. No manager can ignore them. Whatever else you do, whatever programmes or interventions you opt for, you'd better be sure they embrace these basics:

1. **If you don't make a difference, you don't matter.** The 'value' you offer must be clear to customers, and it must matter to them. You have to stand for something in their minds.
2. **You can't make a difference for everyone.** Resources are limited. Opportunities abound. To be successful, you have to aim a critical mass of resources at a critical mass of opportunity. This focus decision is the most important business decision.
3. **You have to keep redefining your 'value proposition'.** No matter how you segment a market, you're unlikely to have any customer to yourself for long. If you don't give them new reasons to buy from you, they'll lose interest and buy elsewhere.

Not very complicated, is it? Not new, either. Like most executives, you probably look at these principles and say, 'Oh, I know that.' And of course you do.

But pause now, and take this test:

1. My firm matters to customers because: ________________
2. We have chosen to focus on the following customers: ____________
3. This is how we've changed/improved our value proposition (from the customer's perspective) in the past 6 months: ________________
4. This is how we intend changing/improving our value proposition (from the customer's perspective) in the next 6 months: ________________
5. This is how we've reduced costs in the past six months: ____________
6. This is how we intend reducing costs in the next six months: ____________

Happy with your performance? When I give managers this test in strategy workshops, they usually see that there are huge gaps between what they're doing and what they need to do. Some try to justify the difference or make excuses. Many argue from their point of view rather than their customers'. Most underestimate the impact that progress in these areas would have on their bottom-line results.

The First Principles of business competition have been described in many ways. They have been buried in countless 'new' concepts. They have been captured in slogans and songs, and endlessly repeated in visions, missions, values, philosophies, policies, and action plans. Yet look around, and you'll see smart executives around the world violating these principles all the time.

Everyone knows that the First Principles make sense. But what 'everyone knows' is a business opportunity not to be missed. And the very fact that what you have to do is so clear means that you have to do something else to stay ahead.

If all the players in an industry use the same operating guidelines, the one who implements them most imaginatively and aggressively will win.

It's human qualities that matter most

Understanding and applying the First Principles is the key to competitiveness. But it's essential that you see this as a process and not a one-time activity. The focus decision you make today will be wrong for tomorrow; improving value and costs is an ongoing quest. Today's analysis and hard choices may point your organization in the right direction, but that's just a first step; it's what you do next that really counts.

The First Principles of business competition offer a framework for thinking about how you compete. They are mandatory if you want to succeed. Violating them is lethal.

It's not enough, though, to just be aware of them or even to apply them diligently. For sooner or later, your competitors will learn about them too.

Long-term advantage is a product of knowledge and how you apply it. Bottom-line, this means that the two most important characteristics of winning firms today are imagination and the human spirit.

Of course, you need money to pay for growth. You probably have to sign up for research and development programmes, invest in state-of-the-art technology, spend on capturing customer information and building your brands, and gain access to key distribution channels. Many factors add up to competitive strength.

But there is a real danger that in your quest for success, you'll fail to see the wood for the trees. You'll be distracted from the basics by the clamour of seductive ideas and demanding stakeholders.

Lessons from warriors

Corporate strategists have had a long fascination with military strategy. Von Clausewitz is often cited. Sun Tzu *(The Art Of War)* and Myamoto Musashi *(A Book Of Five Rings)* are favourites. Leading business thinkers have used battlefield analogies to describe ways to compete. Executives liven up their presentations with words and phrases – 'tactics', 'attack', 'kill', 'troops', 'campaign', 'hit them where it hurts', 'take them out' – that have a battlefield ring.

As in war, business strategy usually emphasizes the importance of avoiding head-to-head conflict. 'Supreme excellence consists in breaking the enemy's resistance without fighting,' advised Sun Tzu. Heinz boss Tony O'Reilly explains his strategy as 'niche leadership', building on the philosophy of the company's founder, Henry John Heinz, who believed it best to choose markets carefully and 'hit 'em where they ain't'.[13]

Philip Kotler, the renowned marketing author, suggests that managers think in terms of five possible attack strategies: flanking, frontal, encirclement, bypass, and guerilla.[14] Of these, the flanking, encirclement, and bypass options all are calculated to avoid head-to-head confrontation with competitors; their objective is rather to seize unserved segments of the market. Even guerilla fighters seek to grab territory that is undefended or weakly defended, to avoid having to commit serious resources or engage in major combat.

As a manager, it's important to consider how you might conserve resources by sharing territory with your enemies, and how you might avoid bloody and bruising conflict. Bruce Henderson, founder of the Boston Consulting Group, reminds us that 'continued coexistence' rather than the elimination of the competitor is a desirable outcome in both diplomacy and business.[15] Furthermore, some competitors may be classified as 'good' competitors, and having them around is better than killing them off.[16]

In unexploited markets, it's easy to steer clear of competitors – there are few of them. But when things heat up, it gets much harder. Chances are, your company has to fight many others, on many fronts.

Endless possibilities

Organizations are powered by human imagination and energy. These are infinite resources. So companies can compete in many ways, and the winners do.

Those that perform well over time are both single-minded and adaptive. They hold their course for years, but they also change their minds as fast as they need to ('If this strategy doesn't work, let's try that one.').

Of course, there are examples where the core strategy has remained constant over time. Some that spring to mind: Marks & Spencer's commitment to its own brands; Caterpillar's quality and service; Mercedes-Benz's dedication to engineering and safety; Hanson's acquisition of under-performing companies in basic industries; and Coca-Cola's 100-year promise of good times. But in every one of these cases, we've also seen a never-ending stream of adjustments, improvements, and shifts.

It's impossible to label a strategy 'right' or 'wrong'. What's best depends on a host of factors. One firm will sell through wholly owned channels; another will use independent distributors. One will succeed by offering lifetime guarantees; a competitor will do equally well even though it provides no after-sales security at all.

Or watch the way firms are structured. Organizational design is widely held to be a key factor of success. There are strong advocates of every option. But what's ideal? In 1994, Shell re-organized its head office, and abandoned its matrix structure. Ford shifted from a geographic structure with 'functional chimneys', and re-organized around a matrix. Troubled Apple Computer replaced its hardware/software structure with divisions dedicated to engineering, manufacturing and distribution, marketing and customer solutions, and to sales and customer support.

If flexibility is one characteristic of high-performing companies, another is that they're able to wrap their minds around many issues at once. On the one hand, they attack from many directions. On the other, they keep changing direction, and sharpening their attack. They embrace paradoxes and turn them to advantage, so they can accept a customer's need for both low prices and extra value, and deliver in both areas. They advance on many fronts.

A study of Germany's small and mid-sized companies, the much-admired *Middelstant*, concluded that they don't aim to beat the competition on every dimension; instead, they concentrate their strengths on delivering what customers value most. What might that be? 'Product quality, closeness to the customer, service, economy, quality of employees, technological leadership, and innovativeness.'[17]

Or read a recent Texas Instruments ad in the *Financial Times*:

> Dataquest has just named Texas Instruments its European Semiconductor Vendor of the Year for 1995.
>
> We're extremely proud.
>
> Proud that so many customers have voted us number one for delivery, quality, responsiveness, support, price, flexibility and overall performance.
>
> And proud too that our entire organization continues to rally around a single cause: Total Customer Satisfaction.
>
> But we won't stop there.
>
> Our quest for perfection is a perpetual one. Every TI employee in every corner of the world is committed to doing things better. Faster, lower cost products, higher levels of integration with customers, accelerated production cycles, better support, revolutionary new technologies, and the list goes on.

What the hell is left?

What can you do to win against these new competitors?

The answer lies in simplicity and complexity. In grasping that what you must do is remarkably simple, but that how you do it should be as complex as possible (Figure 10.2).

The easy way out can kill you

Either/or strategies may confer vital advantages. But that is less and less likely as competition intensifies. By staking out a clear price/performance position, you obviously simplify your decision-making process and your to-do list. It's far easier coming to work each day knowing you must either slash costs or invest like crazy to add value. There is much to be said for single-mindedness.

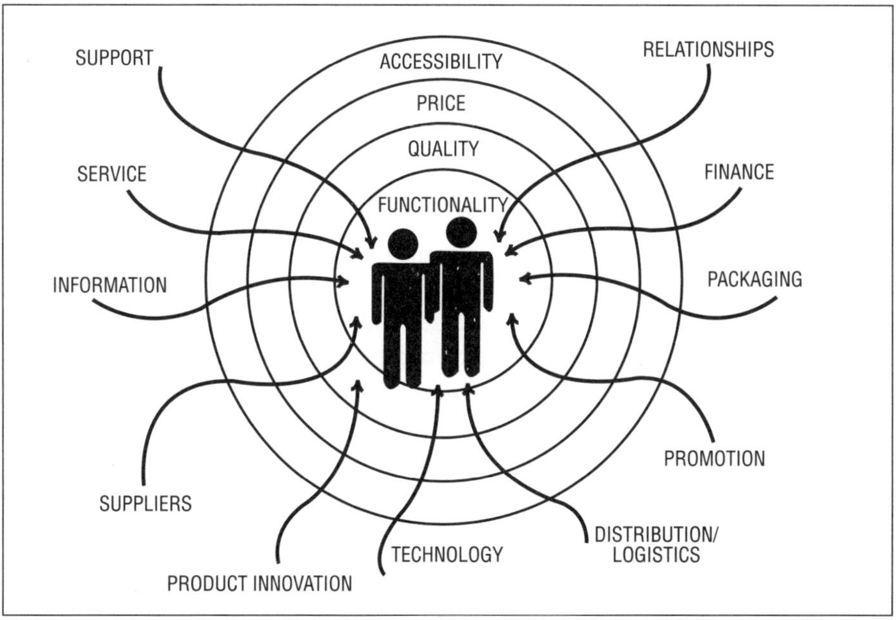

Figure 10.2: *Strike with a flurry of blows*

But the downside is that a one-dimensional strategy exposes you to competitors who can embrace the cost/value paradox. It also depends on competitors backing off from the position you choose, and making different claims for themselves.[18] *If they're stupid enough to copy you, or too obstinate to move, you might not be able to convince customers that you're unique and better.*

The most aggressive competitors have transcended yesterday's favourite concepts.

First, they no longer think in terms of the mass market, but rather in terms of 'de-massification', 'mass customization', and 'production runs of one'. Their goal is to get as close as possible to customers, to develop intimate win-win partnerships with them, and to tap a long-term stream of income from them.

These firms don't see customer intimacy as an optional extra; they know it's an entry fee to the business game. I can't name a company that's not working furiously to improve in this area. They're not all delivering, but they are getting better. The promise of exceptional customer service will not prove a long-term advantage for anyone when everyone's pursuing it.

Second, instead of competing either on cost or on value, aggressive companies compete on both. They drive down costs even while they drive up the value that they offer. And they relentlessly pursue improvements in both directions.*

* Note that I've talked about *costs*, not *price*. When you lower costs, you have many options: you can cut prices, of course; or you can invest more in R&D, training, sales promotion, service, and so on; or you can pocket the extra margin. If you concentrate on value alone, you run the risk of creating an umbrella under which other players can carve you up.

Of course, delivering more for less can be extremely hard to do, and goes against the conventional wisdom of many managers. 'Value costs money,' they argue. 'We can either cut costs or we can add value, but we can't do both.'

But as we see from the Dell example, companies can do both. Canon and Nikon captured sales from Leica with cameras that combined exceptional quality with affordable prices; Toyota attacked Mercedes-Benz and BMW with its Lexus; and steel minimills beat big integrated producers in niche markets. All these challengers offer a superior customer experience; all fund that added value by ruthlessly pruning costs.

In the past, western companies mostly competed through differentiation rather than cost. Positioning, not implementation, was at the centre of their strategies. 'Stake out your turf and stick to it' was their dictum. Japanese companies, in contrast, were less concerned about where they fitted in relative to their competitors, and more committed to the implementation of their strategies.[19] Today, however, everyone's playing the same game.

And if every competitor is racing to capture the same customers, it's little wonder that they adopt the same strategies, that their 'unique selling propositions' quickly become generic claims, or that their newest products and services become commodities. In this age of temporary advantage, world class competitors know that the only way to compete is to drive value up and costs down faster than the enemy. That, in turn, demands radical changes in everything they do and the way they do everything.

Mental agility is essential to keep your organization growing. Mental toughness is needed to keep you going. But competitiveness doesn't end there. Equally vital is the ability to organize and reorganize your resources for each new thrust.

This is a competence that's seriously under-estimated. But watch it get more attention as strategies continue to converge.

First and fastest

Ironically, in their efforts to gain a competitive edge, strategists raise the level of conflict. By segmenting markets, they create more targets, some of which will attract new competitors. By narrowing their range of core capabilities, they expose themselves to competitors with a wider array of strengths and ambitions in many areas.

When firms diversify, they meet more competitors. Managers who once had to keep an eye on just one competitor suddenly have to watch many. Anglo American used to be a mining company; now, it operates in industries as diverse as chemicals, paper, wine, and motor manufacturing.

In a perfect world, you'd have no competitors. In the real world, you have lots. Even in mature industries – cars, colas, supermarkets, watches, PCs – the level of competition is likely to stay high and keep rising in the future. 'Non-competitors' are a growing threat to almost everyone.

As a first step, it makes sense to focus your attention on a specific customer, and tailor your value delivery system to satisfy that customer's needs. But that is only a first step. Head-to-head battles are inevitable. No matter how finely or creatively you segment your market, sooner or later you'll bump up against someone offering the same satisfaction – or better – to the same customers.[20]

This brings us to a radical shift in thinking. If it's impossible to avoid competitors or stay ahead of them, should you try? Can you continually side-step them? Should the main purpose of your strategy be to position yourself in a different space?

The answer to all these questions is yes and no. It may be possible to differentiate yourself through product design, quality, distribution, or price. Creative promotional messages may give you a lift. First prize is to tap these advantages.

But if clashes are unavoidable, positioning is a non-strategy. In this case, you should plan to trigger conflict, and sustain it. The timing and force of your attack becomes your strategy.

A self-defence expert once taught me that when someone invades your space, and you're not sure why, it's safest to attack fast and hard. James Carville, the aggressive and highly effective strategist for the U.S. Democratic party, operates on the principle that 'speed kills'.

The value of surprise is immense. The fact that you strike first can cause an opponent to back off and flee. When you show you won't be bullied, and that attacking you is costly and dangerous, you gain both respect and time. Your enemy loses control of the fight, loses confidence, and momentum.

If it seems excessive thinking about business competition in these hostile terms, take a moment to reflect on the alternatives. Your customers are a target for many firms intent on growth. You're a sitting duck if you expect competitors to play by the Queensberry rules. You either take the fight to them, or you won't be around to fight.

Only by thinking in this aggressive way will you access the imagination and mental resolve you need in the business climate of the 1990s and beyond. Only by turning your competitive paradigm upside-down will you build the skills and resources you need to own the future.

A flurry of blows

Martial arts experts don't rely on one punch to win a fight: they hit, kick, slash, jab, and gouge. Generals wage war with an array of weapons and a range of tactics. And aggressive companies compete in many ways, all at once.

- A May 1992 article in *Forbes* asked: 'What is Compaq Computer Corp.? A clonemaker that sells on price or a market leader that sells on technological prowess? It's somewhere in between, and that's a dangerous place to be right now.'[21] But is 'in between' the wrong place to play?

  Compaq launched a price war in 1992, which forced the entire industry to slash margins and sent sales soaring. The company then switched strategy, to emphasize features and benefits.

Compaq was founded by a group of former Texas Instruments managers who were proud of their engineering, design, and manufacturing skills. Its products were once over-engineered and expensive. Now, it buys laptop and consumer PCs from outside suppliers. Among other reasons, it hopes to adapt faster to fluctuations in demand. But will this give it an edge? Not likely. H-P has a new build-to-order programme that does the same.[22]

Hewlett-Packard, well known for its pricey, high-quality products, is attacking the home computer market with three lines of multimedia Pentium PCs sold through consumer electronics stores. In a pre-emptive strike, Compaq launched 12 Presario machines equipped with Pentium chips and quadruple-speed CD-ROM drives, the top performing CD-ROM drive.[23] But H-P undercut Compaq and almost matched the prices of Packard Bell, the leader in this market.[24]

H-P (a 'product leader' by Treacy and Wiersema's definition) dominates the printer market, which is basically a commodity area. Its products are consistently rated tops by reviewers, but prices are down with the also-rans.

Once a laggard in the PC business, H-P is now one of the world's fastest-growing PC companies. According to a former executive, 'It took us a long time to figure out some fairly fundamental rules of the game.' Rule 1: cut prices. Rule 2: win dealer support. Rule 3: differentiate products.[25]

Says an admiring Dell executive: 'They have been very good about eating their own young.'[26]

- Watch IBM's current PC strategy: prices drastically down, multimedia facilities built into most new PCs and notebooks, and thousands of rands worth of software bundled with these products. 'We will continue to have people buy off-the-shelf pieces of technology,' says chairman Gerstner. 'And you compete there on the basis of who has got the best technology, best price, best delivery.'[27] IBM cut its staff from a high of 430,000 to about 150,000. People who worked in clerical jobs are making sales calls. Where once sales teams were concentrated on product lines, now they're moving to an industry focus, and Gerstner expects the company to earn more from consulting in future.
- Arianespace, a consortium of 40 European aerospace companies, builds rockets that launch customers' satellites into space. It only entered the business in 1984, but it won almost half the launches between 1989 and 1994, and holds 55 per cent of future launch bookings.

  Unlike competitors such as Lockheed Martin and McDonnell Douglas, which grew as military contractors, Arianespace has always had a commercial focus. It keeps costs down and prices aggressively. Staging operations are kept lean, with just 200 people preparing a rocket for launch, compared to 500 or more involved in American launches. Its rockets are reliable. It provides excellent facilities where customers fit their satellites onto launchers. And, the company even keeps French chefs on the staff at its launch site in Kourou, West Guiana, to spoil customers while they wait for the final blast-off.[28]

- Look at what's happened to the prices of Mercedes-Benz cars: the C-Class was launched in 1993 at the same price as earlier models; the 1994 E320 was launched in the U.S. for 15 per cent less than its predecessor, the 300E. The upgraded 1995 S-Class was seven to ten per cent cheaper than 1994 models.[29] A slew of new low-cost/low-price models is on the drawing boards.
- 'Our objective,' Rubbermaid CEO Wolfgang Schmitt recently told *The Economist*, 'is to bury competitors in such a profusion of products that they can't copy us.'[30] The most admired company in America introduces new products fast, makes a huge range of products, makes them better than anyone else, and improves them rapidly.[31]
- Here's Percy Barnevik, chairman of ABB: 'With lower costs, shorter cycle times, a relentless push for higher quality and a high product innovation rate, ABB has substantially improved its competitiveness.'[32]
- Dominic Cadbury, chairman of Cadbury Schweppes, reports: '1994 saw new sources of competition and lower prices. We met this challenge by successfully increasing sales and margins. This was the result of product improvement and innovation, higher efficiencies and lower costs.'[33]
- Or consider the intentions of David Sainsbury, chairman of much-admired Sainsbury retailing group, as he describes changes under way in his organization: '... strengthening the price competitiveness of the Sainsbury brand ... reinforced quality by improving over 200 existing products and introducing over 1,000 new products ... far-reaching review of the central and support functions of our supermarket business ... concentrate effort on providing outstanding service ... simplify and rationalize operations ... efficiencies in procuring equipment, materials and services ... improving productivity ... improve customer service ... change working methods and manage resources more effectively ... implementing several new computer systems ... opening an average of 20 stores a year over the next three years ... increasing expenditure on remodeling and refurbishing existing supermarkets ...'[34]
- Within months of being appointed chairman of British Airways in 1981, John King (knighted in 1983) chopped the workforce from 59,000 to 36,000, sold surplus planes and various properties, fired the insurance brokers who'd held the business for 60 years, moved the advertising account to Saatchi and Saatchi, brought in some heavyweight new board members, and started work on a programme of cultural change called 'Putting People First'. Later, BA signed alliances with a number of other airlines, fine-tuned global routes, spruced up its aircraft, invested heavily in technology for marketing and operations, and started selling services as brands (for example, 'Club World').
- Southwest Airlines, the only major U.S. airline to keep profits up in recent years, does many things to keep ahead. All its planes are 737s, so it saves a fortune on training and upkeep. Whereas other airlines favour a hub-and-

spoke system and long flights, Southwest focuses on frequent flights between cities that aren't too far apart, uses airports that aren't too busy, and cuts frills to hold down fares. CEO Herb Kelleher is highly regarded as a strategist, and other carriers work hard to copy him. But, says one analyst, 'The real difference is in the effort Herb gets out of the people who work for him. That is very, very hard to duplicate.'[35]

- '... we shall manage the federation of Cable & Wireless companies in a way which aims to ensure that the value of the whole is greater than the sum of the parts,' says Lord Young, the chairman. 'This will be underpinned by a ruthless commitment to world class customer service and innovative product development and marketing which will run parallel with productivity improvement and tight cost and cash control.' [36]

Race without end

In the face of competitive innovation and pressure, every management team must constantly reassess what customers value, and reinvent both products and processes to satisfy them.

If exceptional quality in products and services once was a big advantage, now it's taken for granted. TQM programmes are so widespread that standards have risen in every industry. Customers are no longer 'surprised and delighted' by boasts that you deliver what you led them to expect. They've become intolerant of shoddiness, breakdowns, and lousy service. If you fail to deliver, they shop where they will be satisfied.

Many companies are proud of their ISO9000 quality status. But the world's really tough competitors are chasing Six Sigma quality (3,4 mistakes per million). Motorola aims to cut its error rate tenfold every two years, and cycle times tenfold every five years. Some Motorola plants have already gone way beyond measuring defects per million, and aim to measure defects per billion.[37]

If you shout about 'zero defects' in your promotional slogans, it's time to deliver.

If you accept that your service staff 'occasionally' screw your customers around or let them down, it's time to make that 'never'.

And even as you work on your promise today, think about what you'll offer tomorrow.

From minor skirmishes to all-out war

Consider how petrol companies will compete a year from now. They're selling parity products, so there's little reason for motorists to favour one over another. And now they're all promoting their customer service, so wherever you stop, you get the same smiles, the same quick attention, the same offers to wash your windscreen and check your tyres. Yesterday's surprise is today's 'So what?' or 'Ho hum!'

Or watch the battle between hotels. No-frills operations offer perfectly comfortable rooms with good beds, a bathroom, TV, and a coffee maker. Their rates are almost identical. But they also strive to improve customer service perceptions. To gain custom, one of them will sooner or later be tempted to add something else – free newspapers, rusks with your coffee, or holiday specials. So others will retaliate. Guests will get more for less.

Or take car-hire. It's hard to see the difference between, say, Imperial and Avis. Their cars are the same. Their airport desks are side-by-side. Their staff are smart and friendly. Their rates are similar. They all issue credit cards and offer a range of convenient services. They both strive to do better, all the time.

Customers are a moving target, because competitors relentlessly change, upgrade, and improve their offerings. More than one person has said to me, 'I use XYZ hotel because it's perfectly adequate. I'm only there to sleep, anyhow. I never use any of the extra facilities in more expensive places.' But the same people aren't going to refuse new goodies from City Lodge. They'll happily accept more personal attention from the manager, an expanded breakfast menu, help with their luggage, and the bonus of free air miles every night they stay.

Today's special becomes tomorrow's norm. The products and processes that surprise and delight customers on one occasion are quickly taken for granted.

A critical goal of your strategy must be to render obsolete not just your organization and its offerings, but how you think about what you do. To beat the enemy by breaking with your own past.

Who's responsible?

Openness and involvement are vital in high-performing companies. As I've suggested, you should include as many people as possible in key discussions. But as with all rules, there are exceptions to this one.

Focus decisions are perhaps the most difficult that any organization faces. They involve tough trade-offs and imply huge risks. The changes they trigger are costly.

These decisions demand the broadest possible perspective of an organization and its environment. The people who make them need a great deal of information, plus the experience to know what to make of it. Only a handful of individuals in top management fit this bill. Specialists may add valuable input, but their relatively narrow expertise limits their ability to consider a range of issues. Other employees are even less competent to deliver quality verdicts.

Focus decisions tend to be for the medium to long term. They might be made once in the life of some successful firms. In your tenure as a CEO, you might need to make them no more than two or three times. (Note that the switch from your Chinese take-away shop to a health food bar is not a change of focus; it's a change in how you serve the same customer.)

Some decisions about costs and value might be of the 'big-bang' variety – for example, shut a factory, launch a new product, reposition a service. Here again, special expertise is essential. It makes little sense to involve masses of people in such conversations.

But continuous improvement and change are also needed. Responsibility for both should be shared with the teams or individuals closest to the action.

Cost control, in particular, is everybody's business. It's not enough to hope that costs will fall far enough or fast enough if you simply do the right things. Costs accumulate effortlessly. They're easily rationalized. So they demand specific, relentless attention.

If the job is left to finance people they'll always be at war with the rest. And hard as they might try, they'll always be more out of control than in control. They simply cannot see what's happening at the edges of the organization. They don't know enough about processes to know if there's a better way. Information technology may help, but it'll never be the total answer; costs are best managed by the people who incur them.

An even more important reason to make costs everybody's business is that doing so forces them to think. Instead of being seen as a negative chore, cost management becomes a vital spur to challenging the status quo, to testing conventional wisdom, and to innovation. It gets people asking, 'Why are we doing this at all?' rather than 'How can we do it cheaper?'

Costs come effortlessly. Profits are elusive. If executives do not constantly focus on high-yield activities, and on squeezing the last drop of performance from every cost, failure is certain. Effective turnaround strategies are rooted in the idea of doing the right things and doing them right. Effectiveness and efficiency. Leadership and management. Stuff we all know – but all too easily forget.

Connections that count

The focus decision requires knowledge, perspective, and judgement, plus a willingness to take risks. No matter how much faith you have in your people, chances are that only a few have these strengths. No matter how democratic your organization might be, some decisions are best left to these rare birds. So strong leadership is a prerequisite.

But winning in business takes more than one person. To leverage those first principles, you have to involve and inspire others. Your strategy must not only be understood by everyone on your team, it must also be lived by them. For this to occur they need to know what you aim to do, and why. They need to understand the pressures and challenges your organization faces. And they need to know exactly what's expected of them.

In most companies, strategy is still a top management issue. But while senior people might be best able to set a company's course, they cannot push value up and costs down on their own. This is a job for everyone. It must be delegated as far down the line as possible. (To see why, walk around your own organization now. Chances are, too many people are driving costs up and value down.)

Today, a growing number of firms give more people a role in shaping strategy, as well as making it happen. I encourage my clients to invite people from all levels in their companies to strategy retreats. Some resist, using stock arguments:

'They won't be able to contribute.'
'They won't understand the full picture.'
'They'll be out of their depth.'
'There are too many sensitive issues.'
'The group will be too big.'

Bottom-line, there's a lack of trust and of confidence in the ability of people to add value. But the only way to foster trust is to show it; and the only way to make people more capable of adding value is to involve them in the key conversations.

Magnificent obsessions

If focus, value, and costs are so important when things go wrong, why isn't more attention paid to them when a company is growing, and when things are okay? Why are these not obsessions? Why do managers persist in believing that one of these three factors should dominate their strategies? Why do all three not feature on every meeting agenda?

When they are 'headline' issues, people have a sense of purpose. They understand what's needed, and why. Everything they do is clearly connected to the bottom line.

In the past, you could survive with vague strategies. You could afford to be lax about where you focused your resources and about costs and value. From now, however, you have to be exceptional on all three dimensions. So you have to be specific and clear about what's needed on each. You have to communicate your intentions. Focus, value, and costs have to be the central topics of conversation in your organization.

Endnotes

1. James L. Heskett, W. Earl Sasser, Jr., and Christopher W.L. Hart, *Service Breakthroughs*, New York: The Free Press, 1990.
2. Robin Cooper, *When Lean Enterprises Collide*, Boston: Harvard Business School Press, 1995.
3. 'Three CEOs share their tested formulas for speedy recoveries of sick companies', *Wall Street Journal Europe*, July 24, 1995.
4. 'Kodak focuses strategy on photography', *International Herald Tribune*, March 28, 1995.
5. 'Kmart fails to beam out of a 1960s time warp', *Financial Times*, March 28, 1995.
6. Corporate advertisement: 'The BNP group in 1994: preparing for the future under difficult operating conditions', *Wall Street Journal Europe*, March 28, 1995.

7. 'Lyonnais focuses on restructuring, improving European units' profits', *Wall Street Journal Europe* April 6, 1995; 'The gilt-edged rescue package', *Financial Times*, April 5, 1995; 'Lyonnais cites weak loans leading to loss', *Wall Street Journal Europe*, April 10, 1995.
8. 'Sandoz will firm core focus by shedding chemicals arm', *Wall Street Journal Europe*, March 24–25, 1995.
9. 'Schering emerges in strong shape', *Financial Times*, April 4, 1995.
10. 'Volvo shelves start to look bare' and 'Volvo to sell food arms but retain interest in drinks', *Financial Times*, April 4, 1995.
11. Zeneca Annual Report 1994.
12. 'Goodyear to name Gibara president amid global push', *Wall Street Journal Europe*, April 10, 1995.
13. '125 Years at the Heinz table', Anthony J.F. O'Reilly, *Journal of Business Strategy*, May/June, 1995, Volume 16, No. 3.
14. Philip Kotler, *Marketing Management*, New York: Prentice-Hall, 1984; Philip Kotler, Liam Fahey, S. Jatusripitak, *The New Competition*, New York: Prentice-Hall, 1985.
15. Bruce D. Henderson, *The Logic Of Business Strategy*, New York: Abt Books/Ballinger, 1984.
16. Michael E. Porter, *Competitive Strategy: Techniques For Analysing Industries And Competitors*, New York: The Free Press, 1980.
17. Hermann Simon, 'Lessons from Germany's midsize giants', *Harvard Business Review*, March–April 1992.
18. William G. Egelhoff, 'Great strategy or great strategy implementation – two ways of competing in global markets', *Sloan Management Review*, Winter 1993, Volume 34, No. 2.
19. Egelhoff, 1993.
20. Robin Cooper, *When Lean Enterprises Collide*, New York: The Free Press, 1995.
21. Julie Pitta, 'Identity crisis', *Forbes*, May 25, 1992.
22. 'Where Compaq's kingdom is weak'; 'Hewlett-Packard heads for the home', *Business Week*, May 8, 1995.
23. 'Hewlett-Packard to produce home PCs', *International Herald Tribune*, April 4, 1995.
24. *Business Week*, May 8, 1995.
25. 'PC turnaround at Hewlett', *International Herald Tribune*, February 16, 1995.
26. 'How H-P used tactics of the Japanese to beat them at their game', *Wall Street Journal Europe*, September 8, 1994.
27. 'We won't stop … until we find our way back', *Business Week*, May 1, 1995.
28. 'Arianespace soars on its top-market launchers', *International Herald Tribune*, April 7, 1995.
29. 'Mercedes can't shift into cruise control yet', *Business Week*, April 17, 1995.
30. 'Producer power', *The Economist*, March 4, 1995.
31. 'Small-town values make a big firm', *International Herald Tribune*, April 6, 1995.
32. ASEA Annual Report 1994.
33. Cadbury Schweppes Annual Report 1994.
34. J. Sainsbury Annual Report 1994.
35. 'Is Herb Kelleher America's best CEO?' *Fortune*, May 2, 1994.
36. Cable & Wireless Annual Report 1994.
37. *Fortune*, April 18, 1994.

11

Value Systems

The purpose of business activity is to put together a set of relationships which maximize added value.

— John Kay, *Foundations of Corporate Success*[1]

The logic of value innovation starts with an ambition to dominate the market by offering a tremendous leap in value.

— W. Chan Kim and Renee Mauborgne[2]

A business design is the totality of how a company selects its customers, defines and differentiates its offerings, defines the tasks it will perform itself and those it will outsource, configures its resources, goes to market, creates utility for its customers, and captures profit.

— Adrian J. Slywotzky[3]

Contrary to what many managers seem to think, sustained superior performance is not the product of a SWOT analysis. It does not come from your ability to tell 'cash cows' from 'question marks', 'stars', or 'dogs'. It is not guaranteed by your fine mission statement or your passion for 'excellence'. What it does depend on is your ability to identify the 'right' customers for your company and to lock them into your business system.

Of all the factors that affect long-term financial performance, customer loyalty is far and away the most important.[4] 'In some industries,' says Frederick Reichheld, a director of Bain & Company, a management consulting firm, 'reducing customer defections by as little as five points – from, say, 15% to 10% per year – can *double* profits.'[5]

But customer loyalty does not come cheap. Earning it is much harder than most managers realize. There's a big difference between getting customer satisfaction right 'often' and 'always'.

Research by Xerox Corporation showed that 'totally satisfied' customers were six times likelier to repurchase the company's products over the next 18 months than merely 'satisfied' ones.[6] What's more, totally satisfied customers are the only ones you can rely on to talk well of you; and their recommendation is the most valuable promotional tool of all.

Anything less than 100 per cent rating from your customers is very expensive. In this age of hyper-competition, it's a cost no company can afford. So customer satisfaction is not just a topical idea or a theme you can promote for a year or so; it is the reason your business exists. Every person in your company needs to know this. Your organization must be designed and managed to deliver with total consistency.

If you want to bring customers back, you've got to wow them every time!

Outside-in

All business strategy begins with a choice of which customers you'll serve (and thus which competitors you'll take on), and how you'll do it. This familiar product/market decision defines your value delivery system. What you do within it determines how successful you'll be.

This, in turn, is possible only when your strategy is driven from outside rather than from inside; by the needs of your customers rather than of your company; by a marketing approach, rather than a selling (or production) approach.

Ted Levitt offers a useful view of the difference between selling and marketing: 'Selling,' he says, 'is getting rid of what you've got. Marketing is getting what you can get rid of.'

By Levitt's definition, a sales-driven company says to a customer, 'Here's our widget; you should buy it.' No options. No unusual frills. No tailoring to suit the customer's needs. In short, this company is rigid and inflexible. It's more concerned with maintaining the status quo than with change; satisfying its own needs is more important than satisfying the customer. Its competitive logic is motivated by its past investments; yesterday's systems, policies, and philosophies; and the personal desires of managers.

In contrast, a market-driven firm asks, 'What are your needs? How can we satisfy them?' It then finds a way to deliver exactly what the customer wants, time and again. This organization has no sacred cows; it abandons the past just as fast as it must. Its competitive logic springs from a deep desire to understand customers, and to create a future with them.

The implications can be painful and costly: award-winning advertising campaigns are abandoned; yesterday's state-of-the-art plant and equipment are sold off; people with outdated skills are retrained, replaced, or let go; offices in the wrong place are closed. Hard decisions, all of them, but taken with tomorrow in mind.

Lifetime partnerships

Today, every executive claims to be a champion of customer service. It's a headline issue in most firms. However, it's usually just one intervention in a long list, and is so superficially treated as to be virtually meaningless. The chairman writes about it in the annual report, posters exhort staff to answer phones 'in three rings or less', and trainers offer courses on how to deal with complaints. But place plans on a scale with 'smile school' at one end and corporate overhaul at the other, and the tilt is towards the trivial. Front-line behaviour gets attention; deep-down radical change in the value delivery system is avoided.

Too many people keep busy with tasks that please people in Accounts, but do nothing to help customers. Too many departments exist because they always have. Too many products are poorly designed or defective. Too many processes are fine-tuned when they should be abandoned.

Despite the fine words chairmen use, and despite the money spent on raising customers' expectations, too many companies work harder on internal housekeeping than on external partnerships. It's no exaggeration to say that, all too often, both customers and competitors fall into a single camp – the 'enemy'.

If this is bad news for customers, it's a golden opportunity for ambitious companies. There are untold possibilities for reinventing 'value' and how it's delivered. Untapped profits await when you foster durable, win-win partnerships with your customers.

To customers who are on your side, it's a hassle – financially, emotionally, and in terms of time and effort – to shop around. They know what to expect from you. They know they can trust you to help them buy wisely. They know you'll stand by them if a product fails or if they want to exchange it. In contrast, what competitors promise is untried and unproven, and customers know that switching has risks.

Symbiotic partnerships raise customers' costs of buying elsewhere and raise competitors' costs of attacking you. The tighter the bonds, the higher the barriers.

Raising these barriers should be your explicit objective. Customers are costly to get. It's much cheaper to keep them. And loyal customers provide not just a long-term stream of revenue, but also of 'invisible assets' – word-of-mouth recommendation, learning, ideas, and so on.

Companies that understand this use a variety of strategies to hold on to customers. The logic behind their actions is so clear it's hard to understand why their less successful competitors ignore it.

Prospecting – whether through personal calls, advertising, telemarketing, or whatever – remains a hit-or-miss affair aimed mostly at new customers. Sales staff get a wealth of potentially useful information when they serve customers, but it stays in their heads and isn't used; when they leave, they take it with them.

Database marketing has become a familiar term, yet few companies 'mine' their databases for new selling opportunities. They invest heavily in advertising, but screw up on after-sales service. They hire more sales people, yet make little effort to sell more than once to a customer.

Though I've bought many motor cars, I've never had a dealer call me to offer a trade-in or sell me a car for my wife. Insurance brokers are taught to exploit key events in clients' lives – birthdays, marriage, the purchase of a new home, starting a business – as opportunities to sell more cover. But though I've dealt with many intermediaries, most have vanished after the first sale. Recently, when I instructed a broker to cancel insurance cover on three motor vehicles, they didn't even ask why.

The lifetime value of a customer is impossible to calculate. Making them 'missionaries' for your business has to be your most important task. Every business conversation should be dominated by this issue.

From everyone to one-to-one

Mass production and mass marketing went hand-in-hand. When goods are scarce and customers are plentiful, you can blast away shotgun-style. 'Everyone' is a customer. And because their choices are limited, almost anything keeps them happy.

Managers like the idea of mass markets because it suggests a vast pool of unexploited business. Lots of customers, they think, means lots of profits. Besides, if 'everyone' is your audience, you don't have to do special things for anyone. Being average is okay.

The whole notion of global marketing was built on exactly this premise. As Ted Levitt explained it in his seminal 1983 *Harvard Business Review* article, 'The Globalization of Markets', firms could reach out to customers everywhere if they cut out the specifics that made their products attractive to particular groups – for example, Belgians, Bostonians, or the British aristocracy.[7]

'The globally oriented competitor,' said Levitt, 'will constantly seek opportunities to achieve global scale by globally standardizing everything he does in order to maintain his cost competitiveness ... The most endangered companies are those that produce largely for, and dominate, relatively small domestic markets with high value-added products for which there are small markets in all countries.'[8]

As we now know, however, relatively few firms succeed as true global marketers. Products that are acceptable to people across the planet provide cover for those that are tailored for specific buyers, and which offer superior performance benefits. New technologies will ensure that customization becomes even easier and more necessary in future. Knowing who your 'right' customers are, and being able to satisfy them over time, will make or break your business.

The focus decision is a tough one, because it always requires sacrifice. To concentrate on one customer, you have to ignore others. So when you do choose, you have to be sure you'll get your money's worth.

How you define customers makes all the difference

Which customers are right for your company? Where should you focus? How do you choose?

These are all tough questions. They're easy to avoid. After all, when you aren't specific, anything goes. Everyone is a potential target.

However, no company has the resources to chase after everyone who might buy. There's no way you can satisfy everyone. The wider your audience, the less you can customize your product and your promotions. And the more you ask customers to 'satisfice', the more you sacrifice.

Customer definition is a basic business task. But it also offers you the possibility of doing radically different things, in radically different ways. Examples:

- In the early days of cellular phones in South Africa, Vodacom and MTN both went after credit-worthy customers. That quickly became a constraint on their growth. By shifting the focus to people who *couldn't* pass a credit check, and selling pre-paid airtime, they scooped hundreds of thousands more people into their net.
- Spartan Computer Rentals started out selling PCs and peripheral equipment. But when the market became over-crowded, the company redefined its customers as those who wanted to rent, not buy. This took it out of the dog-fight and gave it a niche of its own.
- When most hotels assumed that their customers wanted a full range of services, City Lodge saw a gap in serving those who wanted no more than a clean room with a shower and bed. Formule 1 Hotels went even further in stripping out the frills – and cutting the price.
- Pierre Cronje saw the opportunity in selling new furniture based on old designs. His Furniture Manufacturing Company makes a range of high-quality pieces that appeal to people who want hand-crafted, classical items, but don't want antiques.
- Old Mutual has traditionally sold through intermediaries, so they were its immediate customers. Mutual Direct focuses on buyers of insurance. By cutting out the middleman, the company can reach an audience that might never have come to it for cover.

In all of these cases, defining the target customer was just a first step. After that, every aspect of the value delivery system had to be tailored to satisfy those customers. The tighter the fit, the more robust the relationship.

You and your team should be engaged in an ongoing dialogue about customer focus. The opportunities shift. Customers are bombarded by new offerings and their needs and wants change fast. Either you manage their perceptions of value, or it'll be done by someone else.

The first question in choosing customers is: where is the critical mass of results you seek? Which customers, in other words, will give you the financial returns, the learning, the insights, and the market presence that you want, for the least cost?

The obvious way to define your market is by demographic factors such as age, income, education, location, and so on. But psychographic factors might be far more important – even if you sell to industrial buyers. These include attitudes, values, hobbies, and other 'soft' factors that may be much harder to discern.

Every buyer of everything is a human being. Their purchasing decisions are not purely rational. Facts matter, but so do feelings.

The clearer you can be about who the individual is that you're targeting, the better. One-to-one marketing is, at its best, an intimate, person-to-person affair.

Capture their profit potential

Getting more customers is necessary to fuel your growth. Also, you will inevitably lose some existing ones. But if your company is typical, you should give lots more attention to *earning more profits from present customers and to extending your ties with them*. You know them and they know you. You've already paid the high cost of getting them. It's easier for them to stay with you than to move.

There are five ways to capture the full profit potential of your customers:

1. **Sell more units to them.** The easiest way is simply to ask for more orders, and to increase the size of each order.
2. **Increase the margin in each sale.** By clearly explaining the value you offer, and by constantly improving it, you may be able to charge maximum prices. And the more loyal your customers are, the less it costs you to re-sell to them.
3. **Send them away singing your praises.** Word-of-mouth is the most potent form of promotion. Every customer should be a missionary for your company and your products. The more marketing they do for you, the more valuable they become and the less you have to spend on other activities.
4. **Reduce the cost of support.** New customers need a lot of product information before and *after* they buy from you. They also need training. And they are most likely to need intensive support while they learn to use your offering. Long-term customers, on the other hand, tend to need less of all of these.
5. **Learn from them to innovate for the future.** Customers are a valuable source of information and insights. The better they know you, the more likely they are to share what they know. They're also more likely to feed you intelligence about competitors, so they become your eyes and ears in the marketplace.

Thanks to new information technologies, it gets easier to connect with customers. On-line product information, sales, and support all add value and cut costs. But I've made the point before and I'll make it again – IT is just the enabler. It can only enhance the competitive advantage you design into your business.

Capturing the full profit potential in every one of your customers begins with a philosophy. It involves every person in every part of your organization. Marketing is not a task you can leave to the marketers. It's everybody's responsibility.

Battle for the high ground

To get customers' attention, you have to stand out in the marketplace. They have to believe that what you offer is different and better. Your name and your promise have to hold a unique space in their minds.

Competitive strategy defines that space. The position you occupy is always relative to that held by your competitors. In positioning yourself, you position them. This makes it imperative that you make clear what you stand for, that you spend enough to own that claim, and that you consistently and persistently reinforce it.[9]

Companies and their products are perceptions in customers' minds; how they see you determines whether or not they'll buy from you. Customers, in turn, are perceptions in the corporate mind; how you see them affects the way you treat them.

Attracting customers' attention is easier than holding it. A good first impression is quickly negated by poor follow-up. Your image rests less on what you say than on what you do. In a marketplace where myriad competitors fight, and customers are confused by a blizzard of messages, execution is all important. Business in the Information Age is not conventional war.

What's your 'value' worth?

Strategy is the process of thinking and acting to build relationships through the creation and delivery of value. Value is a perception. It's a customer's ideal price/performance mix for a particular product or service.

Customers use three criteria to make their buying decisions (Figure 11.1):

- Function (What does this product or service do for me?) It may perform a task, such as drill a hole, transport goods or people, or heat a room; or it may provide an emotional benefit, such as a feeling of confidence, sexiness, or fun.
- Price (What will it cost me altogether?) Not just the initial purchase amount, but also all the other costs of ownership – installation, training, supplies, service, support, resale, disposal.
- Friendliness (How easily can I get it and use it?) Availability, packaging, assembly, clarity of instructions, time to get started, etc.

While customers do make trade-offs between these factors, they have less need to do so when markets mature and offerings converge. Early in the life-cycle of

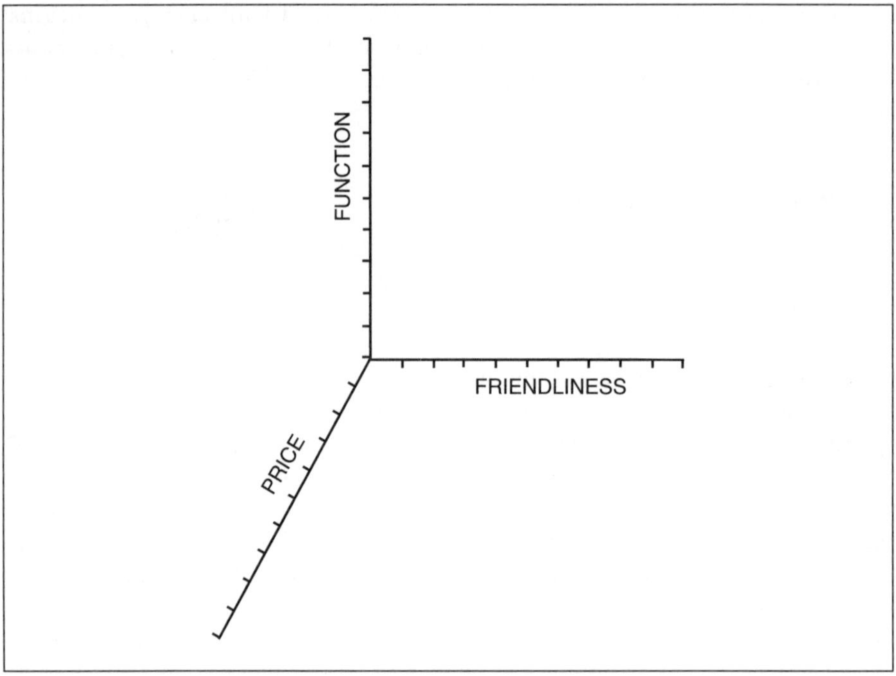

Figure 11.1: *Purchase criteria add up to the value proposition*

a product you may get away with exceptional performance in one area; but competition quickly forces you to push the envelope in all directions.

The price you get for your offerings is a direct result of the value customers think they get from you – of the way they perceive your total value proposition. When you deliver more value than your competitors, you earn a 'value premium'. When you deliver less, you pay a 'value penalty'. When you earn less than the customer would pay, there's a 'value gap' to exploit.

In the illustration opposite (Figure 11.2) Company A earns higher price than Company B so it gains a value premium. Company B pays a value penalty. There's an opportunity for both to add value and boost their prices.

Whether you earn a value premium or pay a value penalty depends on how you manage your value proposition. That, in turn, is a product of the way you manage your value drivers.

Your goal should be to redefine your value proposition to increase the value premium you earn and to narrow the value gap.

Competing value systems

Today most companies boast about their customer service. 'Customer intimacy' has become a cliché. Yet companies continue to spend fortunes trying to capture and keep customers, and customers leave them in droves.

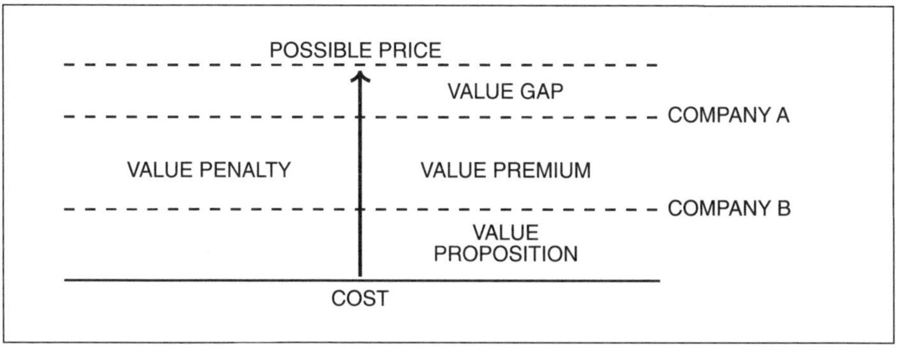

Figure 11.2: *Value premium, value penalty*

This dismal state of affairs will continue as long as managers think their view of the world is the *only* view. Too much strategizing in companies is aimed at persuading customers 'to see things *our* way' rather than to clearly understand '*their* way'. Mostly, its goal is to leverage current strengths rather than develop new ones.

Companies and their customers live in different worlds. Each have their own ways of thinking and seeing, their own mental models, their own value systems, and their own needs and wants. Strategy must connect the customer's value demand system and your company's value delivery system, and bond them tightly to ensure your future earnings and profits (Figure 11.3).

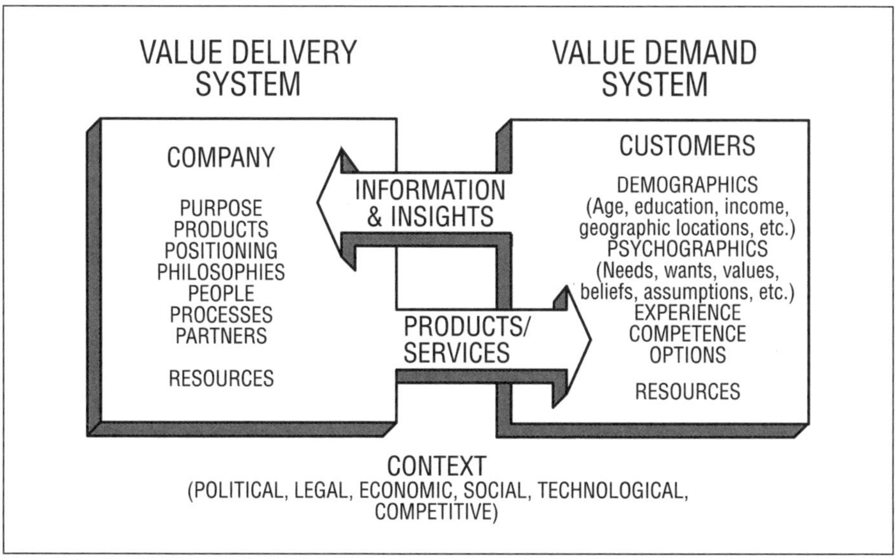

Figure 11.3: *Value systems*

The customer wants to know:

- Why do you want me?
- What can you do for me?
- What makes you special?
- Is this the best offer I can get?
- Why should I believe you?
- What will you do for me later?
- What happens when I have problems with your product?
- How far will you go to make our relationship work?

Companies, in turn, need to know:

- Who are you?
- Where are you?
- What can you afford?
- What do you buy?
- How do you buy?
- When do you buy?
- Where do you buy?
- How do you pay?
- Why do we want you?
- What are you worth to us?
- When can we expect a payback?
- What can you teach us?
- What can we expect from you as part of this deal?
- What could we gain or lose from you opinion of us?
- How will you measure us?
- Why might you ignore us?
- What would make you leave us?

Connecting these different 'worlds' isn't easy. Just being near one's customers doesn't make a company their supplier of choice. If a firm doesn't make a difference that matters, it won't attract or keep customers.

The two value systems change over time. When the customer's changes faster than the company's, divorce is certain. For a while, customers might put up with products or service that don't quite meet their needs, but sooner or later they'll seek value elsewhere.

To forge a binding relationship, you need to clearly understand your customer's needs. Then, your value delivery system must be designed to satisfy those needs.

But no firm can stop at there. All too often, customers don't *know* what they need or want. They have no idea what is possible. They cannot imagine the company's capabilities. Contrary to what we've been told about listening to 'the voice of the customer', listening too closely can be the kiss of death!

Which customer, for example, demanded Netscape's Navigator, Boeing's 747 jetliner, a BayGen wind-up radio, a Palm Pilot personal organizer, or a plastic hip joint? Where were the suggestions for titanium spectacle frames, 3M's Post-It notes, cellular phones, or disposable cameras?

But those all high-tech products, you say. Okay, so what about Kellogg's Corn Flakes, Club Med resorts, Gardena's range of gardening equipment, or the wonderful Leatherman pocket tool? What about steakhouses, massages on Virgin Atlantic's flights, or SAA's Voyager loyalty programme.

Literally every human need and activity offers a marketing opportunity. Wherever you see ho-hum products, there's the prospect of profits through revolution. Every 'me-too' service points to a gap for innovation. But the push for change must come from within as well as from without. It must be driven by your team.

Customers are not all-knowing. They are often conservative. Their imagination is limited and they are technologically ignorant. But they are also an invaluable resource. To shut out their ideas and insights would be utterly foolish. In the quest for competitive advantage, you need all the help you can get.

Customers should be as much a part of your strategic conversation as your own people are. The more you count both in, the more you're likely to discover. The more they all know about your ambitions, the better they can help you get there.

The profit barrier

I talked earlier of the need to raise the cost of customers leaving you and of customers attacking you. Now, let's look at the matter of barrier-building in detail.

Every company with less than 100 per cent market share must face a simple fact: for some reason there is a barrier between it and some – or all – of its potential customers. Customers and competitors are together on the far side of that barrier. Your task is to move that barrier – to get on the same side as your customers, and to shut competitors out (Figure 11.4).

The only way to do this is to offer a better, more attractive value proposition. You have to make a difference that matters. Fortunately, there are infinite ways to do this. But to find the ones that are best for your company, and to bundle them in the most meaningful way, you have to understand branding.

In the mind of the customer

It is not good enough in business just to make a difference. You have to be *seen* to make a difference. And you have to keep reminding customers why your difference matters. This is where branding comes in. And it's why branding is today more important than ever, even though customers increasingly shop for the best price.

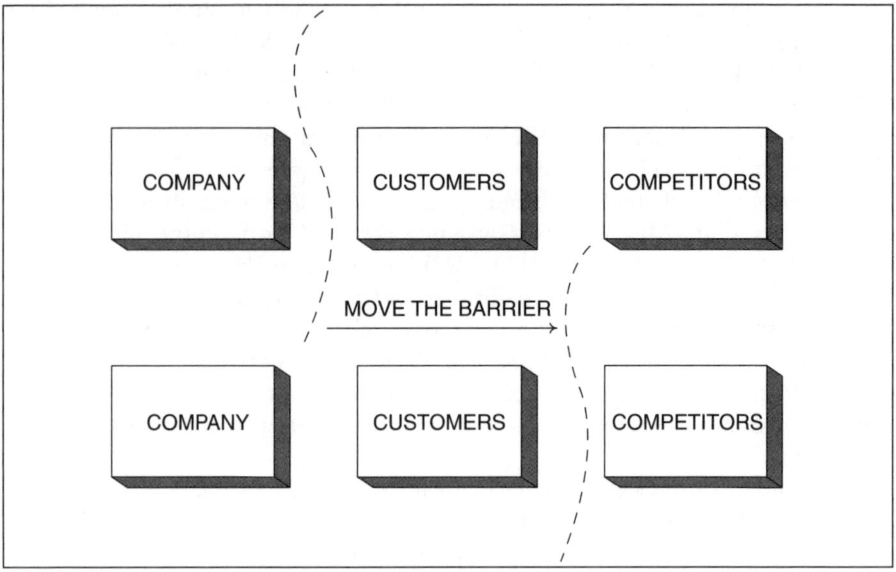

Figure 11.4: *Move the barrier*

Branding makes your value proposition visible and credible. It is an essential factor in building your competitive edge. But you have to get on with it fast as it will become more costly and difficult over time. What's more, building a brand is not an overnight matter; it takes concerted effort over a long time.

Branding is a notion that is overworked and misunderstood. The term is used carelessly to justify almost every corporate activity. Executives boast in the financial press about 'the value of our brands', when what they have is a bunch of products that could vanish overnight without anyone noticing. Marketing people pontificate about 'building our brands', even as they spend their promotional funds in ways that will gain no more than a day of fame.

So what is a brand? Is it a product? A famous name? A corporate logo or a catchy phrase?

It's all these, and more.

- A brand is an *attitude*. It is a customer's attitude towards a product or company, but also a company's attitude towards the customer.
- A brand is a *bond*. It's the shared meaning between company and customer and a vow of loyalty between them.
- A brand is a *symbol* of quality, a performance guarantee.
- A brand is a *statement* about the values of both company and customer.
- A brand is a *feeling* of confidence, self-worth, and pride.

While a brand name says a lot about a firm or its products, it also tells you about the customer. The Mercedes-Benz three-pointed star conveys one kind of image; Opel says something else. Caterpillar boots ('machines for walking') suggest toughness, while Bruno Magli slip-ons promise comfort and sophistication. Chivas Regal 12-year-old Scotch promises one kind of satisfaction, while Klipdrift brandy is for other people, other occasions.

People who wear gold Cartier spectacle frames want to make a loud fashion statement. Those who wear frames by Oliver Peoples are more laid back. Motorists who tool around town in four-wheel-drive vehicles are probably telling you, 'I love the outdoors. I do tough stuff.' And when housewives take home Royco or Knorr soup rather than a cheaper unbranded product, they want their families to know, 'I love you and care for you, and I prove it by paying more for the best.'

Branding a company, a product, or a service adds value to it. It's a task that demands the most serious attention from your most senior people because it involves every part of your organization. The payoff is huge – and the penalty for failure is equally huge.

Some firms have made tentative efforts to place a value on their brands. Some have made brands a factor in their balance sheets. But this remains an unusual practice and brands are more often hidden under the general heading of 'goodwill'.

In future, as companies pay more attention to their invisible assets, and as they try harder to value – and manage – their knowledge about customers, processes, and so on, brand value will rise to the top of their agendas.

You cannot watch winning firms like Coca-Cola, Disney, CNN, Intel, or Sony, without marveling at what their names are worth. Replacing their visible assets – buildings, equipment, and other stuff that you can see and touch – would be relatively easy, but the soft knowledge component of their businesses is worth a fortune. If it were lost, it might never be regained.

But here's the rub. While a brand is nominally the *property of a company*, its entire value lies in *the perceptions of customers*. They alone decide what it is worth. And when customer behaviour changes, and they define 'value' in new ways, sellers beware!

Facts and feelings

Buyers' perceptions are shaped by both hard and soft factors. On the one hand, customers want to know that a product offers specific advantages and will do what's promised; on the other, they need emotional assurance that it's 'right for me'.

To effectively build a brand, you have to deliver in terms of functionality. It obviously helps to have a 'unique selling proposition' (USP) – a meaningful advantage that others can't or won't match.* But as this gets harder to do, imagery becomes an important differentiator. In fact, it may be the only one.

* The idea of the USP was invented by the Ted Bates advertising agency in New York in the 1940s. Rosser Reeves, a famous copywriter and later head of the agency, made it famous in his book *Reality in Advertising* (London: MacGibbon and Kee, 1962).

Marketers often work hard to produce different products, then lose their advantage through weak promotion. They either fail to explain what sets them apart, or their message doesn't resonate with customers.

Marketing messages are communicated through advertising, public relations campaigns, packaging, logo design, and in many other ways. Yet vital as they are, these creative inputs are often delegated to junior or inexperienced people, or to suppliers who're more concerned with winning awards from their peers than with building an asset for their clients.

(One South African ad agency is said to spend R500 000 a year entering its work in awards contests. As a fine collection of certificates and statuettes shows, this 'marketing investment' clearly pays. But no one knows what the agency's creativity does for its clients' sales.)

While there's no foolproof way to create effective promotional materials, and while creativity can lift a product from 'me too' to 'most wanted' status, the one thing you can do is be emphatic about how customers should see your offering. So ask:

- In what way should you look different to them?
- Why should that difference matter?
- Why should they believe you?

These are profound and difficult questions. Glossing over them is foolish and expensive. You need to think about them from the moment you start making strategy right through to the 'moment of truth' when a customer uses your product.

Value perceptions are a product of value delivery. That, in turn, is a consequence of *value design*.

The costly disconnect

Every company faces a central challenge: How to create congruence between customer demands and organizational capabilities (Figure 11.5). This is the key to building, promoting, and protecting products in the marketplace.

Just as an individual will fail to reach his or her potential by trying to be something they're not, so will a company fail to reach its goals if it tries to 'fake it'. Integrity is the characteristic that makes winners in every field.

In practice, few firms achieve the necessary integrity – or alignment – between themselves and their customers. They spend fortunes doing things that do not support the image they want to present in the marketplace. They waste their resources on unimportant things, and neglect the activities that will boost profits over the long term. They send mixed messages to customers.

Strategizing is a quest for integrity. It's an ongoing search for the essence of an organization, and the process of building connections between what's expected outside (your value demand system) and what happens inside (the value delivery system).

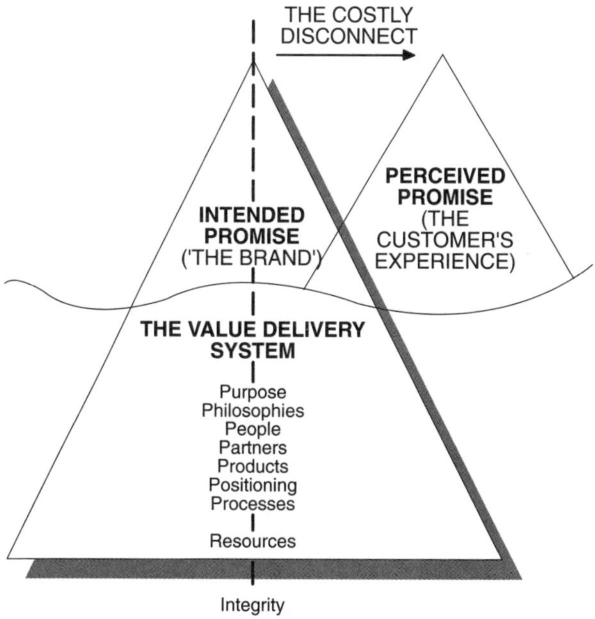

Figure 11.5: *Image and reality*

Integrity as lodestar

Choices about focus – which customers you'll aim for and how – are choices about 'what's right for us'. That they're easy or comfortable is not enough. You must be able to commit to them. You must feel strongly about defending them. You must be both intellectually convinced by them and emotionally affiliated to them.

Managers talk a lot about integrity. It's a favourite word in mission and values statements. Mostly what it means is don't cheat the company, and try to be ethical in dealing with outsiders.

But there's more to it. Listen to Emerson:

> *Insist on yourself; never imitate. Your own gift you can present every moment with the cumulative force of a whole life's cultivation; but of the adopted talent of another you have only an extemporaneous, half possession. That which each can do best, none but his Maker can teach him. No man yet knows what it is, nor can, till that person has exhibited it. Where is the master who could have taught Shakespeare? Where is the master who could have instructed Franklin, or Washington, or Bacon, or Newton? Every great man is an unique ... Do that which is assigned thee, and thou canst not hope too much or dare too much.*[10]

Integrity has to do with being true to others. But it begins with being true to yourself. You don't become another Ernie Els or Tiger Woods by trying to copy the swing of one of these champions. You can't clone yourself to stardom. Everyone who ever makes a difference is, first and foremost, an original.

Just as people are unique, so are companies. And just as you and I should be driven by our search for the essence of ourselves, so should managers seek the specialness of their organizations.

Effective strategy is a product of integrity. Your performance in each area of the strategy process is a direct reflection of how committed you are to your own reality, to finding your own truth, to carving your own niche, and to putting your own stamp on things.

Consider what this means when you study your competitors, or benchmark yourself against other organizations, or borrow strategies from them. By taking the easy way out, you are almost sure to achieve less than you're capable of.

Other people's answers might teach you something and might even be an intermediate goal, but they should never be accepted as *your* answers, or as *the* goal.

When you and your colleagues think about strategy, test yourselves continually against these questions:

- Is this really us?
- Is this the very best we can do?
- Are we absolutely comfortable with it?
- Are we proud of it?
- Does it deserve our ©, ®, or ™ stamp?
- Is our strategy as unique a 'fingerprint' as our products and services?

The point is not just to be *different*, but to be *yourself*. Not to be *another* Microsoft or McDonald's, but to be the *original* Netscape or Starbucks.

When one organization copies others, it can only copy what it sees. But the tip of an iceberg is not all there is; a fine suit is not a man. It's what you don't see – and can't copy – that counts.

Finally, remember that the test of your strategy is not whether you make *more* profit than a rival, or win *more* market share or invent *more* new products. It's whether you achieve your potential and do what's right for your company.

The discipline of value design

Value design involves both radical thinking and discipline. One the one hand, you need what the Zen masters call 'beginner's mind'. You have to empty your thoughts, escape the hold of 'what you know', and set your imagination free to explore possibilities. But you need to do this in a systematic way, or you'll simply flail about.

Sportsmen practice hard to develop what my father, a professional golfer, called 'muscle memory'. Come the big contest, they have to rely on their bodies to do the right thing. Conditioned instinct separates the winners from the also-rans.

Building a company's competitive capability is, in many ways, the same as preparing for a big match. You have to work at your moves until they're second nature. You may dissect them and fine-tune them separately, then put the lot together again. Afterwards, you can let instinct take over.

Empowerment efforts fail for many reasons. One of them is that people aren't sure enough about what's expected of them. Telling people to 'be innovative' or to 'improve things' is too vague to be useful. What's more, my experience in many groups shows that while people do want freedom they also want guidance.

Coaching has become an important leadership skill because people want counsel. Effective coaches carry in their heads a model – a 'teachable idea' – of what it takes to excel in their particular sport. By helping athletes understand the building blocks, they help them develop a smoothly integrated swing, stroke, stride, or whatever; and by helping team members understand what each one must do, they enable the group to function harmoniously.

'To be a practitioner,' writes psychologist Guy Claxton in his book *Hare Brain, Tortoise Mind*, 'it may be best not to be able to think too much about your skill or your art. But to be a coach is different. A whole new phase of learning may be required if the virtuoso wants to become a teacher, for she may have to laboriously to unpick her seamless expertise and turn it into the descriptions and explanations that, judiciously administered, help learning to happen.'[11]

It may come as a surprise to some people that creativity requires discipline. As amateur writers know, if you wait for your muse you may wait forever. Professionals don't have that luxury; they have publishers and deadlines between them and the paycheque. So how do they write books or articles? They draft an outline, describe the main concepts or characters, agree on a delivery date ... and start writing. They know where they're going, and they invent the details as they go.

The famed advertising man, David Ogilvy, relied on hot baths and 'John Barleycorn' to warm his creative juices.[12] However, he built Ogilvy & Mather on a set of well-researched principles about advertising. And he was fanatical about delivering creative work to his clients on time.

The most innovative companies – 3M, Sony, Chrysler, Glaxo – invent new products in a systematic way. If they have a 'culture of innovation', it's supported by disciplines, deadlines, reviews, and budgets. Structures and processes are in place to ensure that new ideas actually see the light of day.

Following the same logic, I developed a powerful new model (Figure 11.6) to help you design your business for the future.* Let's explore how you and your team can use it.

* I make no apologies for the fact that it is built around seven words all starting with 'P'. Research shows that seven is about the number of concepts we can handle at one time. And my experience in advertising taught me the value of simple, catchy ideas.

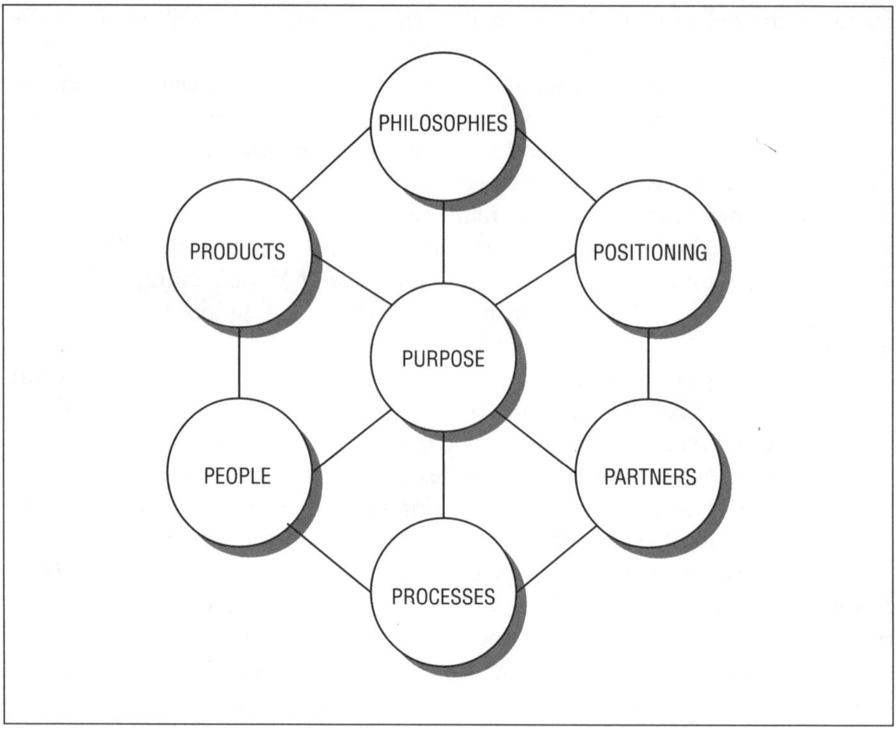

Figure 11.6: *Seven Ps in the value delivery system*

A holistic view

Doctors check your physical health by taking your temperature, blood pressure, and pulse rate, and by looking in your throat and ears and listening to your heart and lungs. In the same way, you need to examine your organization and re-think your value delivery system from various perspectives. You also need to see how the bits connect.

Here are the factors to consider:

1. The central – and ongoing – question all executives must answer is: What is our corporate **purpose**? Why does our company exist? What do we aim to achieve? What ultimate goal must we reach to think of ourselves as successful? What should our legacy be?

   These questions embrace both the vision and mission of the firm. The answers describe not just 'the hill' you aim to seize, but also what products or services you'll sell and which customers you'll sell to. They should describe what makes your firm special for customers and other stakeholders, and what your ambition is.

   Naturally, your organization's purpose will change over time. But it should have an enduring quality to keep you from zig-zagging. It should reflect a higher ambition than just making a profit. It should appeal to both head and heart. (More about this on page 251.)

Your purpose, in turn, is shaped and made possible by these factors:

2. Customers are increasingly discerning, demanding, and disloyal. To capture and hold them, you have to offer **products** (or services) that redefine 'value' – 'killer apps', as computer buffs say. The questions to ask:
   - What products can we make better than anyone else?
   - What unique satisfaction do our products offer – and what could they offer?
   - What technology might they embrace?
   - How should they be priced, promoted, distributed, and supported?
   - What should our product mix look like?

3. The 'value' a product offers is a matter of customer perceptions – of your **positioning** relative to competitors. To capture and keep customers, you should aim to separate yourself apart from your competitors, and 'own a slice of customers' minds'. The questions to ask:
   - What does our product mean to them?
   - What is its positioning relative to direct and indirect competitors?
   - What makes our product stand out from the crowd?
   - How will we communicate the difference?
   - How will we defend it?
   - How will our positioning evolve as demand changes and competitors attack with new ideas?

4. Executives have to make 'hard' decisions every day – about people, investments, safety, the environment, R&D, training, sales promotion, customer service, and so on. These decisions are made more difficult because all too often the 'soft' factors that underpin them or are affected by them haven't been addressed. Organizations often don't have explicit **philosophies** to guide everyday thinking and action; people arrive at particular choices 'because that's the way it's always been around here'. The questions to ask:
   - What do we stand for?
   - What principles do we believe in?
   - What kind of place do we want our organization to be?
   - What do we want people to think of our firm?

5. As I've emphasized throughout this book, **people** make the big difference between success and failure in any company. The questions to ask:
   - Do we have 'magic people' in the pivotal positions in our organization? (More on them in the next chapter.)
   - Do we hire people for the new strengths and fresh thinking they can bring to the party? Is our induction process thorough?

- Do we train, manage, promote, and pay people for performance?
- Do the best stay long enough to make a difference?

6. Every company has its own special mix of **processes**. These include technologies, systems, procedures, and everything else you do to produce and market your products. The questions to ask:
   - What must we do to deliver customer value?
   - Why do we do the things we do?
   - What should we stop doing?
   - Do our processes all drive value up and costs down?
   - Are there better ways of doing things?
   - What do we do now, that if we changed it radically, would put us ahead of the competition?
7. Finally, there are the **partnerships** that magnify the strength of a company. Every stakeholder relationship has positive possibilities. Managers should see them in this light, and aim for win-win relationships with all stakeholders. By aligning your entire 'ecosystem', you gain a vast amount of power that your company could never create on its own. The questions to ask:
   - Are our stakeholders all aligned behind our purpose?
   - Do we shove enough responsibility for our success onto their shoulders?
   - Are there other ways we could involve them?
   - Are there possible partners we don't know yet – and how can we attract them?

This model doesn't have a starting point, or a logical end-point; you can begin anywhere and work through it in any order. Nor do you have to seek a 'conclusion' to any of the 'Ps'. As you work on one, you'll probably find that it's somehow linked to others; by moving back and forth between them, you trigger further ideas and insights.

Paradigms and paradoxes

To get even more from the 'Seven P' model, you might find the following framework helpful. This time, there are four Ps (Figure 11.7).

1. First, there are the **paradigms** that limit creativity. Inevitably, your knowledge of 'what is' gets in the way of imagining 'what might be'. Companies need to understand their paradigms, and their industry's paradigms, in order to break free of them. The questions to ask: What do we 'know' – about the environment, our company, our products, our industry, or whatever – that, if we turned it on its head, would give us an advantage? What are 'the facts' about our purpose, products, positioning, partnerships, processes, and philosophies that we should ignore or rewrite? What is 'true' from where we stand, that may look different if we changed our perspec-

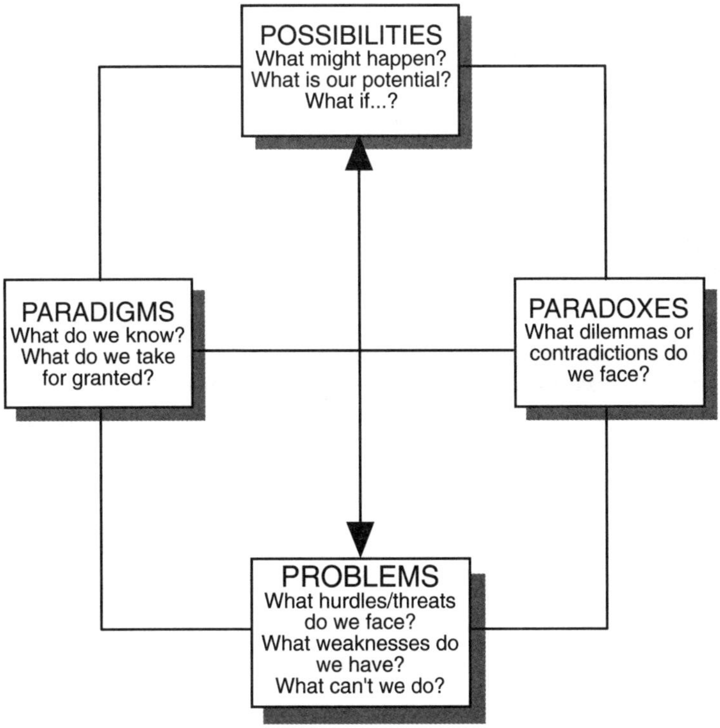

Figure 11.7: *From problems to possibilities*

tive? What do we take for granted that someone else might not agree with or care about?

2. Second, there are the **paradoxes** that surround you. If once you could get away with either/or choices, now you cannot. You're faced with a multitude of issues that don't let you easily pick one direction or another. Stakeholders with conflicting interests all clamour to be heard. By embracing rather than denying paradoxes, your company gains huge advantages. The question to ask: What paradoxes face us, that, if we could embrace them, would give us an advantage? Addressing it systematically and deliberately often highlights issues that hold back or even cripple progress. When you surface and discuss the issues that could tear your company apart, you often find imaginative ways of dealing with them.
3. Third, are the **problems** that face you. Do any of the seven Ps fit into this category? Are there external factors that threaten you or stand in your way? Are those problems really problems – or is that just the way you view them? What makes them problems? How serious are they?
4. Fourth, are **possibilities**. Your goal should be to move issues from the 'problems' area into this territory. What could you do if you forgot 'what

we know'? What's possible when you embrace a paradox (accuracy vs. flexibility; minimal inventory vs. convenience and responsiveness; rapid new product launches vs. reliable old favourites, etc.)? What might you achieve if you shifted your team's attention or refocused your resources? Which problems could you simply ignore?

These tools are designed to shape and focus your corporate conversation. Use them with all your people, and right across your company. Use them regularly. Share the ideas that they inspire. You might have all your people tackle a single 'P' each month, or allocate all seven of them across your organization. How you do it is up to you. But make the process deliberate, with deadlines and a review process, and do something about the results.

Like any business tool, this one will only produce results when it's applied. When you do use it, you'll almost certainly find many new ways to compete.

Which model is best for you?

Two different retail models point to a new direction for your business. The following descriptions are not based on what managers in those companies say, but on what I as a customer see. The details may not all be correct, but think about the concepts.

The company on the left is Pick 'n Pay. The one on the right is Woolworths (Figure 11.8).

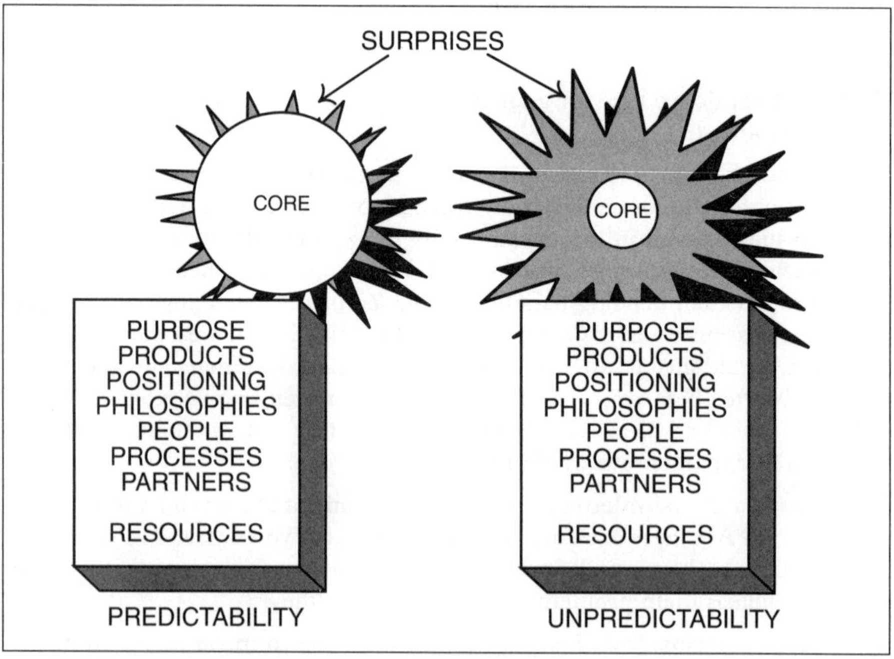

Figure 11.8: *Predictability vs. surprise*

Pick 'n Pay has a well-earned reputation as the consumer's friend. The prices compare well with those of other groups. The shelves of its stores are always full, and it carries a huge range of items. Housewives know that they can shop here at the end of a month, and get everything on their lists. Convenience is a big plus.

Pick 'n Pay's value proposition is essentially one of predictability. The company's value delivery system is designed to deliver on that promise. Every one of the Seven Ps is managed to reinforce it. Suppliers know they have to get their goods onto the shelves at a particular time. They know they have to keep their prices down. Credit policies give Pick 'n Pay the margins it needs. IT systems track sales to avoid out-of-stock situations. Promotions consistently position the firm as the one that offers the best value for money.

But predictability alone isn't enough to keep pulling in customers. So Pick 'n Pay does many things to keep them interested: price cuts on selected items, new displays, new merchandise. Stores are regularly refurbished. Most have butcheries, bakeries, fish counters, fresh fruit and vegetable departments, and deli areas.

Contrast this model with the one on the right – Woolworths.

A more different shopping experience you couldn't imagine. In contrast to Pick 'n Pay, 'Woolies' offers some certainty, but lots of surprises. Some are irritating, as when you go in too late on a Saturday, say, and find that the shelves are empty. But customers tolerate them, because the gaps send a powerful message. You know that on Monday, fresh-picked items will be back.

Woolworths carries a much smaller range of foodstuffs and household products than Pick 'n Pay. But it rings the changes much faster. Every time you visit a store, there's something you've never seen before. It may be a new winter soup mix, ready-to-roast stuffed butternut, pasta sauce, or French wine.

Woolworths works hard to act like a corner store. Products are displayed to show off their quality and goodness; many fruits and vegetables are ready-washed and pre-packaged, while customers can pick and pack others to suit their needs. Suppliers are valued for their inventiveness. Stock levels are kept low, to ensure freshness and fast turnaround. Staff are friendly and helpful.

Now, which model will endure into the future? Will Pick 'n Pay become more like Woolworths, or will the shift be the other way? And which model is best for your business? Should you offer lots of predictability and a few surprises, or less predictability and lots of surprises?

My guess is that while predictability will always be important, and you have to offer a minimum level of it to satisfy customers, surprise will become increasingly important. The evidence is all around us already, in a range of industries. The best competitors work hard at the basics, but they also relentlessly pursue 'irrationalities'. The management of surprise will be the weapon of the future.

Summing it up

While simple models can blind executives to the complexity of the real world, they do help cut through the confusion. In an early critique of U.S. President

Bill Clinton's foreign policy, Henry Kissinger wrote: 'Where the administration has created problems – for itself and its interlocutors – is in failing to articulate an operational theory and to relate individual events and crises to it.'[13]

In the previous section, I deliberately simplified two complex companies to make a point. The business model you choose (your value delivery system) must be designed for the customers you want (your value demand system). You need to think of each of the Seven Ps in terms of what they mean to your target customers. And you need to ensure that together they add up to a single-minded, compelling message.

This is what branding is all about. And this is how you win or lose in the age of hostile competition.

Einstein once said that a theory should be as simple as possible, but as complex as necessary. And that's the way organizational theories or models need to be.

The purpose of any 'operational theory' (or model) is to make a situation or a problem understandable. Ideally, it should put things into context, tidily lay out the factors that must be considered, and offer a clear and logical way to tackle problems.

One criticism of any model is that it suggests there's 'one best way' to deal with a particular challenge. Another is that models provide a frame for issues and ideas – and the frame gets in the way of lateral thinking. And thirdly, because models specifically set out to neaten a messy world, they leave out lots of stuff.

At best, models offer one way to start thinking. But they do help get the process started, and they do guide it.

There's truth in the adage that a picture is worth a thousand words. So if there's a way to explain your company and its strategy, grab it. Pick models to provoke thinking, challenge sacred cows, and drive key messages through your organization. Use them with care. Use just a few. Use them often, so people understand them clearly. And use them for long enough to convince people you're serious, but not after they've served their purpose.

Endnotes

1. John Kay, *Foundations of Corporate Success*, Oxford: Oxford University Press, 1993.
2. W. Chan Kim and Renee Mauborgne, 'Value innovation: the strategic logic of high growth', *Harvard Business Review*, January–February 1997.
3. Adrian J. Slywotzky, *Value Migration*, Boston: Harvard Business School Press, 1996.
4. Thomas O. Jones and W. Earl Sasser, Jr., 'Why satisfied customers defect', *Harvard Business Review*, November–December 1995.
5. Frederick F. Reichheld, 'Learning from customer defections', *Harvard Business Review*, March–April 1996.
6. Jones and Sasser, 1995.
7. Theodore Levitt, 'The globalization of markets', *Harvard Business Review*, May–June 1983.
8. Theodore Levitt, *The Marketing Imagination*, New York: The Free Press, 1983.

9. Bruce D. Henderson, *Henderson On Corporate Strategy*, New York: Abt Books, 1979.
10. Emerson, *Essays*, J.M. Dent & Sons, 1906.
11. Guy Claxton, *Hare Brain, Tortoise Mind*, London: Fourth Estate, 1997.
12. David Ogilvy, *Confessions of an Advertising Man*, London: Longmans & Green, 1963.
13. Henry A. Kissinger, 'At sea in a new world', *Newsweek*, June 6, 1994.

4

LEADERS AND OTHER STRATEGISTS

12

Leadership and Magic People

Why is it I always get a whole person when what I really want is a pair of hands?

— Henry Ford

Giving planners responsibility for strategy is like asking a bricklayer to create Michelangelo's Piéta.

— Gary Hamel[1]

Leaders have the capacity to mobilize lower-level leaders within the system and to reach out to potential allies at all levels … Leaders can turn on green lights throughout the organization with a minimum expenditure of energy.

— John W. Gardner, *On Leadership*[2]

Napoleon once said, 'A leader is a dealer in hope.'

Top executives must talk things up, not down. They have to appear confident, certain, in charge. Their people's performance depends on it (as does the value of their own stock options!). But while they focus attention on opportunities rather than problems, on what might be possible rather than what is impossible, on learning from failure, overcoming hurdles, and creating the future, they have to also beware of deluding themselves. They must be intensely aware of their 'lenses', so they're aware of their own distortions. They must question their assumptions and the assumptions of others. And they must challenge the simplistic solutions that come their way every day.

Perhaps the most difficult challenge today is to maintain a sense of perspective. Leaders must:

1. Show that there's light ahead.
2. Help people accept that they can create the future.
3. Hold a course in the midst of turmoil and pressure to change direction.

The leader's job is never done. Just when you think you've got things 'under control' and everyone headed roughly the same way, you have to stick a high-explosive charge under them and turn your plans, your organization, and your activities upside down.

This leads us to tricky questions:

1. First, how long do you stay with one direction, and when do you change? Investments in technology, training, brands, and core competencies take time to pay off. Some of what you did in the past does have value today and will pay off for some time. But there's a growing risk that it'll outlive its usefulness.
2. Having seen a new reality, and with people starting to accept it, how do you get them to change again? And again? And again? Human beings, like all living organisms, seek stability. Every organization needs a measure of it. But too much of it, and you're in a deadly rut.
3. How do you get people to trigger change themselves? Top-down direction is important, but even the brightest boss cannot see every problem or opportunity on the far horizon. Nor can she come up with all the answers all of the time. To pick up faint signals, virtually every employee must be the firm's antennae – its eyes and its ears. They must also invent responses that work.

Effective leadership is a blend of many things. You need to know when to play it safe and when to go for broke; when to milk your old 'cash cow' and when to spend on tomorrow's 'rising star'. There is seldom 'one best way'. No manager in his right mind writes off past efforts without good reason. No one can be sure that a new opportunity is 'the best' opportunity.

Strategy is driven by perceptions. The way we read the world shapes our responses to it. Competition is fought in the mind. Conversation is a key weapon in this battle.

But where do you begin? How do you create the radical strategy that will take your organization into the future? How do you enlist a critical mass of people in support of the effort?

Everyone a change agent!

Not long ago, a large industrial company asked me for help with their strategy. The top team expected a workshop at which they'd hammer out a plan. But there were so many sensitive issues involved, that I proposed another course.

We invited 600 managers to a series of briefings. I explained what we were trying to accomplish, and gave them a 90-minute presentation on changes in the environment that were likely to affect their business. Then I asked them to go away and do their own scan, and feed it back to their bosses.

The top 12 executives and I used the input to paint a broad-brush strategy. We then took it back to the larger group, and for the sake of consistency, I presented it to them. Given the issues at stake, there were sure to be tough questions, lots of resistance, maybe some anger.

In fact, the response was quite different.

In every meeting, when I asked for comments, there was only one. It was the same one every time. 'You guys aimed too low,' said the group.

Too *low*? We thought we'd aimed way too high. What happened?

What happened was quite simple. The response should not have been surprising. Those 600 managers had been involved in the debate right from the outset, and had spent time thinking about the world around them. The inevitable result was that they told us that there were serious problems ahead, and that things had to change. *We* didn't have to change their minds; *they* changed their own minds.

This corporate conversation started early, with huge benefits all around. But too often, they start too late. Vital people are left out. Decisions are taken for them. By the time they get brought in, they've made up their minds that they don't count. Winning their support is an uphill battle – and may prove impossible.

Wanted: volunteers

Wal-Mart, the world's biggest retailer, keeps growing at the pace of a start-up. Its extraordinary success is due to a host of factors, from legendary logistics to the ability to pick good locations, from its leverage over suppliers to its 'customer greeters'. But what really drives it is a 'hyper-productive' culture. 'Wal-Mart,' reports *Fortune*, 'gets everyone, from CEO to clerk, to work like a dog for relatively low wages and then brag about it.'[3]

People commit themselves for many reasons. Money may be an important turn-on, and it's usually the first one that management turns to. Plenty of companies offer a wide range of financial incentives, and more and more employees are becoming shareholders.

But money is far from being the only motivator. In fact, there's evidence that in some cases it may not prompt better performance at all – and might even have negative consequences.[4]

One problem is that bonuses may cause short-term hikes in output. When this happens, you have to keep awarding them to keep growth going. The likelihood is that people will see today's incentive payment as tomorrow's base package.

The best workers contribute because they want to. They are not pitted against each other or against manipulative managers. Rather, they commit themselves to a meaningful purpose.

During World War II, women, minorities, and even partially disabled people were hired to work in General Motors' factories. With little experience and few supervisors, they drove productivity far above the norm. There are any number of similar examples from other companies and countries. Come the crunch, people do wondrous things.

Pride and a sense of contribution are enormously important to human beings. We all need meaning in our lives. Viktor Frankl concluded that individuals who survived the horrors of Nazi death camps had something to live for.

Warren Bennis has written endlessly about the need for leaders to provide a sense of meaning for their followers. There is too much solid evidence to ignore – yet we ignore it all the time.

Being part of a winning team is also a big turn-on. A study of global business by the *Harvard Business Review* revealed that executives in growing companies 'think more highly of their own jobs, their employers, and their people than do those from stagnant companies'.[5]

One reason American business leaders value their corporate reputation, and like to score well on *Fortune*'s 'Most Admired' list, is because they believe it motivates their people. Jamie Houghton, CEO of Corning, set his organization the specific goal of making the Top Ten. Intel's Andy Grove says reputation 'gives people extra energy. It gives you that extra lift to do the tough stuff our life consists of day in and day out.'[6]

A purpose must be clear and meaningful. It needs to be both well understood and deeply felt. It should engage both the mind and the gut. It must suggest a worthwhile reason for being – for turning up each day.

Strategy provides meaning to individuals. Strategizing is thus a core leadership function. Whom you involve and how you do it makes people feel counted in or counted out.

Strategy is much too important to be left to ivory-tower strategists. They might get it precisely 'right', in the sense that are able to pick a perfectly sound route to the future. But in another sense, they'll definitely get it 'wrong', because there's no way on earth they can provide the fuel that makes it go.

First comes context

Getting more from people is the most urgent challenge for business. To do it, you probably have to start by re-thinking your assumptions of their worth, and then change virtually everything you 'know' about managing them.

The process has to start with whom you hire and how you do it. Then it extends through induction, training, communication, rewards, and promotion. Firms need to take far more responsibility for the total well-being of their people, which means they have to get involved in literacy and numeracy training; provide transport, health care, and child care; and reach out into the community to help establish a sound social infrastructure.

Until recently, you could hire and fire at will. There were plenty of people in most skills categories. You could get away with a cavalier attitude towards training. You could be autocratic and rude. Bullying behaviour was okay.

'In the past, if a person could walk and wasn't sick, we'd hire them,' says the training manager of a manufacturing company. A supervisor in another firm complains: 'When we need a worker, we hire whoever is at the gate. They come in, often having been out of work for years, maybe drunk, maybe smoking dope, straight onto our highly automated production line. I'm expected to get productivity from people like this. If I push them, they threaten to kill me.'

Alex Trotman, chairman and CEO of Ford talks of 'achieving the lowest possible coefficient of bureaucratic drag'.[7] Firms everywhere have to achieve the lowest possible 'coefficient of human drag'. They have to enable their people to innovate and act at light speed.

Empowerment – a favourite word in business and society right now – is one part of the answer. But it doesn't help to put power in the hands of the wrong people; or poorly-trained or inexperienced people; or people who don't know enough about your company, its strategy, and its philosophies. Without proper rewards, and the prospect of career advancement, no one will be motivated to take responsibility. Without appropriate systems and tools, they cannot be responsible.

Human performance depends in part upon the individual, and to a very great extent upon the context in which that person functions. Finding the right person is vital. But in this age of unlimited possibilities, it's increasingly important to manage them right.

The power of the human spirit

According to *Fortune* magazine, Herb Kelleher, CEO of Southwest Airlines, may be the best business leader in America. When he hires people, he looks first and foremost for 'a sense of humour', then 'for people who have to excel to satisfy themselves and who work well in a collegial environment'. We don't care much about education and expertise, because we can train people to do whatever they have to do. We hire attitudes.'[8]

Attitude – or spirit – is the ultimate performance driver. It's an intangible /tangible something that only a few have. You can't create it by boardroom dictate, you can't train it into people, you can't measure it. But somehow it's there, alive in the air. A sense – when you walk into a company's reception area, meet a sales person, or deal with a clerk – that 'this organization has got it! ... These people are different! ... This team means business!'

Spirit is what makes the best 'go for it' when a new opportunity is still faint on the horizon, when serious problems arise, or when a final burst of energy is called for at the end of a long task. You sense it as you enter the front door: in the receptionist's smile, in the look of offices, and by the spring in people's step. It impacts on the way they run meetings, make presentations, deal with requests, and handle complaints. When it's missing, you also know. Lethargy hangs in the air and people drag themselves from 'problem to problem'.

The top executives I know are all workaholics. They may have many interests outside of work, but they take their jobs seriously. They get to the office early and stay late. Often they follow a long day at the office with a business dinner or late-night meetings. They tackle dozens of problems at once, and seem to thrive on the challenges that pour over their desks. But watch carefully, and you often get a sense of desperation: they seem to be alone in their determination to make the business survive and grow. There seems to be a battle by the few to haul the many into the future.

Outside of the executive suite, a different sense of purpose prevails.

Heredity or environment?

If companies like Dimension Data, The Hollard, Momentum Life, and Imperial Car Hire stand out, it's because they're all led by rare individuals who make a difference. But as you look deeper into these organizations, it's clear they have a great depth of talent. There are exceptional contributors at every level.

Strategy obviously affects an organization's fortunes. Technology, raw materials, patents, brands, and distribution – and a host of other things – all count. The more of them in your favour, the better your prospects. (But you can have every one of those advantages and still fail.)

With exceptional people, however, you can succeed despite a lack of other resources. You can transcend your limitations in other areas. You can travel beyond the bounds of reason.

The question is, what's most important: the people you hire, or the context you create for them? The answer, of course, is both. You should always aim to hire the very best people that are available. But you must also manage them for performance.

What about people you already have? It pays to begin with the assumption that they can do incredible things, they do want to excel, and they will if you'll let them. Change the context, and they, too, will change.

For the vast majority of people, work is simply a way to pay the rent, buy groceries, or take a holiday. They're not driven by their jobs. They feel real relief when they say, 'Thank God it's Friday!' Nor are they deeply committed to their companies; changing jobs is easy as long as they can transfer to a new pension fund and medical aid with no loss.

Many CEOs are bewildered by this. In their view, the gap between them and their employees has nothing to do with the way people are managed, and everything to do with personality. 'I just don't understand the bastards,' said one executive. 'They're not interested in anything but themselves. You give them an inch and they take your whole arm. Any chance for time off, and they take it. Walk around this place during the day, and you'll see private conversations everywhere. Walk around at five o'clock in the afternoon, and it's like a bloody morgue.'

But what's the real problem? And whose fault is it? Do the people who've made it to the top bring different purpose to their jobs, or do they get a different sense of purpose *from* their jobs. Are we talking heredity or environment?

Human beings are different from each other. Some are born with wonderful talents and just never get anywhere; others battle every obstacle in the world to achieve incredible things. We all have different agendas. We're turned on by different things. But people, with all their foibles, are what management must work with. The task of a manager is get the most out of them by plumbing the depths of their spirit.

This has nothing to do with exploiting them or pressuring them to do impossible things. It has everything to do with opening their minds and encouraging them to explore their potential, and with providing whatever push and resources they need to be their best.

Human beings are the raw material of management. Just as there are 'good' and 'bad' people in every society, so you find them at work. The character of your company depends on what you, as the leader, make of them. Where you point them is one issue; what you do to free their spirit is an equal challenge.

'You have to make people proud of their company,' said Jac Moolman, former managing director of Nashua. 'You have to allow them not just to grow, but to blossom.'

'People must want to get up and come to work in the morning,' says Piet Steyn, chief executive of the Rennies Group. 'Unless they really want to be there, they're going to spend the day thinking about going home. I want them to think about our company and our clients.'

Make them important

Most advice about motivating people has to do with making them feel good about themselves. You can do that, says conventional wisdom, through praise, pay, or perks. But research shows that these incentives all offer short-term benefits. Unless you keep giving more of them, motivation soon falls and performance slumps.

The real key to sustained high performance requires that managers make the quantum leap from making their people feel important to making them important.[9]

This may sound like a *semantic* shift, but for most people it's actually a *seismic* shift. Consider what it means.

You can make people feel important through quite superficial acts: a pat on the back, a thank-you note for a job well done, a bigger car, or a new desk. But to make them important takes something else entirely. To achieve that, you have to give them power, which means control over meaningful resources and responsibility for meaningful tasks. You have to share confidential information. You have to invite their opinions on important matters, involve them in key discussions, and leave them to make major decisions.

This is what empowerment is all about. So it's easy to see why so few people are empowered. The task – and the perceived risks – are simply beyond most organizations. And they'll stay that way as long as most people are shut out of the most important conversations.

Prepare them for another life

If 'excellence' was yesterday's favourite word, today's is 'empowerment'. Women, we are told, must be empowered to deal with discrimination in the workplace, with health and education authorities, and with dangerous husbands.

Communities must be empowered to use funds, build roads and clinics, and get electricity, water, and houses. And of course, workers must be empowered to improve working conditions and pay, and to have a say in how their organizations are run.

When business leaders talk about empowerment, they have a narrow definition of the concept. What they usually mean is that people must be managed in ways that make them more productive, innovative, and responsible in their current jobs. What they don't mean is that people should be set free to do their own thing. The organization's goals are always paramount. Job descriptions limit what individuals may do; supervision is always necessary; control is vital.

These assumptions affect hiring practices, training programmes, the shape of the organization chart, and management practices. Conservatism is more common than liberalism; it's regarded as safer to keep a 'tight rein on things' than to let go.

As long as managers think this way, companies will under-perform. The people in them will not reach their potential. Good ideas will not surface, or if they do, they won't be implemented. Problems will go unsolved. Conflicts will remain unresolved.

As long as empowerment means letting someone do a particular job to a narrow set of standards, it will mean little to individuals, organizations, or society. In fact, it will be self-defeating, in that people will quickly realize that it does not change their lives.

To make empowerment meaningful, you need to redefine it. You need to go beyond 'giving people the information, resources, support, and freedom they need to do their present job in this company' to '... making it possible for them to leave and do better somewhere else'. Empowerment, in other words, means putting individuals in charge of their lives, not their jobs.

Imagine what you would have to do to make this reality. Imagine the new kinds of training you'd have to introduce – and how much more you'd have to spend on training. Imagine how you'd have to change your management style to give them the self-confidence they'd need. Imagine how you might set targets with them, coach and cajole them, give them positive feedback, and reward them.

Empowerment means ... grow them to go!

Anything less means you short-change them, your organization, and the whole of society.

A special gift

To reach their personal potential, human beings need a sense of purpose. Companies, too, must be purposeful. People make them that way. They set winning organizations apart from the also-rans, make them strong in the face of adversity, and innovate to create the future.

So what is the human purpose?

That's a tough one, and it has tested philosophers throughout the ages. But perhaps the answer is simpler than we think.

As human beings, we have two abilities unique in the animal kingdom: the gift of choice and the gift of creativity. Other animals are prisoners of their environment: they cannot consciously anticipate how it will change, so they can at best only react to it. Presented with challenges, they have few choices as to how to react.

Human beings, on the other hand, can look ahead, make assumptions about the future, and make almost infinite choices. We can explore options in our heads and pick the ones that seem best. We can then act in ways that shape the world to suit our needs.

Blessed with these abilities, it seems to me that the human purpose is a clear one: *we are here to make a difference*. Every one of us is a change agent. None of us has been put here to keep things as they are.

This is a huge responsibility. If we are to live up to our potential, we need to ask ourselves daily: 'What will I do today to make a difference in my family?' 'In my company?' 'In my community?' 'In my country?' 'In the world?'

Companies, in turn, should do whatever it takes to enable people to be their best.

Where's the magic?

When I interact with people in companies, I have an unspoken question in my mind: 'Is this a person who makes a difference?' (Not, please note: 'Is this someone who *can* make a difference?' We all can. But few do, and those are the ones to find.)

I've taken to calling these rare individuals 'magic people'. These are the ones who make a difference. They're our best hope for the future.

First prize for any organization, of course, would be to fill every post with a magic person: someone who could be trusted to make a difference. But in the real world that's unrealistic. Most people are far more interested in keeping things the way they are. Their energies go into blocking change.

So the next best course, and the only practical one, is to make sure that the few pivotal jobs in the organization are filled by magic people.

To identify these jobs, think of your organization as a system of cogs. Now locate the handful of those cogs that make the biggest difference to performance. These 'pivotal' jobs are the ones that need people who make a difference. Fill them right, and other gears start turning; energy soon radiates throughout the whole organization.

How do you define 'magic people'?

By defining, first, the job-specific attributes that will make a difference in your particular company, in your particular industry. If you need a rugby player, don't hire a soccer star. Your organization might need experts in a key technology, people with special sales skills, or financial whizzes.

Hiring well is perhaps the most important thing management does. The task deserves utmost care. To raise the odds of hiring the best people, try starting with these four questions:

- What results are needed in this job?
- What skills, knowledge, experience, and character does it demand?
- What traits will lead to exceptional performance?
- What is the time horizon?

Now, how would you define your 'magic people'? What characteristics do you need in your organization? Think about them. List them. Rank them. And be tough applying them.

Having identified individuals with promise, ask:

- Is this absolutely the best we can do?
- Will they bring something extra to our enterprise?
- Can we afford *not* to hire them?

Of course, at this stage you'll probably say, 'Hold on. This is South Africa. There's a shortage of skills. And what about transformation?'

Your only option

As I mentioned in Chapter One, our ability to develop people has been hurt by our assumptions about what it takes. Before you decide that all is lost or that what you have to cope with is impossible, consider what you need from your people.

To be effective, they need four things (Figure 12.1):

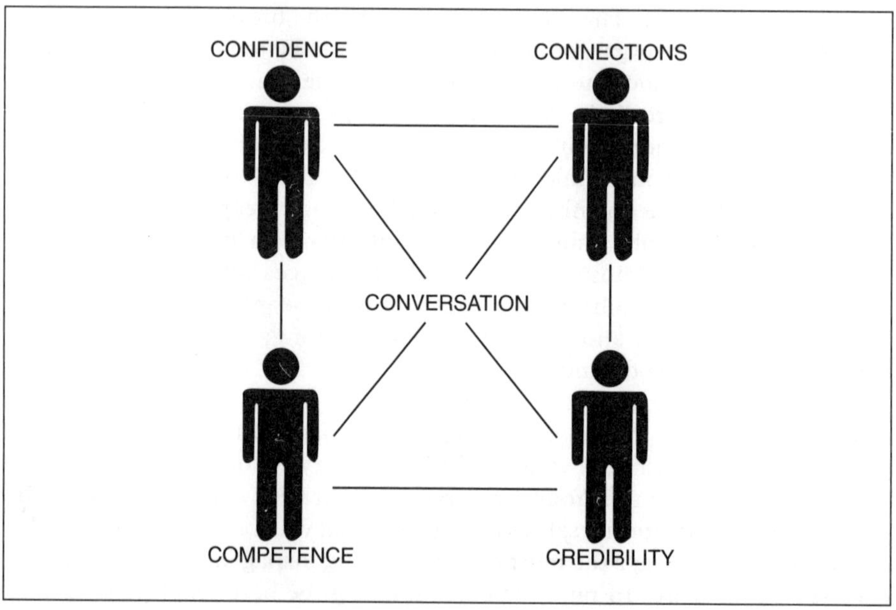

Figure 12.1: *Basic attributes people need*

1. **Competence.** They must have basic skills necessary for work. Some of these may be gained in the classroom or brought in from outside experience. But the most valuable learning usually takes place on the job.
2. **Confidence.** If they are to take on important tasks, to take part in tough debates, and defend their point of view, people must be confident. Some are naturally this way – they don't know when they don't know. But most gain confidence as they progress through life and tackle a succession of challenges with some degree of success. Action leads to learning, which in turn leads to a sense of self-worth – a virtuous cycle.
3. **Connections.** Networking is being recognized as a vital skill. People with the right connections can get things done; those who don't know who to call, who can't get through to the right person when they do call, or who can't ask others for favours, are at a great disadvantage.
4. **Credibility.** Past training or experience may give someone credibility. Their track record helps when they walk into a new job. But it's what they do on the current job that really counts.

If you're lucky, some of the people you hire will arrive imbued with these four vital qualities. What's more likely is that you will have to assist in their development to one degree or another. Even the most promising of individuals have room for growth.

The surest way to help anyone advance along these four paths is through your corporate conversation. Count them in, and they will make progress; leave them out, and they'll go nowhere. Expose them to the 'small stuff', and you'll slow them down, and maybe frustrate them and cause them to leave.

There is a strong argument for hiring people with potential. Obviously, this has risks. But given the realities of the South African situation, you simply have no choice. So when you do accept this course, it's best that you follow up by doing what it takes to get results.

Provide adequate induction. Offer training, support, and exposure to various functions. Conduct regular performance reviews, and give honest feedback. But above all, involve people in high-level conversations.

When you get down to it, this is the only course open to you. Other approaches simply are not bringing success fast enough. All the evidence says that conversation makes the difference – and it's the one way to get people to make a difference.

Leaders or managers?

The people who give companies direction are usually different from those who keep them in motion. Currently there's a danger that we're focusing on the first (few) at the expense of the second (many).

The criticism that too many companies are 'under-managed and over-led' is a favourite attention-getter of conference 'infotainers'. The phrase sits well with managers under siege, because it's a clarion call for heroes, for feisty visionaries who thumb their noses at the establishment. The notion of leadership is exciting; mere management is boring. After all, whoever heard of a bureaucracy with balls?

However, to say that everyone in every firm should be a leader is a ridiculous and unfounded generalization – a silly 'urban legend'. And while the idea may be to foster change, the result may be stagnation and failure.

Peter Drucker long ago noted that some people are especially good at 'doing the right things', while others are better at 'doing things right'. Bennis and Nanus, Noel Tichy, John Kotter, and many other leadership gurus use these differences to define leadership and management. Leaders, we are told, do the right things, while managers do things right.[10]

But we should beware of assuming that people either are leaders or managers. 'Leaders,' says Harry Levinson and Stuart Rosenthal of the Levinson Institute, '*are thinkers as well as doers*'[11](my italic). Managers, you might counter, are doers as well as thinkers.

Some companies might well need more leadership and less management. Others are under-managed and over-led. Just look around, and in many firms you see plenty of excitement and lots of brilliant ideas, but too little attention to detail.

What's really needed, of course, is people who make a difference – whatever you choose to call them. Diversity of talent, ability, inclination, and motivation is not only a reality within organizations, but also a necessity. The fact that people are different is precisely what makes companies work.

Many CEO's have a great ability to spot opportunities, and are very good at creating unique strategies. But they're not always as good at following through. They have a short attention-span. Their butterfly minds take them from one project to another. Their people are turned on by the hype of occasional breakthroughs but are less interested in the need for relentless improvement. Their organizations lack persistence. They give up too early on new possibilities.

Entrepreneurs usually get together to start businesses because they have different strengths. They hope that what the one does well will be magnified by what the other brings to the party. Partnerships are about multiplication, not addition. Companies should recognize this fact and exploit it. Far too much time and effort are spent trying to iron out individual idiosyncrasies, and in getting people to 'fit into our culture'.

Compromise doesn't pay

Hard decisions about people are easily avoided. The new labour relations climate makes getting rid of them complicated and often costly. Old loyalties get in the way. The need for trust and teamwork often cause bosses to put off what must be done.

In addition, the wrong people get important jobs. Those appointing them don't ask, 'Is this the *best* person for the job, or the *easy* one?' The challenge for which the new person is needed isn't clear. Past loyalty or long service win too many points.

A CEO once justified promoting a colleague to a key post by telling me: 'I have to look after him. He's due for a directorship.' But one thing companies don't owe their employees is promotion to where they'll fail. That is irresponsible, stupid, and immoral. When people in powerful jobs fail, they take others with them. Resources are wasted in mopping-up operations. Future opportunities and profits are lost.

Nothing hurts a company more than the wrong people in pivotal positions. As long as they're there, you incur two costs:

1. **The cost of managing them.** You have to second-guess them, cover for them, and fix what they get wrong. This soaks up more time and attention than you can imagine or afford. And the wrong people will screw up a lot!

2. **The cost of lost magic.** When the wrong person is in a job, you never discover what the right person might have brought to it. And the difference might be huge.

   A study in the *Journal Of Applied Psychology* compared the output of the top one per cent of workers in a range of organizations with that of average workers. In simple jobs, the best people were 50 per cent more productive. In jobs of medium complexity, the difference was 85 per cent. In highly complex jobs, it was 125 per cent. When top performers were compared to the bottom one per cent, the gap widened to 300 per cent for simple jobs and 1 200 per cent for medium-complexity jobs. In the most complex jobs, the differences were so big they couldn't be measured![12]

   But productivity alone is not a measure of magic. The best people bring insight, imagination, resourcefulness, passion, and many other invaluable qualities to a job. They anticipate problems. They sniff out opportunities. They find shortcuts. They take hurdles in their stride. And most important of all, they keep going when the going gets rough.

   These people might not be easy to get on with. They might not be team players. They might be hard to manage. But one thing is obvious: the world is a better place for having them around. When they're not there, they're sorely missed.

A company has to function as a community. Every member needs to have a purpose, and should be there because they add, not subtract, from the group effort. One wrong person can imperil the jobs and lives of many others. It's unfair to everyone to make excuses and duck the issue.

If the purpose of the individual is to make a difference, the leader's purpose is to create a climate or an environment in which people can make a difference. In fact, most organizations seem somehow to conspire *against* performance. To cause even the most extraordinary people to do only the most ordinary things. Their systems, policies, procedures, and management style all get in the way of magic people. Following the rules scores more points than breaking a few of them. Playing it safe is more sensible than testing the limits. Mediocrity is the norm.

How leaders hurt themselves

Companies everywhere are having to change their human resources practices to satisfy a new breed of worker. Today's workers insist on respect – and on the training, involvement, communication, and power that comes with it. No longer can you treat adults like children. No longer can you see 'the workers' as your enemy.

Companies have to radically change their view of people, the way they employ them, and the way they tap their potential. Managers need to wake up fast to the new realities and to their own shortcomings. Many of the people problems they've had to cope with in recent years have been of their own making. If the workforce is hostile or obstructive, that is only partly due to external forces or union actions. Many problems have been created right in the workplace – by managers themselves.

- In one management workshop, I suggested to a group of administrative workers from a factory that they should take responsibility for changes in their area. Asked one: 'How are we supposed to do it? Our managers aren't interested in change. They're comfortable the way things are. If you push new ideas, you may not get promoted. You get labeled a "trouble-maker". It's just not worth the risk.'
- When the managing director of a large industrial company – let's call him John – was promoted to chairman, and a new man arrived in his place, there was a sigh of relief from the other directors. 'John knows the industry like the back of his hand,' said one, 'but he doesn't know people. When he was MD, no one ever offered an opinion at a board meeting. If he asked what had happened to sales in the past month, you gave him the numbers – no view of why they might be up or down. If he asked, "Is the latest industrial relations issue resolved?" you said "Yes" or "No". Nothing else. He didn't want to hear anything else. Now, everyone is involved, everyone is expected to speak up, and we all do.'
- 'Management expects us to go the extra mile, to feel as committed to the company as they are,' said a supervisor in a manufacturing plant, 'but they treat us as if we're invisible. Many of them don't greet us. They never ask for our ideas or opinions on the things that affect us. They lecture, but they don't listen.'
- When I conducted a seminar with a group of senior bank executives, I argued that they should aggressively pursue strategic change. They shook their heads. 'When I made some suggestions,' said one, 'I was told, "Don't mess with strategy. It's not your job." ' One of his colleagues added that being too pushy was a sure way to kill one's career.

The message is clear. People across organizations tell us the same things. Managers search vainly for clever new ways to earn their loyalty, to make them more enthusiastic, energetic, and entrepreneurial. Yet managers themselves stand in the way.

The first principles of business competition are worthless without spirited people to apply them. This is where the leverage comes from. This is the ultimate edge. And the only way to take advantage of it is to show the way … and get out of the way!

Endnotes

1. Gary Hamel, 'Strategy as revolution', *Harvard Business Review*, July–August 1996.
2. John W. Gardner, *On Leadership*, New York: The Free Press, 1990.
3. 'And the winner is still … Wal-Mart', *Fortune*, May 2, 1994.
4. Alfie Kohn, 'Why incentive plans cannot work', *Harvard Business Review*, September–October 1993
5. Rosabeth Moss Kanter, 'Transcending business boundaries: 12,000 world managers view change', *Harvard Business Review*, May–June, 1991.
6. 'Corporate reputations', *Fortune*, March 6, 1995.
7. 'Senior managers face a gruelling eight months', *Financial Times*, April 23/24, 1994.
8. 'Is Herb Kelleher America's best CEO?' *Fortune*, May 2, 1994.
9. *The Human Side Of Enterprise*, New York: McGraw-Hill Book Company, 1960.
10. See Bennis and Nanus, 1985; Noel M. Tichy and Mary Anne Devanna, *The Transformational Leader*, New York: John Wiley & Sons, 1986; John P. Kotter, *A Force For Change*, New York: The Free Press, 1990.
11. Harry Levinson and Stuart Rosenthal, *CEO: Corporate Leadership in Action*, New York: Basic Books, 1984.
12. John E. Hunter, et. al., 'Individual differences in output variability as a function of job complexity', *Journal Of Applied Psychology*, Volume 75, 1990, referred to by Alan W.H. Grant and Leonard Schlesinger in their article, 'Realize your customers' full potential', *Harvard Business Review*, September–October 1995.

13

Crafting the Conversation

A good facilitator, good facilitation, is a way of accelerating the process of creating shared understandings.

— Michael Schrage in *The New Business of Design*[1]

... anyone seeking to be a leader should always tell the truth if for no other reason than it is simpler.

— Marvin Bower, *The Will To Lead*[2]

What matters most today is the ability to think together, not alone. To think imaginatively about matters of substance, incorporating many perspectives and reaching beyond conventional categories. To create new concepts that make new connections.

— Rosabeth Moss Kanter, *On The Frontiers of Management*[3]

The purpose of an organization is to leverage human potential. To enable individuals to achieve more than they might on their own.

An organization's results are the product of its people's imagination and spirit and the resources it can call upon. A firm in which 1 + 1 = 2 is clearly worse off than one in which 1 + 1 = 3 or more. Conversation is the multiplier.

Managing the corporate conversation is the strategist's most important responsibility. Nothing else matters as much. And fundamental to that task is the use of language – of words, phrases, concepts, metaphors, emphasis. The 26 letters of the alphabet can be combined in many ways. How you use them determines how well you do in the marketplace.

This seems incredibly obvious, yet there are few mentions in the literature of strategy about conversation as a competitive weapon. Hardly ever is it discussed in books and articles on change management. Yet you only have to watch almost any successful change leader in action to see the importance of conversation in what they achieved.

'Companies need overarching themes to create change,' says Jack Welch. 'If it's just somebody pushing a gimmick or a program, without an overarching theme, you can't get through the wall.' Executives must 'set an objective, one central theme to run through every bone in the company, every corner of it, every person in it'.[4]

Walter Wriston defined Citicorp's strategy in three words: 'World financial intermediary.'[5] Roberto Goizueta reduced Coca-Cola's strategy to 'acceptability, availability, affordability'. Steve Jobs made Apple Computer famous for delivering 'insanely great' products.

Strategic thinking is an ongoing process. Many of its outcomes unfold over a long time. But it should also have an immediate outcome: a set of words that sum up what an organization must do to attain its purpose. These 'key themes' guide people and focus their actions.

Whatever you aim to achieve from your strategic processes – from breakaways, scenarios, SWOT analyses, planning, or whatever – the single most important job is to arrive at these themes. Until you have them, you won't easily be able to guide your firm into the future. Without them, you won't be able to keep it on course.

Stories shape the context

Every society is a product of its stories. Fables, nursery rhymes, legends, and lore all mould our values and beliefs – the core of culture. Shared meaning gives groups a 'shorthand' which lets them cut through long explanations or descriptions and speeds up communication.

According to Harvard psychologist Howard Gardner, 'Leaders achieve their effectiveness chiefly through the stories they relate.'[6] Their stories suggest what's important and what's not. They focus people's attention. They establish priorities.

Former U.S. president Ronald Reagan turned America around by telling Americans different things than his predecessors had done. Jimmy Carter was fond of appearing at 'fireside chats' in an old cardigan. Reagan wore a tuxedo, bought new crockery for the White House, refurbished the presidential yacht, and talked about 'Star Wars'. His message was, 'Walk tall! Be proud! Be great!' And to the Soviet Union, 'Don't mess with us!'

Microsoft's extraordinarily competitive culture is an extension of Bill Gates' words. He never tires of repeating his vision, 'A computer on every desk and in every home.' He constantly travels to tell his story at major conferences and he repeats it *ad nauseum* in the media.

Gates is a legend. He is the Microsoft message. When he retires one day and hands the reins to someone else, you can bet the company will keep asking, 'What would Bill think about this?' 'How would Bill deal with this situation?' 'What would Bill say?'

It's well known in the Seattle software firm that screwing up will earn you a dressing down from the boss – a fearsome experience known as 'a Bill'. As the story has spread, the event has become more awful.

When Microsoft staff started talking about the Internet, not much happened. But when Bill Gates 'got religion', things changed overnight. When he began telling different stories, the whole company changed direction overnight.

Essentially the same thing happened when GM spun off the Saturn Motor Corporation and told the new management to pursue a different dream. Forget about Detroit's war stories, they were told. Start afresh. Build a new car from scratch, one that Americans will love. Hire people who have no history in the car business, and weld them into a community with a cause.

Saturn's success has been little short of sensational. Saturn stories are mostly about people. You see them on TV, you read them in the company's ads. The community now embraces not just employees and their families, but also suppliers and customers.

The leaders of Coca-Cola never tire of their story. When they make speeches, they sip from a bottle of Coke on the podium. Again and again they relate how pharmacist John S. Pemberton stirred up the original caramel-coloured syrup in a brass kettle in May 1886. They tell how Asa Candler bought the recipe for $2 300 in 1891, how the famous contour bottle was designed in 1915, and how Robert Woodruff set about making Coke available 'within an arm's length of desire' after he assumed leadership of the company in 1923.

Coca-Cola lore is about the secret formula, 7X, which is locked in a basement vault. It's about how Coke was sent to American soldiers on foreign duty in World War II. And it's about famous ad campaigns such as 'I'd like to buy the world a Coke' and 'Mean Joe Greene'; the 1985 'new Coke' debacle; and the way a major Pepsi bottler in South America was snatched away and recruited by Coke.

Woodruff used to paraphrase Oscar Wilde, saying, 'The world belongs to the discontented.' That's a story. But for a long time it was just a quote on plaques around the office. Then Roberto Goizueta started talking about why the company should be discontented, and about the need for radical thinking. The new generation of Coke people take it seriously. They're a restless lot and it shows in the company's results.

What's talked about gets done

The old adage says, 'What gets measured gets managed.' But what managers overlook is that the only things they measure are those they talk about.

When return on investment is the big issue, the corporate conversation centres on asset management, cost containment, managing debtors, and how to improve margins. You hear about these things in every forum. Managers are judged by how they measure up. So they do things that will drive the numbers.

When customer service is the topic, managers talk constantly about improving products, cutting response time, streamlining delivery systems, and so on.

Their measures focus on these matters. They spend their time on things that will make their customer service ratings rise.

Issues that aren't high on the agenda don't get management time and attention. They're swept aside in favour of those that do.

Watch what happens when a new CEO beats the drum about, say, productivity or Six Sigma quality in every meeting, and when he refers constantly to these issues in his public speeches and his notes to colleagues. In no time at all, the people around him start saying the same things. The issues that concern him soon concern them. His words become their words.

The behaviour of any organization is a direct result of its conversations. Who says what, to whom, and how, is the cause of every action and the most potent influence on the group's culture. Organizations become what they talk about.

Of course, there's a lot of lip service paid to slogans and buzzwords. If you want to progress in any organization, you quickly find out what to say in order to win brownie points. Many teams parrot one theme while doing something else. But the fact remains that the most important issues are the ones that get talked about, measured, and thus managed. The other stuff is just a distraction.

The proof is everywhere

Read corporate success stories in the business press or listen to consultants, academics, or business leaders, and you get any number of interpretations of what happened. You'll hear about bold visions, exceptional leadership, restructuring, downsizing, new technologies, innovative marketing. But what you'll miss unless you listen carefully is the most vital insight: *success is ultimately a product of conversation.*

This message comes through with relentless consistency:

'The conversation started to change ...'
'We started talking about ...'
'The CEO began preaching a new gospel ...'
'You heard the same thing in every speech ...'
'A change in management changed our focus ...'
'Results came when we started singing the same tune ...'

Things kept changing at General Electric as Jack Welch defined new imperatives. Jürgen Schrempp steered Daimler-Benz in a new direction when he started preaching 'value-driven management' (with every unit earning at least 12 per cent on capital employed), and when he pushed engineers to bring new cars to market two or three years faster than they had intended.

Closer to home, Derek Keys transformed Gencor when he got his team to focus their attention on major, capital-intensive projects. Later, he dared to speak of 'unbundling', and sparked another revolution which led to the break-up of Gencor – and of many other firms. Carol Scott, chief executive of Imperial Car Hire, is passionate about customer service, and it shows in everything the company does.

When a company is dominated by accountants, they tend to talk about the things they're most comfortable with: costs, margins, profits, returns on investment (ROI), economic value added (EVA) , the stock price. Engineers talk engineering. Designers talk design.

It's no accident that folk in Marketing often clash with those in Finance or R&D. Nor is it a surprise that customer service is a foreign concept to people who aren't in daily contact with customers, or that quality but not administration might be a big deal on the production line. An organization's purpose and its priorities must be shared, understood, and embraced. If they aren't, people will go their own way.

So ask:

- What do you talk about in your organization?
- Do a few themes dominate?
- Are the same themes discussed by everyone?
- Are they repeated and reinforced in your speeches, reports, advertising, press releases, newsletters, awards, celebrations?

'Rules of the meeting'

How you say things is as important as what you say. When I start a strategy workshop, I always ask the participants to tell me what 'rules' should govern the process. 'How must we act,' I ask, 'to make this discussion as constructive and productive as we want it to be?'

The answers are consistent:

- Everyone participate.
- Be open and honest.
- Be positive and constructive.
- Attack problems, not people.
- Listen to other people's views.
- Respect them.
- Consider all possibilities.
- Focus on the future.
- Keep the process moving forward.

The questions then are: 'If these factors will make this meeting worthwhile, won't they be equally helpful back in the workplace?' 'Aren't they the basics of every interaction?' 'Shouldn't they be written up and displayed everywhere, so we can continue to be guided by them?'

This list is nothing more than a reminder to act with dignity, decency, fairness, and integrity, and to respect other human beings. Surely, these are the most important ideals we can bring to work.

Quality counts

Talk about the quality of a conversation, and most people would probably think about delivery. But while good manners are always a good idea, there's more to effective conversation than being polite and eloquent.

The big question for strategists is: are your conversations 'nourishing' or 'toxic'? Nourishing conversations are informative, positive, future-oriented; people are enriched by them; they feel okay for having been included. Toxic conversations, on the other hand, are short on details, negative, political, and oriented to the past; they leave people feeling worse off.

NOURISHING	TOXIC
• Open • Honest • Based on facts • Robust • Positive • Interesting • Inspiring • Future-oriented • Focus on opportunities	• Secretive • Dishonest • Based on opinions • Information shared on 'need to know' basis • Political • Boring • Backward-looking • Focus on problems

To do a simple health check, ask:

- Who's involved?
- Who gets listened to?
- How widely is information distributed?
- Who has access to it?
- What secrets are shared?
- How much tolerance is there for conflicting views?
- How hotly are issues debated?
- How rigorously are ideas tested?

In any conversation, how you say things matters as much as what you say. Body language and symbols send powerful signals.

Who's allowed in your office, and what do they get to talk about? How often do you go to your people, rather than summons them to you? Who do you stop and talk to when you walk through your factory? How do you respond when people offer suggestions – particularly uncomfortable ones? Who knows that you're making a presentation to customers, not playing golf with your buddies?

The corporate conversation never stops. Any single day presents infinite opportunities to align and inspire your team. Even a short meeting offers phenomenal possibilities for eliciting ideas, sparking new thoughts, and exciting people.

Particularly important is the way you strategize. For this is such a key process that it sends especially potent signals. In most organizations, strategy is made by a few 'important' people. They go away to a suitably luxurious retreat, discuss things in great detail and then come back and try to get their ideas implemented. But excluding people from the initial strategy debate sends a powerful signal about who counts and who doesn't. And while the few lucky participants develop a 'fingertip feel' for the nuances of their situation during their getaway, others aren't as well informed. So it's little wonder there's resistance to decisions. No surprise, either, that few people come forward with ideas. By keeping them 'out of the loop' in the early conversations, there's little chance of 'counting them in' later.

Creating winners and losers

The workplace is a unique forum in which individuals with different backgrounds, values, and views meet in pursuit of a common purpose. They spend most of their waking hours there. They share ideas, argue, and play power games.

The adults who come to work make life and death decisions for themselves every day. They worry about the welfare of their families, about health, housing, and community matters. They're even allowed to choose who governs the country. But at work they're mostly treated like ignorant and irresponsible children.

Managers expect a lot of these people. They know they have to motivate them. They talk teamwork and understand the need for 'alignment' between all the elements of their organizations. They're hot on company dinners, bonding at retreats, and 'shared values'. But the communities they create are dysfunctional; they create winners and losers.

Most companies I work with consider themselves 'learning organizations' or aim to get there. Yet hardly any have learned the first lesson: to value all their people. The 'mind' of most organizations is an exclusive club. Few people are part of it. Though managers talk about participation and empowerment, they mean it in a limited way.

Most companies are deeply secretive places. Information is doled out carefully, grudgingly. Strategy is usually made by a few for the many. It's a boss-down process. Ideas and action are clearly separated. (Some business schools still teach planning and implementation as distinct subjects.) There's a compartment for complexity at the top and many others for simplicity lower down.

This division of labour, says Harvard Business School professor Shoshana Zuboff, is sustained by a 'moral vision at its heart' – a 'division of love'.[7]

The familiar managerial hierarchy makes some people more important than others. Information is shared on a 'need to know' basis. And since there's a belief that most people don't need to know most things (and in any event can't be trusted with information), most of them are kept ignorant.

But if this division of work, and its dangerous assumptions about the value of various people, made sense in a machine age, it no longer does.

In a topsy-turvy world, strategy is made on the run. It emerges in bits, rather than as a complete and tidy document. Action may precede insight or understanding. 'Emergent strategy' is a reality.[8] *No company should risk pigeon-holing its people, and none can afford to shut off insights and ideas or quench the spirit that brings them to life.*

To be able to perform, people obviously need information about their jobs. They must know what they're responsible for (their job description), how to do their allotted work, and what standards are expected of them. And of course, they need feedback on how they're doing, so they can adjust and improve.

But that's not enough. If people are to excel, if you expect them to 'go the extra mile', and if you expect them to turn up every day as 'volunteers' committed to your cause, they must understand not just the narrow details of their tasks or the narrow context in which they operate, but more importantly, *the total context in which your company functions.*

They need to know what you're up against, where you're headed, why that goal is important, and how you intend getting there. By enlarging their world-view, you set them free.

And that brings us to another factor which is consistently overlooked. *Knowing* is one thing. But *caring* is what finally gives winners their edge.

Kinds of knowledge

Learning takes place both tacitly and explicitly. Some 'sneaks up on us', without our being aware that it's happening. Ideas arrive, and we store them without being aware of them This tacit learning is an ongoing process. It occurs as we experiment and work, in meetings and presentations – in fact, from moment to moment in our lives. Tacit knowledge stays 'below the surface' and is taken for granted until we call it up.

Explicit knowledge, on the other hand, comes with effort and attention. We study, we take part in training sessions, we reflect on what others say in conversations. We know we're learning, and we can pass the lessons on to others.

If you think of your collection of knowledge as an iceberg, your tacit knowledge is the large part under the water. Your explicit knowledge is the visible bit. You use both. They are parts of a whole thinking resource.

Now consider what happens in organizations. They too accumulate both tacit and explicit knowledge. The tacit knowledge is in the heads of their people. It comes and goes with the human flow. It is an invaluable resource, but it never belongs to the organization; it 'walks out the door' every day. Yet for all its worth, it's more often than not carelessly managed.

Explicit knowledge – customer data, training programmes, financial information, product specifications, processes, and so on – gets much more attention. It is shared cautiously (after all, you can't trust everyone, and wouldn't competitors love to get their hands on it!) A lot of it is kept under lock and key. When people leave, this stuff stays; if a firm is sold, this stuff goes with it.

Individuals and organizations become more effective when they're aware that they're learning and aware of what they're learning, and when they apply what they've learned. Knowledge and insights are too easily wasted. They can and must be exploited. This means they must be managed.[9]

Learning modes

Our paradigms about education are strongly rooted in a child-based pedagogical model: information must be fed to people; it must be given to them in small chunks; the easy stuff must come first. But an adult or andragogical model begins with different assumptions: people are capable of absorbing a great deal of complex information; they learn best when they choose the material; their inquiry is more useful than a teacher's pat answers.

Pedagogy gives people fish; andragogy helps them learn to fish. The first is about taking responsibility for others; the second is about making them responsible for themselves.

All evidence says that young executives learn fastest when they're 'tossed in at the deep end' and forced to swim. 'Baptism by fire' accelerates learning.

As Charles Handy reminds us, our characters are shaped most powerfully by cataclysmic events: a close brush with death, loss of a job, and so on.[10] On a more basic level, we learn to drive by driving; to read by reading; to think by thinking. Theory and instruction help, *but only practice leads to competence.*

However, given that most managers have been brought up through a pedagogical process of education, it's little wonder that our management paradigms focus on telling rather than discovery. Far from being 'hothouses of new experience', companies deliberately hold people back and slow their learning. If our natural sense of adventure and our creativity have been stifled at school, the process continues at work.

Some people do buck the system. They insist on challenging conventional wisdom, attacking sacred cows, and breaking rules. This is dangerous for them and discomforting to others, but they learn and grow by it. (And thank God, because the world is shaped by those who push the limits!)

'Leaders differ from others,' says Warren Bennis, 'in their constant appetite for knowledge and experience, and as their worlds widen and become more complex, so too do their means of understanding.'[11] If we want more leaders in our organizations, surely, we should encourage that appetite, and pile on the complexity!

Paradoxes again!

If people are energized in some firms and dull in others, it's not just because one lot gravitated to one place while the others went elsewhere. The problem is the environment.

To be motivated and effective, people must know not just the narrow needs of their jobs, but also the broader facts of their context. They must understand

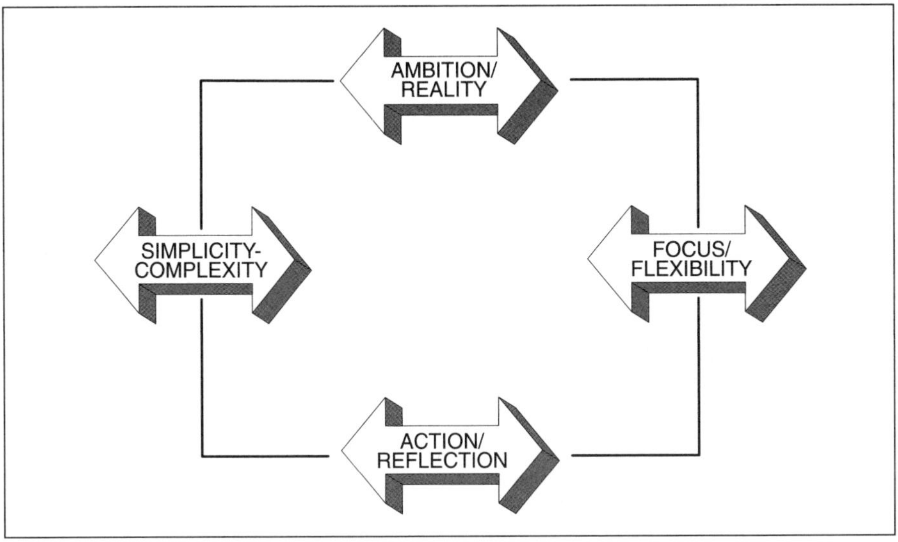

Figure 13.1: *Paradoxes of the corporate conversation*

not just the *what* and the *how* of their work, but also the why – it's importance, its impact, the consequences of doing it well and of doing it badly.

Conversation makes the difference. But to do so, it must embrace four paradoxes. It must:

1. Be based in reality, but also stretch the firm's ambitions.
2. Focus attention on essential goals, but also foster flexibility.
3. Keep things simple, but flood people with information (complexity).
4. Encourage both action and reflection (Figure 13.1).

Here's why these paradoxes deserve your attention:

1. **Reality/Ambition.** Reality is the first requirement, for a simple reason: it's the bedrock on which all else is built.

   Too many people have no idea how important their jobs are. They have no way of placing a value on their contribution. Buried in the bowels of a business, there's no 'line of sight' to the outside world, so they don't know how they affect their employers' competitiveness. They don't have the slightest notion of how demanding customers are or how tough the competition is. What they do know is that if they just turn up most days, they'll get paid.

   To make a difference, corporate conversations need to make clear the realities of life in a hostile environment. They need to give people clear reasons to think creatively, to change, to perform to the highest standards, and to constantly push their limits. Their most basic purpose is to 'turn up the heat' and cause people to say, 'We cannot go on like this. We must change.' And to make change a matter of extreme urgency for which everyone has responsibility. This spurs people to sign up for new adventures; to acknowledge that there will be risks, but that the greatest risk is doing nothing; and to support rather than block new programmes.

Along with those realities, however, people need inspiration. They need dreams, excitement, and a sense of purpose. So the conversation needs to encourage them to experiment, explore, and stretch. It needs to tap that most powerful of all human forces: the self-fulfilling prophesy. For we know that when people aim high, they can fly, but when they aim low, that's where they wind up. And too many people in too many firms aim way too low.

2. **Focus/Flexibility.** Focus is perhaps the most important issue in strategy. No company can afford to take advantage of every opportunity. Clear choices are vital. But flexibility is equally necessary.

   People need to grasp this. They need to understand that it's okay for the boss to say 'head north' today, and 'turn north-west' tomorrow. If they don't know why this is both necessary and sensible, they'll be confused and angry when it happens. Their resistance will be certain.

   They also need to accept that no matter how valuable a particular customer is today, no matter how well a process works, and no matter how much a special skill might be valued, things change. And they personally have to change too.

   Walking the line between focus and flexibility is always tricky. You can easily appear indecisive and inconsistent. The only way to avoid this is by talking openly and early about the realities of business today, and by getting people used to the idea that nothing is forever.

   Centrifugal forces can easily tear a company apart. Attention gets diverted by lawmakers and social activists, by noise in the marketplace. If it's hard choosing a particular path, it's even harder staying the course. Focus decisions must be followed through.

   In even small organizations, the CEO will struggle to fix people's attention in one direction. The problem gets worse with size. The more people in a company – and the more they're encouraged to think for themselves – the greater the problem. Empowerment has a potentially toxic side-effect.

   Executives who've managed successful transitions say that they had to repeat themselves over and over to get their message across. Many say that their biggest error was not being persistent – or insistent – enough. Bored by the sound of their own voices, they fell into the trap that political spin doctors warn about: they went 'off message'.

3. **Simplicity/Complexity.** For people to be effective, they need clear roles and goals. Often, however, they cannot see the wood for the trees. Asked to explain why they matter, they struggle for answers. By spelling out the logic of your organization, the thinking behind your strategy, and how each person will contribute, you begin to empower them.

   But to fully tap their potential, more is needed. Without knowledge about the context in which they work, they will be blinkered and thus constrained. Forced to take a narrow view, they cannot be expected to be open-minded. Shut out of stimulating conversations, problem-solving debates, or brainstorming sessions, there's no reason for them to be creative.

To get the most out of peoplc – even in the most menial of jobs – you have to swamp them with facts, flood them in complexity. The more they know, the richer their context, the better equipped they are to perform.

4. **Action/Reflection.** As I've said over and over, companies need to be more action-oriented. But they also need to allow time for reflection. For in a go-go environment, with all attention on getting things done and meeting deadlines, a lot happens without anyone noticing. Valuable lessons don't stick. Experience slips through the cracks. Learning stays with individuals. It does not get surfaced, considered, or shared. It never becomes a corporate asset.

   Human beings learn not just by doing, but by thinking about what they do. Experience has limited value until you stand back and ask, 'What happened there?' 'Why did that happen?' 'What does it mean?' 'Was it good enough?' 'What else is possible?' Organizations learn when this private introspection becomes an open conversation.

   Making strategy brings a result that few companies recognize, and fewer still aim for. The process itself is a vivid and invaluable learning experience. It's an organization's most important conversation. Being involved in it makes people important and gives their jobs meaning. It also accelerates their learning and growth, making them more valuable for the future.

Messages that matter

Constant change is a given. People must be encouraged to willingly abandon past practices and to leave their comfort zones. So you need to flood them with information and pile on the complexity.

At the same time, you have to help them make sense of what they see, hear, and experience. And the best way to do that is to select a few central themes and repeat them over and over.

Communication may be helped by drama. Some leaders are more charismatic than others, more outgoing, and better presenters. But while these are valuable strengths, they are not essential. What really matters is the clarity, simplicity, and emotional clout of what you say.

No matter how complicated your business may be, you should be able to define its challenges and possibilities quickly and clearly. If you haven't done that already, now is the time. Here's a checklist to help you get started:

- What are your key themes – the core messages you repeat over and over?
- What language do you use?
- What symbols do you use to drive home your point?
- Which 'brave deeds' and 'heroes' do you glorify?
- What virtues and values do you extol?

And most important of all:

- How do you walk your talk?

This last one is the killer.

One managing director insisted that the word 'integrity' should appear in his firm's mission statement, because at 'back-to-school' time, people took home writing pads for their kids. Then he had an affair with a secretary and got her pregnant. He rented an apartment for her and told the ad agency to furnish it and hide the expense in their next bill to his company. But the grapevine works – especially when you don't want it to. In no time, the entire organization knew of his cheating. After that, 'integrity' was the joke word. And whatever the boss said, people knew he meant something else.

The CEO of a bank spent millions on customer service initiatives – speeches, badges, T-shirts, videos, training programmes, and all the rest. One day, after years of effort, an angry customer burst into his office and gave him hell. The executive's response? He bumped up security!

A large industrial company missed its budgets for five years in a row. Part of a conglomerate, there was little pressure on the team to deliver. So while senior people diligently set goals and talked incessantly about meeting targets, everyone knew that delivery didn't really matter.

These things happen too often. Leaders need to be extremely careful of the words they use and the values they espouse. For when they slip, they may never get up again.

Two core questions will help you define your priorities and shape your corporate conversation:

1. Why do we exist?
2. Who are we?

The first question is about purpose. The second is about character. These are not usually matters that rank high on strategy agendas – if they feature at all. But addressing them up front gives you an important context in which to frame many other questions. It also ensures congruence in all that follows.

Beyond vision and mission

At this point, you might ask, 'What's happened to those old favourites – vision and mission?' Do you still need them? And what about more recent notions like 'strategic intent'?

Face it, these are all variations on a theme. But a glance at the statements that companies make shows that too many play with words and too few apply rigorous thinking to their literary efforts.

For many years, I struggled to get executives to be precise and clear. Two conclusions:

1. While vision ('the hill' you aim for) and mission (your product/market decision) are quite different and require different conversations, most people get

the terms mixed up. They talk carelessly about 'our vision', 'our vision/mission', or 'our mission/vision'. Other notions like 'values' or 'philosophy' get thrown in too.

2. It's easy to get trapped in semantic debates that lead nowhere. The question is not what words you should use, but what you should *think* about. What's needed is a simple, clear way of thinking about the critical issues.

Executives face growing pressure to explain why their organizations exist, what makes them different, what they stand for, and why stakeholders should support them. Purpose and character embrace all these questions.

Here at last are two tools that clarify not just your corporate *ambition*, but also your competitive *attitude*. They take into account what you expect from the world, and what you intend contributing to the world. They recognize that while an organization must give investors superior returns over time, it also has other stakeholders: it is inter-dependent, not independent. They define the direction in which you intend moving, but also take into account larger issues such as your management philosophies, stakeholder relationships, social compacts, ethics, and values.

The two frameworks that follow will enable you and your team to make important decisions about both the direction and trajectory of your growth, and the behaviour that underpins it. Other authors have written extensively about the need to consider various questions in this regard. But here, at last, is a pair of tools that give you both a logical approach and the means to link key issues.

Dynamic purpose

Business lore is full of stories about companies which became hugely successful, apparently driven by a simple, single-minded vision: 'Beat Xerox' (Canon); 'Kill Yamaha' (Honda); 'The world's favourite airline' (British Airways). Often, a company's entire reason for being is summed up in a statement like '$100 million in profits by 2005','The biggest in our industry', or 'The leader in our field'. All fine, stirring stuff. But all quite inadequate, given the complex nature of competitiveness.

Purpose is paradoxical, in that it must both endure and evolve. It must stay constant long enough to let you build resources and carve a niche in the world. But it must change when you discover new opportunities, develop new capabilities – and fend off new competitors.

Markets change, and innovation lets you offer new products and services. The future is a moving target, and you have to keep setting new goals, raising your sights and your standards.

A company's spirit is a product of its dreams. A stretching purpose generates energy and enthusiasm; the moment you stop striving, you slump. The threat of inertia is ever-present; to overcome it, you have to keep pushing into new territory, testing your limits, experimenting and learning.

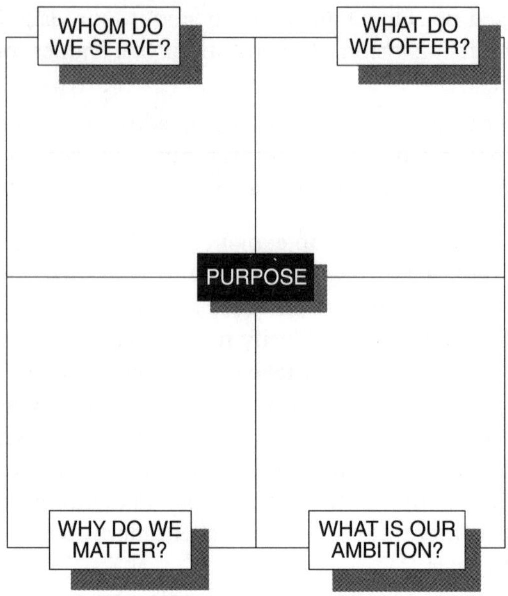

Figure 13.2: *Define your purpose*

Companies do not exist in isolation; they have many stakeholders. Their decisions and actions impact on many people and institutions. Others' moves, in turn, affect them. Managers must be always mindful of how their next step will be seen, interpreted, and responded to. They must also be alert to signals from outside that tell them how much latitude they have, what their priorities should be, and how they should act.

To define your purpose, ask yourself these four questions (Figure 13.2):

1. **Whom do we serve?** What customers do we work with? How do we define the 'right' customers? What makes them special? With whom would we like to work? What other stakeholders concern us? How do we rank them?
2. **What do we offer?** What product/service do we provide? What function does it perform? What need or want does it fulfil?
3. **Why do we matter?** What difference do we make? Why are we special? Why would the world be worse off without us?
4. **What is our ambition?** What do we want to achieve? By when? Which measures count most – sales, reputation, profits, ROI, service levels, etc.?

Questions of character

To provide direction is one thing. But you also need to consider how your organization makes choices and what behaviours are best for it. And once again, four questions give you valuable insights (Figure 13.3):

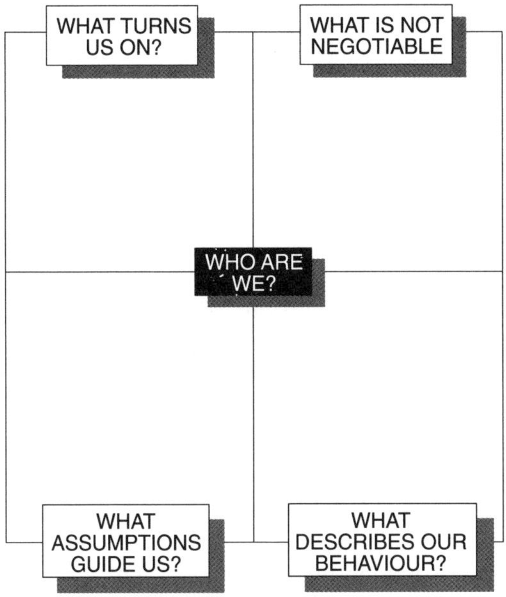

Figure 13.3: *Factors defining corporate character*

1. **What turns us on?** People and companies are motivated by different things. One is obsessed by profit; another gets its kicks from innovation; a third enjoys the cut and thrust of competition. Whatever drives and excites you has consequences. Best you think about these up front, so you know what you'll have to deal with.

   For example, one participant in a strategy workshop said, 'What turns us on is seeing our competitors in pain. Even better is knowing we caused that pain.' The rest of the group agreed with him. But then the question had to be asked: how far will go you in pursuit of that goal? This led to a lengthy debate, in which many other difficult questions came up. The team was forced to confront some of its deepest values, and to consider the effects of such a flip statement on future competition in its industry – and on its potential for destabilizing the industry and causing costly price wars.

2. **What is not negotiable?** For all the talk about freedom, empowerment, and open-mindedness, companies do need discipline. No social group can function effectively without some rules. To say that 'anything goes' is nonsense unless you want anarchy.

   Almost always, 'integrity' is the first word that comes up when this question is posed. But we've seen the risks in using it loosely. The same applies to terms like 'delivery', 'performance', 'innovation', or 'risk-taking'. These may be the right things to say, or the right goals to aim for, but can you live them now? And should you slip, what are the implications?

What happens, for example, when you decide that delivery is not negotiable and a key person lets you down?

What happens when you talk performance but your sales and profits don't improve because of weaknesses in the marketing department?

What happens when someone does take a risk and gets your company into trouble?

It's easy to say you'll act tough. But will you? And will you be even-handed – or will some people get away with things that won't be tolerated from others?

'Not negotiable' is unambiguous. There are no half-measures. When your team signs off on this question, they need to understand that they're making serious commitments. And conformance has to be seriously enforced.

3. **What assumptions guide us?** All behaviour is underpinned by assumptions. By questioning what you currently believe, you may find that you are sustaining dysfunctional behaviours for no good reason. Yesterday's valid views may now be ridiculous.

   Often, teams are divided by the different assumptions people hold. One faction says, 'We'll continue to be successful because our customers love us.' Another says, 'Oh no. We've got some real problems out there.' Or someone in sales lobbies for deep discounts to a customer group that she thinks has great potential, while the marketing manager sees a bigger payback from expensive TV ads aimed at another part of the market.

4. **What describes our behaviour?** Different organizations act differently. In one, people move fast, communicate verbally, take risks, and try lots of things. Another is slower, more cautious, more conservative.

   How do you act now? How should you act? Would you be comfortable with the change? Would the new behaviours be congruent with your values?

   It might be sensible to decide that you have to be more aggressive in attacking competitors. But will your people actually do it? And if not, what then?

   You may agree that your company needs to do things faster. So you set tight new goals for product development; you announce that phones must be answered in three rings or less, and you promise customers that they'll get their orders within 24 hours. But is this reality? Is it possible? Is there the will to do it?

When you debate your corporate character, you lay the foundations for your future corporate culture. This is one of the most important tasks for any management team. The tool I've described here lets you tackle it in systematic fashion.

Spike your fine prose!

By now, almost every company has a vision and/or mission. Values statements adorn the walls. Most of this stuff has much less impact on performance than executives know. A lot of it is garbage.

For one thing, too much effort goes into crafting fine words and too little into the hard thinking that strategy demands. Flowery phrases appear where practical detail is called for.

For another, there's all too often a provocative gap between words and deeds. Management pushes a point of view that it cannot – or simply does not – live up to. It proclaims certain behaviours as 'right', then does something else.

A third reason is that the ideals espoused in many of these statements cannot be measured or managed. They sound just right in the annual report, and everyone nods when the chairman mentions them in speeches, but there's no way to turn them into work. To put it bluntly, they're fluff.

Ricardo Semler boasts that 'Semco has no corporate credo ... and no mission statement. An articulation of company values or vision is just a photograph of the company as it is, or wants to be, at one given moment. Snapshots of this kind seem to hold some companies together, but they are terribly static devices. No one can impose corporate consciousness from above. It moves and shifts with every day and every worker. Like planning, vision at its best is dynamic and dispersed.'[12]

This may be an extreme view. Most companies will gain from spelling out their intentions, if only to remind themselves of what they're about. But before you rush off to the framers, or laminate your mission statement so it fits people's pockets, think about the consequences. If you can't live it, forget it.

Where have you heard this before?

Most vision/mission/values statements are bland, boring, and pointless. The same words and phrases are used by steel makers and hamburger outlets, drug companies and supermarkets. If you asked a roomful of people from different firms to toss their mission statements into a box, mix them up, and then find their own, they'd be lost. Many would pull out someone else's and yell, 'This is it!'

The example below, from a large South African chemical company, could be a template for its competitors in the chemical industry or for almost any other company. (I've highlighted the key words in bold type.)

- Ongoing **growth** and return on investment greater than the Johannesburg Stock Exchange chemical industry average.
- A spirit of **partnership** with customers by consistently supplying quality products and services.
- Technical **excellence**.
- Constructive and enduring **relationships** with suppliers and principals.
- Practising strongly **decentralized** and **participatory management** and fostering the **diversity** of the cultures of its subsidiaries.
- Maintaining a high standard of **integrity**.
- Providing a human resources environment which is **fair**, recognizes the development **potential** of all its people and **rewards** them according to performance.

- Protecting the **safety** and **health** of all its employees and preserving the **environment**.
- Contributing responsibly to the **development of the country and all its people**.

The sincerity of these statements is not in question. No one can doubt their importance. But do they make a difference? This firm's managers would say yes. But all too often, fingers could be pointed at companies saying these things. Their own people know that reality is different. Outsiders are scornful.

Too often, corporate statements of intent don't translate into strategy. Profits stay low. Customer service remains poor. Management is autocratic. People are hurt and die at work. The environment is screwed up in the name of job creation or some nebulous community benefit. The effect of these continuous untruths is devastating. The first victim is trust; the ongoing costs are greater than you ever know.

What sets Land's End apart

One of my favourite companies is Land's End, a mail order company that's a benchmark for firms in many industries. Land's End sells clothing and luggage 365 days a year, 24 hours a day. Here's the formula:

THE LAND'S END PRINCIPLES OF DOING BUSINESS

Principle 1. We do everything we can to make our products better. We improve material, and add back features and construction details that others have taken out over the years. We never reduce the quality of a product to make it cheaper.

Principle 2. We price our products fairly and honestly. We do not, have not, and will not participate in the common retailing practice of inflating mark-ups to set up a future phoney 'sale'.

Principle 3. We accept any return for any reason, at any time. Our products are guaranteed. No fine print. No arguments. We mean exactly what we say: **GUARANTEED. PERIOD.**

Principle 4. We ship faster than anyone we know of. We ship items in stock the day after we receive the order. At the height of the last Christmas season the longest time an order was in the house was 36 hours, excepting monograms which took another 12 hours.

Principle 5. We believe that what is best for our customers is best for all of us. Everyone here understands that concept. Our sales and service people are trained to know our products, and to be friendly and helpful. They are urged to take all the time necessary to take care of you. We even pay for your call, for whatever reason you call.

Principle 6. We are able to sell at lower prices because we have eliminated middlemen; because we don't buy branded merchandise with high protected mark-ups; and because we have placed our contracts with manufacturers who have proven that they are cost-conscious and efficient.

Principle 7. We are able to sell at lower prices because we operate efficiently. Our people are hard-working, intelligent, and share in the success of the company.

Principle 8. We are able to sell at lower prices because we support no fancy emporia with their high overheads. Our main location is in the middle of a 40-acre cornfield in rural Wisconsin.

These 'principles' might be addressed to customers, but anyone who reads them knows exactly what counts at Land's End. What sets them apart is that they're concrete and specific. They tell Land's End people what has made the company successful, and what they must do to keep it that way. In short, they can be made to work.

The word from IBM

IBM's Lou Gerstner made waves in July 1993, when he said, 'The last thing IBM needs right now is a vision.' But in his 1995 annual report, he wrote:

> *... it's with an enormous sense of irony that now, almost three years later, I say this: what IBM needs most right now is a vision. I don't mean a slogan. I don't mean promises and vaporware (announced products that don't exist now and never will.) I don't mean here's-what's good-for-IBM-and-therefore-it's-good-for-you-too.*

Gerstner then described the changes sweeping the computer industry, and particularly the importance of networks in satisfying emerging customer needs. His conclusion:

> *So this convergence of two powerful forces – customer need and advanced network technology – leads IBM to a strategy, or vision, that is simple and clear, consistent with our company mission. IBM will lead the transition to network-centric computing by:*
> - *Continuing to create the advanced products and technologies needed to make powerful networks real; and*
> - *Working with our customers to help them fully exploit these networks.*

The lessons? Clarity. Simplicity. Reality. The hard-nosed Gerstner tackled IBM's turnaround with methodical professionalism. He spent his first months visiting more than 2 000 customers and talking to thousands of IBM-ers. By mid-1996 he'd flown more than 407 000 miles on 464 flights.[13] He slashed costs, abandoned pet projects, and re-focused the organization's energies. By the time he was ready to announce a vision, he had made a huge impact on the company's fortunes. (A lesson for executives who believe that spelling out a vision will fix their problems!)

It's particularly instructive to watch the difference in Big Blue's annual reports before and after Gerstner's arrival. The design, the tone, and the language changes markedly. Under his predecessor, John Aakers, the message was sombre and dull, while Gerstner is chatty and colloquial, and from 1994 the reports have an altogether friendlier feel.

Gerstner took tough action to restore IBM's profits. The head office building and art collection were sold, people were laid off, and the organization was restructured to focus on 14 key industries. But the strategy is not hugely different to that of earlier leaders. What Gerstner is doing is not rocket science. But he communicates it well.

IBM is engaged in a new kind of conversation.

The message and the medium

Most companies would say they have communications problems. They're right. But the way they deal with them is entirely wrong.

When companies call me to help improve communication, they have predictable questions:

'Should we use videos or e-mail?'

'How many people can we include in a meeting?'

'How can we improve our report-writing?'

'Where do we go for help with our presentations?'

These questions must be asked and answered. But they're the wrong place to start. The first issue is *what* must be communicated; then comes *how* to do it.

Conveying the wrong things with skill and flair doesn't help anyone. It does not matter how well you put a bad message across, it remains a bad message.

Perversely, the spread of new communications tools may hurt rather than help corporate conversation. With increasingly smart and user-friendly technology, it's tempting to tart up every message. One reason PCs haven't helped productivity as much as they could is that users waste too much time fiddling with page layouts, adding graphics, and playing with colours. Yet though the results might look great, communication remains poor.

Lou Gerstner understands the danger. According to *U.S. News & World Report*, one of the first things he did on joining IBM was to ban the use of flip charts and overhead projectors in management meetings. Issues that used to be bandied about for 30 minutes are now dealt with in ten.[14]

Jack Welch, too, knows that effective communication doesn't have to be complicated. While he was working his way up through the GE ranks, he toed the corporate line and produced the elaborate presentations that the culture required. But when he became boss, he changed things fast. Out went the fancy slides and thick folders. In came crisp, brief verbal reports.[15]

South African managers, pay attention! If communication is an issue for Gerstner and Welch, it's an even greater issue here. If they see the value in simplicity, maybe you should, too. If you haven't reduced your strategy to 'a teachable idea' – and if you're not out there teaching it with passion – now is surely the time to get to work.

If more time were spent on message content and less on slick words and pretty pictures, companies would soon feel the impact. Their conversations would improve dramatically. There might not be fewer meetings, but there would definitely be different meetings. More people would understand the business, its purpose, and its context. More of them would want to take part.

From intentions to action

Conversations are always more interesting when they paint pictures. Plans are boring when they're packed with facts and figures and footnotes.

I sit through dozens of strategy presentations every year. More often than not, I battle to grasp the point. The insiders may know what's going on, but as an outsider I sure as hell don't. Nor am I interested in ploughing through a document of several hundred pages to try and find The Way.

It's my job to understand strategy. That's not the job of most people in organizations – the people who must make strategy work. So if I battle to grasp what managers mean, those other people surely are in the dark too.

Searching for a better way to make strategy and to make it understandable, I started encouraging my clients to abandon their planning documents, and instead to 'draw' their plans as a wheel (Figure 13.4).* This is a variant on the well-known and widely-used 'balanced scorecard'.

Here's how it works:

1. Your purpose is the axis around which all activities take place.
2. Discussions with many different companies in a wide range of industries suggest eight 'headline' issues which must be managed: customers, suppliers, finance, people, technology, quality, community, environment. (You might want to change some, or add others.) Under each, you need to be more specific. For example, 'finance' embraces turnover, profits, ROI, etc. 'Customers' should be broken down into sales targets, service, distribution, promotion, and so on. 'People' covers issues such as skills, training, and development goals.
3. To roll smoothly and swiftly into the future, the wheel must be round. Its 'spokes' must be of equal length. You won't get away with doing wonderful things for your customers while screwing your suppliers; you shouldn't upgrade your technology at the expense of your people; you won't survive if you do good works for the community but cut into your profits. Quality

* Porter, Hamermesh, and others at the Harvard Business School have used the 'wheel of strategy' to describe a firm's policies.

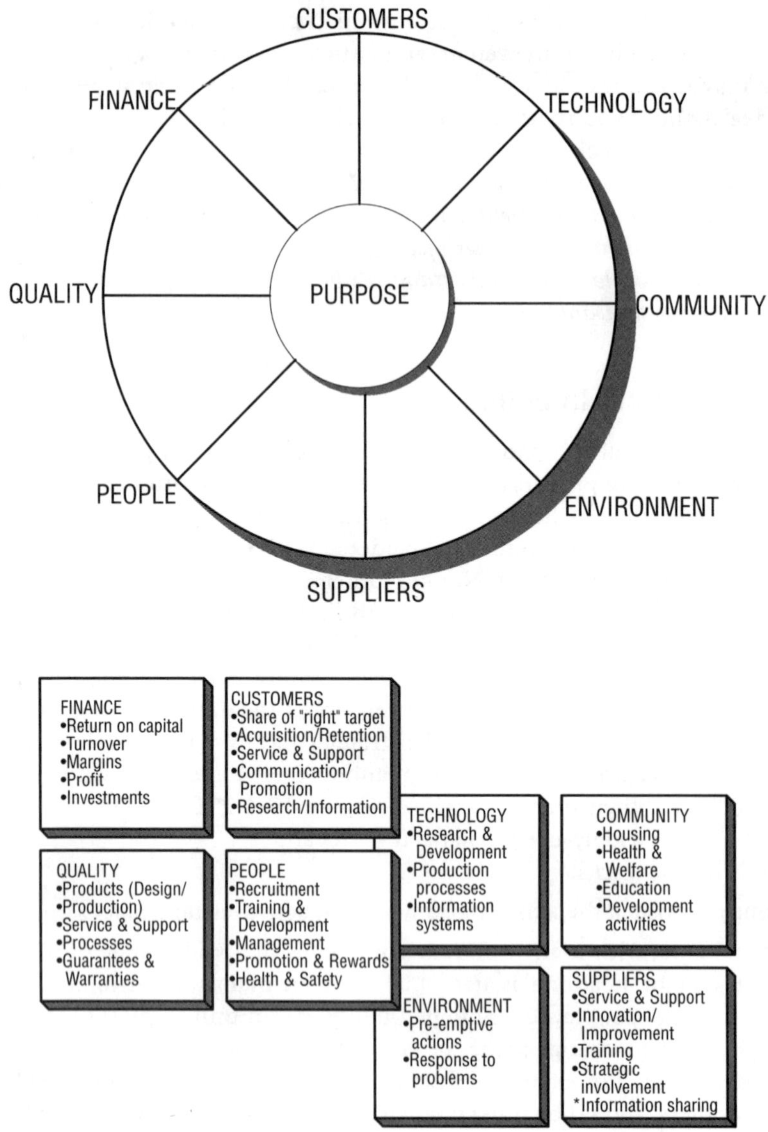

Figure 13.4: *The strategy wheel*

is as important as the environment. The 'strategy wheel' shows that these factors all count, and that managing them is a paradoxical process.

4. For each factor, list your major goals and, if you like, spell out your action plans. A great deal of detail is not necessary. While it's important that you have some idea of how you'll get to the future you want, there's little point in trying to define every step in minute detail. Things will change. Surprises will occur. If you're too specific, you may lock out possibilities.

Using this visual approach, many very large companies have been able to reduce their strategies to no more than four or five pages. Managers have found that explaining the strategy to their people is dramatically simplified. And because every last detail isn't spelled out, there's plenty of room to invent answers along the road.

Of course, it's tempting to be thorough. Managers aren't used to anything less. But don't fall into this trap. You can't have a satisfying conversation about too many things. The more detail you get into now, the less space you leave for other people to create the future.

As CEO, you'd obviously have responsibility for the entire wheel. People elsewhere in your organization would have more specific tasks. The point is to make sure that work is distributed, and each person has both a clear view of what they must do and a sense of the context in which they must perform.

This isn't a 'sophisticated' approach. Neither does it provide much work for strategic planners or typists. But it does get the job done. And it does let you manage in a way that's appropriate to these complex and fast-moving times.

The 'strategy wheel' gives you a balanced scorecard. It helps you create an effective strategy, sell it, and measure it. I know of no other approach that is so simple, so relevant to the times we work in, or so powerful.

Endnotes

1. Gary Hamel, 'Strategy as revolution', *Harvard Business Review*, July–August 1996.
2. John W. Gardner, *On Leadership*, New York: The Free Press, 1990.
3. 'And the winner is still ... Wal-Mart', *Fortune*, May 2, 1994.
4. Alfie Kohn, 'Why incentive plans cannot work', *Harvard Business Review*, September–October 1993.
5. Rosabeth Moss Kanter, 'Transcending business boundaries: 12,000 world managers view change,' *Harvard Business Review*, May–June, 1991.
6. 'Corporate reputations', *Fortune*, March 6, 1995.
7. 'Senior managers face a gruelling eight months', *Financial Times*, April 23/24, 1994.
8. 'Is Herb Kelleher America's best CEO?' *Fortune*, May 2, 1994.
9. Douglas McGregor, *The Human Side Of Enterprise*, New York: McGraw-Hill Book Company, 1960.
10. See Bennis and Nanus, 1985; Noel M. Tichy and Mary Anne Devanna, *The Transformational Leader*, New York: John Wiley & Sons, 1986; John P. Kotter, *A Force For Change*, New York: The Free Press, 1990.
11. Harry Levinson and Stuart Rosenthal, *CEO: Corporate Leadership in Action*, New York: Basic Books, 1984.
12. John E. Hunter, et. al., 'Individual differences in output variability as a function of job complexity', *Journal Of Applied Psychology*, Volume 75, 1990, referred to by Alan W.H. Grant and Leonard Schlesinger in their article, 'Realize your customers' full potential', *Harvard Business Review*, September–October 1995.

Conclusion

The minute we make a decision, we are confronted with our next teacher.

— Charlotte Joko Beck[1]

The first principles of business competition are clear. Now it's over to you.

Getting started on the improvement process is quite easy. Most companies can substantially sharpen up with minimal effort. But after their initial burst of interest, and after they've tackled the easy problems, their improvement curve gets steeper and more costly to climb.

During the 1980s, companies worldwide dashed off 'in search of excellence'. Many made quite impressive progress. But most quite quickly came to a grinding halt. Their initial enthusiasm was killed.

The path from 'terrible' to 'okay' was quite easy and a lot of fun. But from 'okay' to 'exceptional' was a hell of a lot harder, and 'excellence' remained a dream.

The bad news for these firms is that the most aggressive competitors didn't give up. They're committed to both incremental improvements and bold leaps into the unknown. They're setting new standards of quality and productivity – and the bar gets higher every day.

Some firms have seized *kaizen* as the solution to their manufacturing problems. But whereas Toyota spent decades on improvement, these companies want a 'plug and play' result. Not for them the long, slow slog that's fundamental to the notion of continuous improvement – they want a quick fix. And when results don't come fast, they give up and grab another fad.

When Taiichi Ohno was charged with making Toyota's production system world class, he kept at it for 30 years. The much-admired Toyota Production System wasn't dreamed up in a classroom or technical meeting.

As *sensei*, or teacher, Ohno kept challenging his people to do better. Example: changing dies on stamping machines took up to 16 hours in the late 1970s; a decade later it took just *one minute*, and Ohno hinted that perhaps 30 seconds was possible!

The best competitors keep investing in improvement even when their customers stop spending. Take, for example, the commitment that drives Valeo SA, one of Europe's most successful auto components producers.

When European car sales fell in 1993 and car makers pressed suppliers to cut prices, Valeo's turnover fell 20 per cent. But management went right ahead with its policy of hiring 500 to 600 engineers a year and spending 5 per cent of the personnel budget on training. Research and development costs went up to 5,2 per cent of sales, and capex rose to 6,8 per cent of sales. Result: profits rose and the company's share price doubled. Said the president of the company: 'There is no end to improvement.'[2]

Now is the time

Sometimes, you can change just a few things, or change them in a limited way, and be okay for a while. But sooner or later in an era of tumultuous upheavals, every firm must face up to the need for dramatic and radical change. Incremental improvements help you stay abreast of competitors; quantum leaps put you out front.

Business leaders are quite ready to speak out for change, to beat their drums, and to set up project teams and committees to lead the charge. They're sitting ducks for the latest change programme; if it's a package so much the better.

But when it comes to *action* – when they realize how much the changes will cost, how hard they'll be, and how long they'll take – they back down fast. Typically, change programmes are limited in their objectives, starved of funds, and ultimately killed off by executives who keep busy with 'real work'.

Yesterday's customers have enormous value. Today's assets must be squeezed. You have to take care of your people, talk to the lawyers, spend time with major investors. *But the only reason to do any of this is to prepare for the future.*

Companies around the world forgot this. They created business systems that fed off themselves. Instead of shaping the future, they became its victim. Their growing bureaucracies forced them to look inwards rather than outwards. They failed to notice when customers and competitors changed.

By the time they woke up, the cost of responding was unthinkable; when they put off the tough action that was called for, the costs grew. They're now frantically reengineering their business systems. The changes are traumatic.

The lesson: be alert. Act early. Act fast. Have the guts to do whatever you must do in one hit.

'Whatever you can do, or dream you can,' wrote Goethe, 'begin it. Boldness has genius, power and magic in it.'

Endnotes

1. Charlotte Joko Beck , *Nothing Special*, San Francisco: HarperSanFrancisco, 1993.
2. 'Under Goutard, Valeo thrives on pressure', *Wall Street Journal Europe*, May 27–28, 1994.

Appendix

Challenge Your Limits

The results a company delivers arise from the mindset of its people. What is your organization's mindset? What do you believe to be possible? What do you aspire to? What are you planning to do about it?

1. What is your potential?

Life is an adventure in which we test ourselves against the possibilities. Business is similarly an adventure in which we explore 'what might be'. And like individuals, companies have unfathomable potential.

All too often strategic plans are no more than an extrapolation of the past into the future. Yesterday's budget is their base. More of the same – perhaps with a tweak here and there – is the result. Yesterday's organization is fine-tuned for the future.

That this is dangerous is evident. But it's also a tragic waste to be held back by past achievements or by limitations set by someone else.

The 'potential' question forces you to look ahead, rather than over your shoulder. It forces you to think about what could be, rather than replaying what is. It challenges your assumptions about your organization and its environment. And it helps you change from a mindset of negative certainty to one of positive wonder.

You'll probably find it hard to imagine that you could change anything and everything your company does, but try. Everyone has constraints, but visualize your company overcoming those that currently seem to limit your performance. Create a picture in your mind of making a fresh start, being able to change anything you want, having unlimited resources. Be ridiculous; you can get serious later.

If you and your team really gave your business everything, ask:

- What market share could you gain?
- How much turnover could you attain?
- How much profit could you make?
- How well could you do in terms of productivity, quality, customer service, or any other measure?
- How well could you communicate with your stakeholders?
- What could your rate of product innovation be?
- How rapidly could your company become the industry benchmark?
- What contribution could you make to your community, or the nation?

2. How radically must you change to achieve your potential?

The world around us has changed dramatically and will continue to do so. It will become more, not less, hostile. No company is likely to reach anywhere near its potential without changing equally radically.

To build on what you already have is to limit yourself. The assets of the past will not necessarily be valuable in the future. Other strengths will be needed. Some might be bought, so you can acquire them quickly; others will have to be developed, which might take a long time. Either way, you need to make a decision and get to work.

Deciding what to change is always a risk. In times as unpredictable as these it's easy to guess wrong. The 'best' answer can, in hindsight, look idiotic. Making no decision might seem safest – and may even turn out to be so!

Because radical change can be risky, difficult, and costly, you can easily avoid even thinking about it. Simple changes are more palatable. But ask:

- What external pressures must you respond to?
- What's likely to happen next in your environment?
- What will happen if you do nothing?
- What is the least you can do?
- What are the two or three most important 'mega-changes' you should make?

3. How radical are you prepared to be?

Recognizing that radical changes are needed is one thing; making them happen is something quite different. Most managers know they must change. Yet they invest themselves in resisting change.

It sounds crazy, but human beings work hard to fail. We erect defenses against our own greatness. Psychologist Abraham Maslow called this the 'Jonah complex':

> *We fear our highest possibilities (as well as our lowest ones). We are generally afraid to become that which we can glimpse in our most perfect moments, under the most perfect conditions, under conditions of greatest courage. We enjoy and even thrill to the godlike possibilities we see in ourselves in such peak moments. And yet we simultaneously shiver with weakness, awe, and fear before these very same possibilities.*[1]

When some lunatic does suggest new ways of doing things, the responses are predictable:

'Are you mad?'
'Be realistic.'
'Policy won't allow it.'
'We tried it once before.'
'Do you think it's really worth the hassle?'
'Let's do another study first.'

'Whose mad idea is this?'
'Who'll carry the can if it goes wrong?'
'What's the downside?'
'That's not us.'
'Go away and think about it again.'
'It'll never fly.'
'The competition will crucify us.'
'We can't afford it?'

I like to ask top managers, 'What radical changes have you made in the past week ...? 'Month ...?' 'Year ...?' All too often, they cannot name a single shift. And in almost every group someone shoots back with 'change for the sake of change is foolish'.

And of course, they're right. Change for the sake of it *is* foolish. Often, there are good reasons not to change. But given the tumult around us, it's scary to hear smart managers immediately block discussions of change. If *they* of all people aren't provoking it and demanding it – and changing themselves – the future is bleak.

Here are some issues to think about:

- How badly do you want to realize your potential?
- What would you gain from the journey?
- What commitments will be needed?
- What principles or values might be compromised?
- What's to be lost by trying?
- What must you abandon to get where you want to go?
- What are you willing to give up?

4. How will you make the necessary changes?

Knowing you have to do something new is one thing. Knowing *what* to do is another matter. And knowing *how* to do it – and being able to get it done – ultimately stands between you and success.

As we've seen, most change efforts fail. So it's realistic to assume that in the years ahead, firms will flail about, spend a fortune – and make little progress. Managers will seize on slogans, flog new concepts, and wonder why the competition keeps eating their lunch.

Strategy sessions usually end with bold statements of intent. Less clear is who will do what by when. Resourcing is a subject 'for another meeting'. Details about execution are left for later. But in strategy, execution is crucial. Figuring it out deserves more attention. The old saying that 'politics is the art of the possible' applies equally to business.

Ask:

- What are the few things you must do that will make the biggest difference?

- Where are the 'levers' of change?
- Who are the 'pivotal' people – the one's who'll make it happen?
- Who might get in the way?
- What must you do first?
- What are your deadlines?
- Can you afford it?

Endnotes

1. A.H. Maslow, *The Farther Reaches of Human Nature*, New York: The Viking Press, 1971.

Subject Index

Note: Brand names and names of companies are printed in italics.
Foreign or technical terms are underlined.

D

E

F

G